WHAT HAS COME BEFORE...

Concealed beneath the ocean's waves lie[...] [...]rs a war has been raging between undersea [...] threatens to surface, engulfing the entire [...]

It's up to CAPT'N ELI and his allies to sta[...] [...]al destruction.

Traveling through time and space, CAPT'N ELI and fellow inventors and explorers, THE SEASEARCHERS – led by the amazing PROF. WOW, reveal evidence that alien races secretly live beneath the waves. The mysterious hero COMMANDER X guides CAPT'N ELI as he discovers a hidden history of the world as well as clues to his personal past and future.

For centuries, the refugees of Atlantis and Lemuria have been waging a secret war in the sea for domination of the planet. Control of a strange alien power source called THE STARGIFT and a time portal in the Bermuda Triangle are the sources of the conflict.

LORD HYDRO is a blue-skinned nobleman of AQUARIA, the underwater empire founded by mutated, amphibian descendants of Atlantis. He seeks dominance of Aquaria and eventually the world – fulfilling an ancient prophecy that Atlantis will rise again. He also has on old score to settle with his father, BARON HYDRO's, arch enemies COMMANDER X and SEA GHOST.

His weapons of mass destruction are the HYDRONS, an army of artificial eel-men and their fish shaped flying submarine warships called VAIXILI. The HYDRONS were used in the ancient war between Atlantis and Lemuria.

Along with the HYDRONS, LORD HYDRO employs a vast array of exotic, giant war machine robots he discovered in TANTARUS — the underground ruins of the empire of Lemuria.

LORD HYDRO makes a series of actions that force the world on the edge of global war with CAPT'N ELI caught in the middle.

THE PLAYERS

CAPT'N ELI is a 10 year old boy with a brilliant scientific mind and a flair for invention. He also possesses unusual aquatic skills. His past is shrouded in mystery, with links to the legendary hero COMMANDER X and a secret underwater world of ancient empires in conflict. He is accompanied by his dog, BARNEY, who can tie knots and his 200 year old talking parrot JOLLY ROGER. CAPT'N ELI is the junior member of the SEASEARCHERS, a global team formed for aquatic rescue and exploration.

COMMANDER X is the Man From the Future. He is a time traveler who has lost his memory. The man who would be known as COMMANDER X arrived from the future using a time portal in the Bermuda Triangle in the late 1930s using a high tech submarine piloted by a sentient supercomputer called S.H.I.V.A. S.H.I.V.A. guides COMMANDER X who has lost his list of missions that will help avert doomsday some time in the distant future. COMMANDER X takes on the civilian identity of LAMONT DRAKE, millionaire philanthropist, and dons the mask of COMMANDER X to fight evil above and below the waves. Armed with a vast arsenal of high tech weaponry, COMMANDER X frequently joined on missions with CIRCE THE SORCERESS and THE SEA RAIDER.

THE SEA GHOST is the Avenging Spirit of the Sea. Originally THE SEA RAIDER, his real identity is REX NOBLE, a drowned WW2 sailor saved by PRINCESS AQUA from the highly advanced underwater empire of Aquaria — founded by the refugees of lost Atlantis. To save REX's life, AQUA gives him the ancient serum that transforms humans into amphibians. The serum gives REX vast powers such as super strength, speed, invulnerability and limited flight. He becomes an ally of COMMANDER X and they share a bond in defeating their arch enemy and axis collaborator, THE RED OCTOPUS.

Many years later, THE RED OCTOPUS is eventually revealed to be BARON HYDRO, a rival for AQUA's affections and a renegade trying to usurp the Aquarian throne.

After a sneak attack by Hydro on the underwater city of Aquaria, REX is left widowed and his two children, CORAL and TRITON, are left motherless.

To protect his children, REX leaves evidence that they all perished in the attack. He takes them into exile to The Ghost Grotto, a high tech hideout deep within a dead underwater volcano, and dons the new identity of THE SEA GHOST. The spirit of his wife, QUEEN AQUA, appears and grants REX even greater powers, including generating vast amounts of electrical energy and a physical link to Aquaria's power source, the ancient STARGIFT.

LORD HYDRO is the power mad warlord of the underwater empire of Aquaria. He is obsessed by an ancient prophecy that he believes will project him as ruler of the planet. He is bent on revenge of his father, BARON HYDRO's, enemies: COMMANDER X and THE SEA GHOST as well as the children of THE SEA GHOST, PRINCESS CORAL and PRINCE TRITON, the current rulers of Aquaria. LORD HYDRO commands a massive army of artificial beings known as HYDRONS and a group of giant robots used in the ancient war between Atlantis and Lemuria. As CAPT'N ELI assists COMMANDER X with his S.H.I.V.A. missions, LORD HYDRO targets CAPT'N ELI who is thrown into the center of the great conflict.

THE AQUARIANS are the blue-skinned refugees of lost Atlantis who survived the destruction of their continent by means of a serum that converts air breathers to amphibians. The serum was created by the Atlantean scientist, AQUARIA, and the new kingdom is named to honor her. For thousands of years, using super science, the highly advanced empire of Aquaria keeps itself secret from the surface world — until now.

THE SHARK RIDERS are the mystically transformed, fish-like descendants of the refugees of ancient Lemuria. They are a tribal race, named after their domestication of sharks used as mounts for their underwater cavalry. They are in possession of THE STARSOUL and are the savage rivals of THE AQUARIANS. Their domain lies in the Pacific Ocean and they keep their existence a secret to the surface world as well.

THE OUTCASTS are the nomadic, hybrid race of AQUARIANS and SHARK RIDERS. Green skinned and barbaric in appearance, they employ primitive weapons and a giant sea horse cavalry. For centuries, THE OUTCASTS have struggled to gain control of THE STARHEART and THE STARSOUL. They are motivated by an ancient prophecy that predicts their eventual success. CAPT'N ELI plays a key role in their existence and he is worshipped by THE OUTCASTS as a deity.

THE STORY CONTINUES...

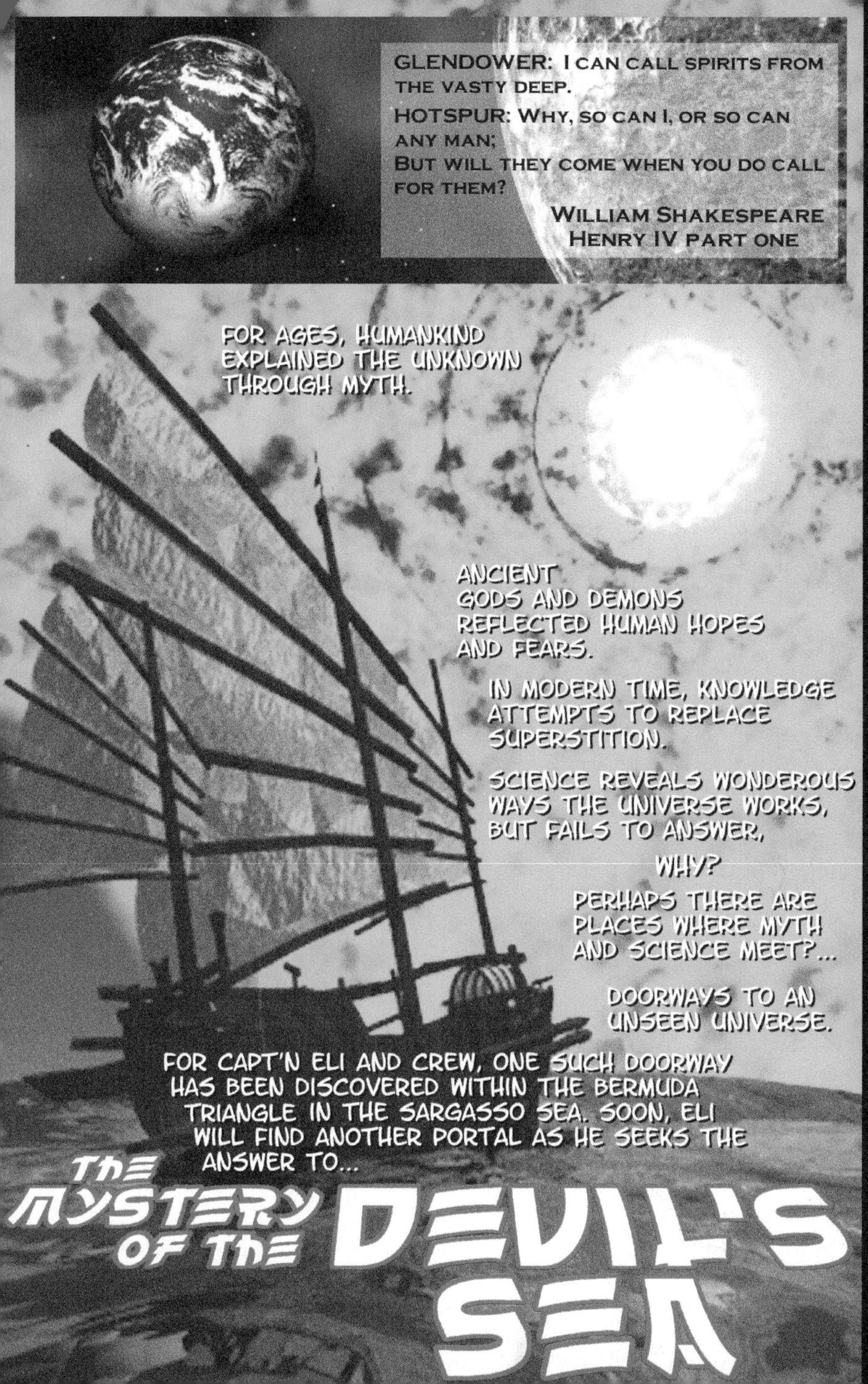
GLENDOWER: I can call spirits from the vasty deep.
HOTSPUR: Why, so can I, or so can any man;
But will they come when you do call for them?
William Shakespeare
Henry IV part one
FOR AGES, HUMANKIND EXPLAINED THE UNKNOWN THROUGH MYTH.
ANCIENT GODS AND DEMONS REFLECTED HUMAN HOPES AND FEARS.
IN MODERN TIME, KNOWLEDGE ATTEMPTS TO REPLACE SUPERSTITION.
SCIENCE REVEALS WONDEROUS WAYS THE UNIVERSE WORKS, BUT FAILS TO ANSWER,
WHY?
PERHAPS THERE ARE PLACES WHERE MYTH AND SCIENCE MEET?...
DOORWAYS TO AN UNSEEN UNIVERSE.
FOR CAPT'N ELI AND CREW, ONE SUCH DOORWAY HAS BEEN DISCOVERED WITHIN THE BERMUDA TRIANGLE IN THE SARGASSO SEA. SOON, ELI WILL FIND ANOTHER PORTAL AS HE SEEKS THE ANSWER TO...
THE MYSTERY OF THE DEVIL'S SEA

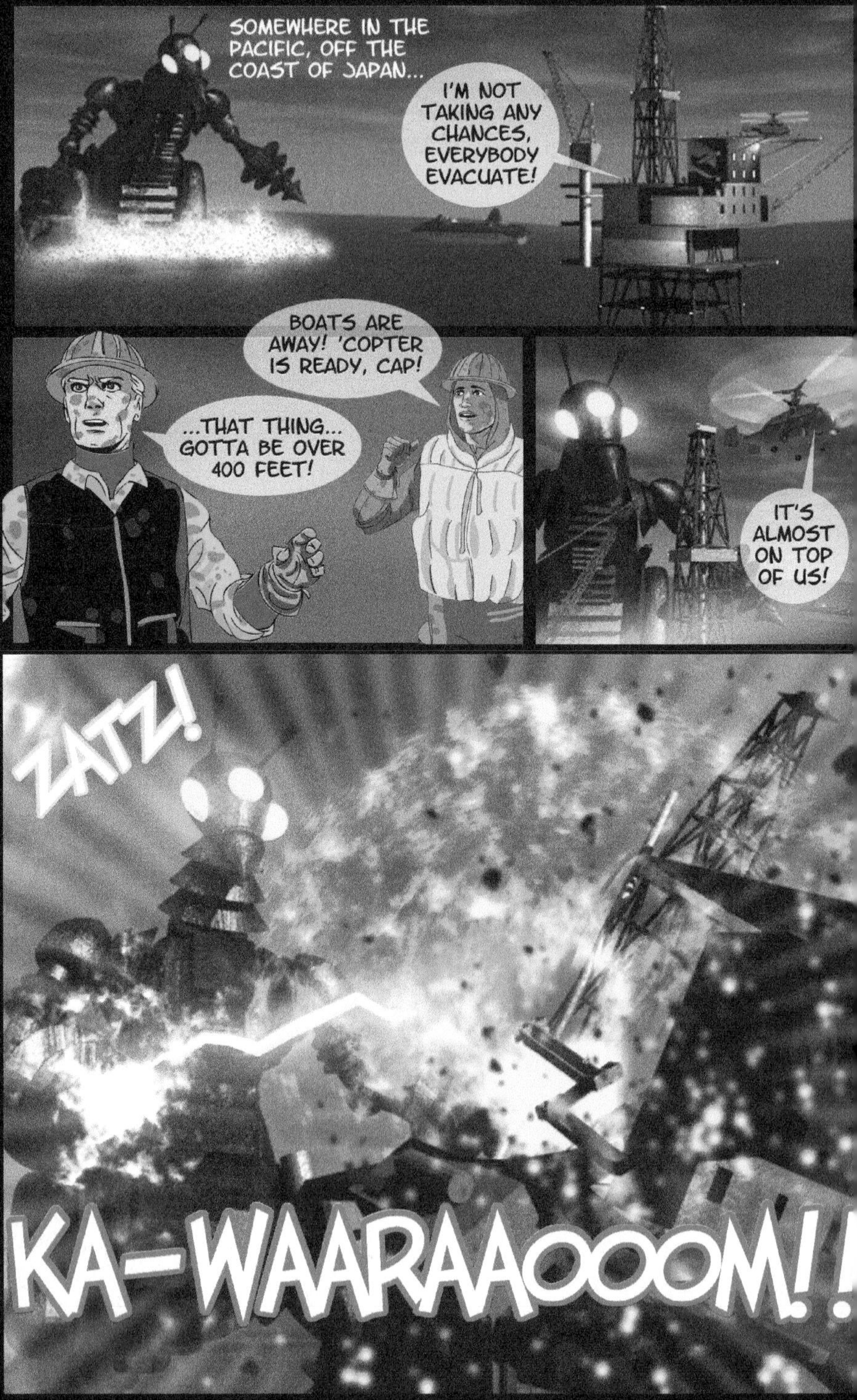
SOMEWHERE IN THE PACIFIC, OFF THE COAST OF JAPAN...
I'M NOT TAKING ANY CHANCES, EVERYBODY EVACUATE!
BOATS ARE AWAY! 'COPTER IS READY, CAP!
...THAT THING... GOTTA BE OVER 400 FEET!
IT'S ALMOST ON TOP OF US!
ZATZ!
KA-WAARAAOOOM!!

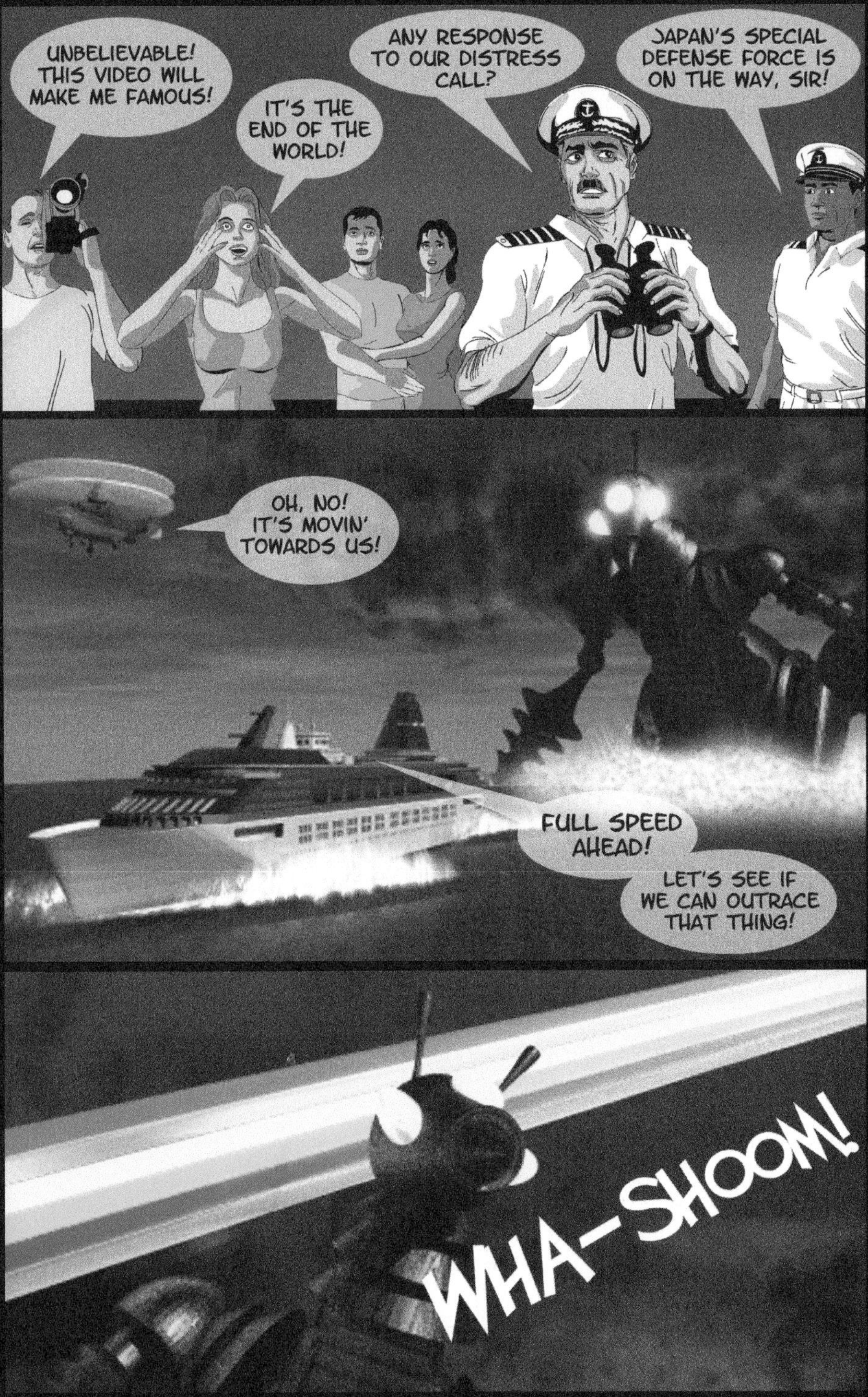
UNBELIEVABLE! THIS VIDEO WILL MAKE ME FAMOUS!
IT'S THE END OF THE WORLD!
ANY RESPONSE TO OUR DISTRESS CALL?
JAPAN'S SPECIAL DEFENSE FORCE IS ON THE WAY, SIR!
OH, NO! IT'S MOVIN' TOWARDS US!
FULL SPEED AHEAD!
LET'S SEE IF WE CAN OUTRACE THAT THING!
WHA-SHOOM!

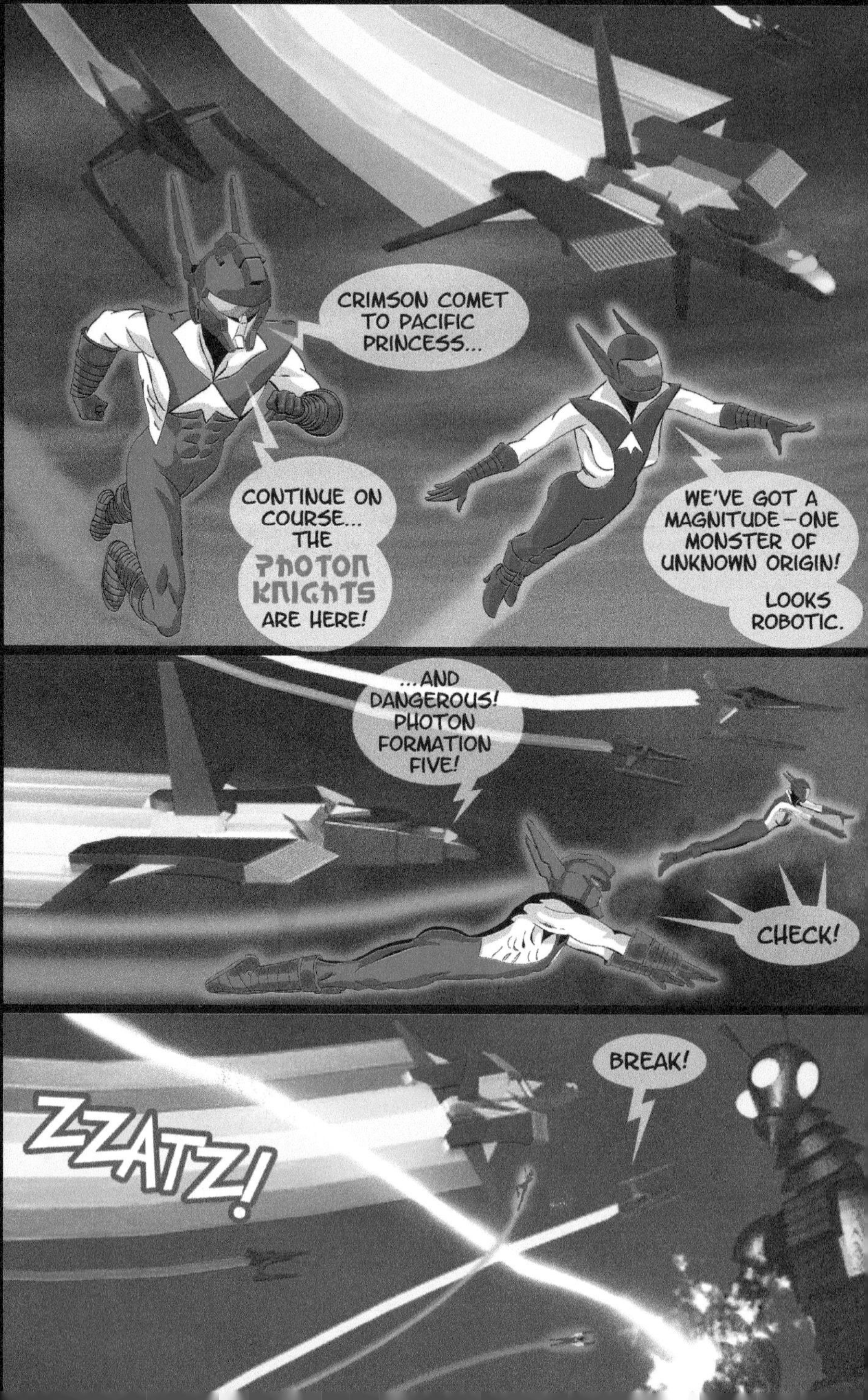
CRIMSON COMET TO PACIFIC PRINCESS...
CONTINUE ON COURSE... THE PHOTON KNIGHTS ARE HERE!
WE'VE GOT A MAGNITUDE-ONE MONSTER OF UNKNOWN ORIGIN!
LOOKS ROBOTIC.
...AND DANGEROUS! PHOTON FORMATION FIVE!
CHECK!
ZZATZ!
BREAK!

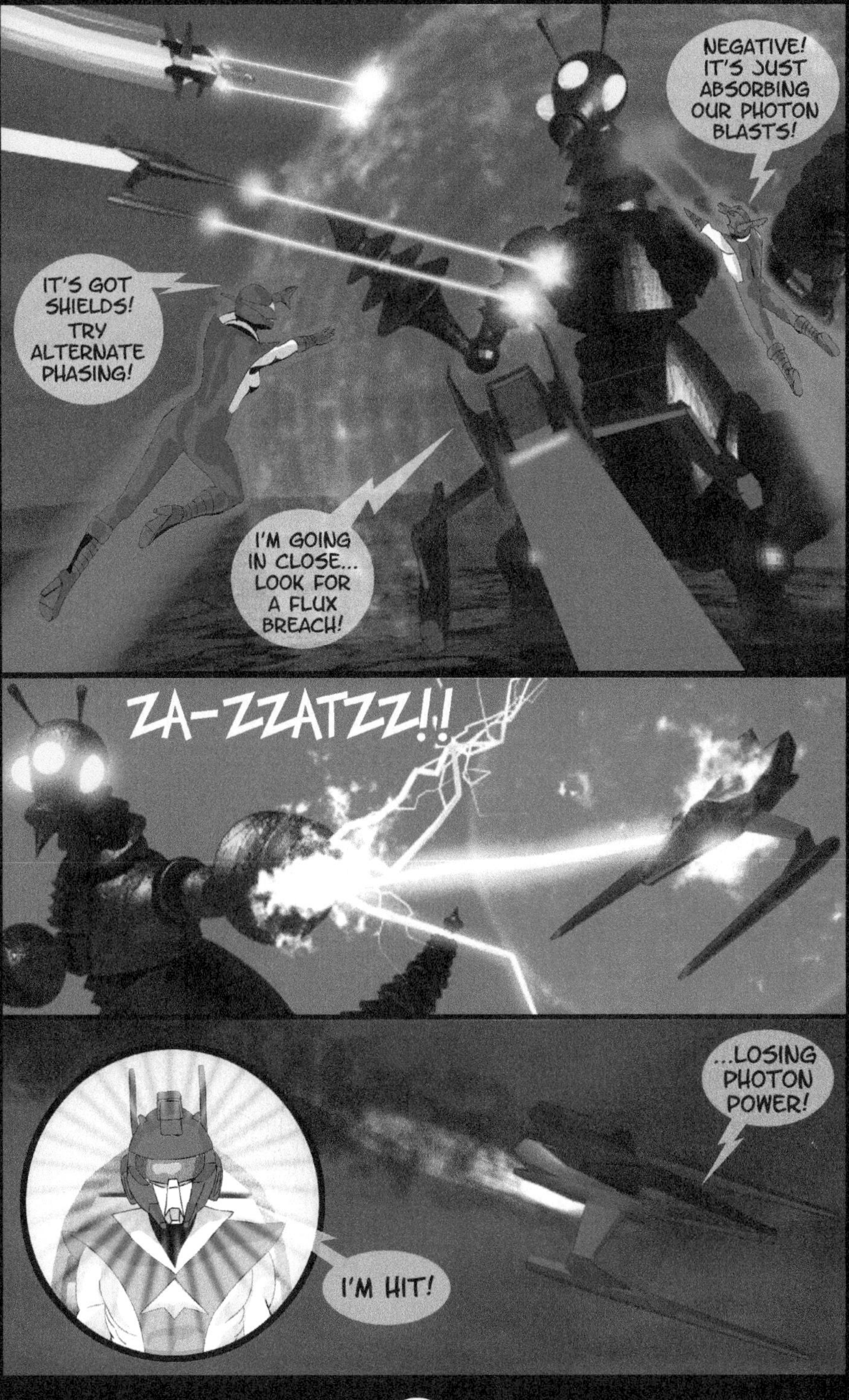
NEGATIVE! IT'S JUST ABSORBING OUR PHOTON BLASTS!
IT'S GOT SHIELDS! TRY ALTERNATE PHASING!
I'M GOING IN CLOSE... LOOK FOR A FLUX BREACH!
ZA-ZZATZZZ!!
...LOSING PHOTON POWER!
I'M HIT!

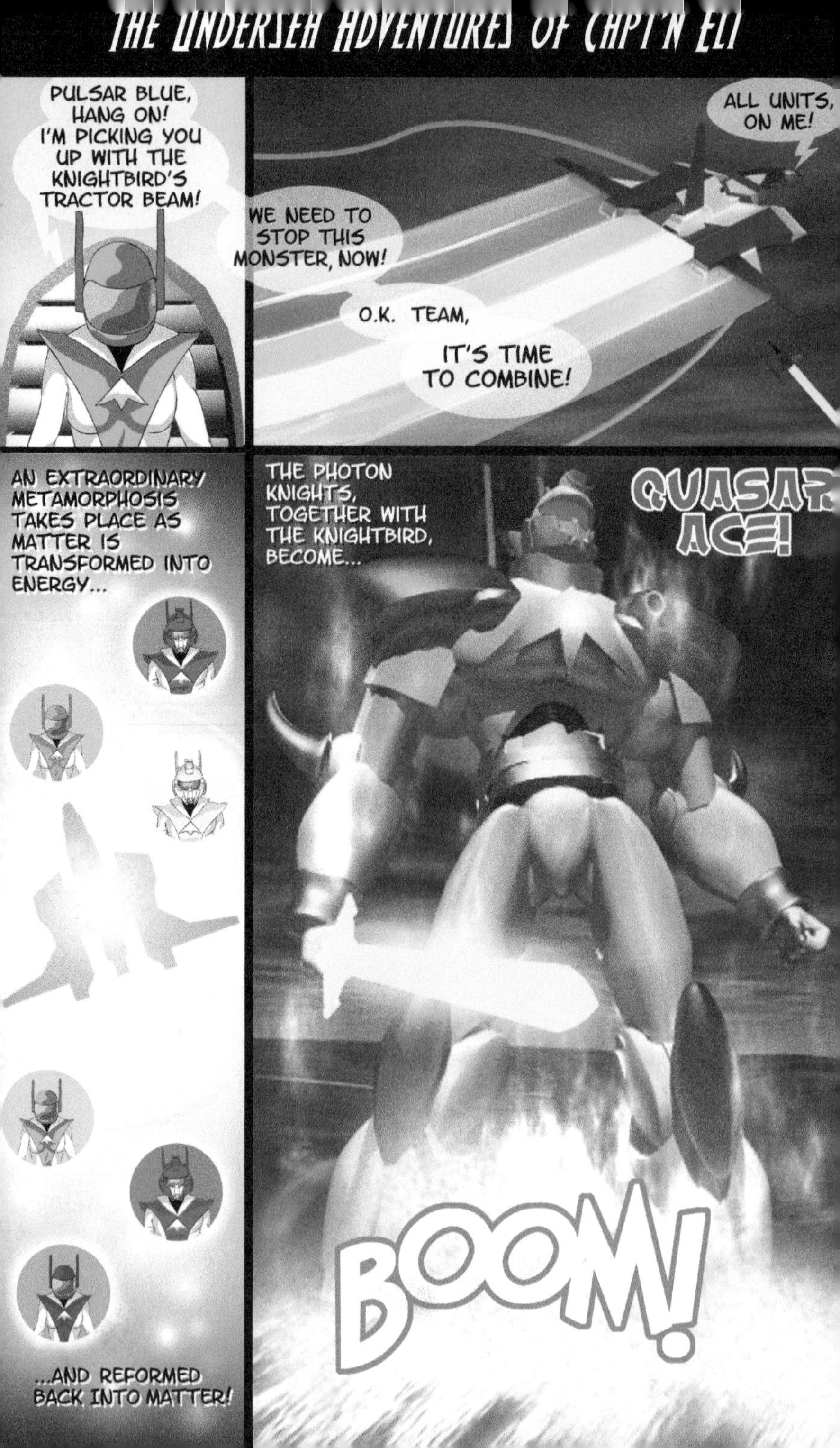
THE UNDERSEA ADVENTURES OF CAPT'N ELI
PULSAR BLUE, HANG ON! I'M PICKING YOU UP WITH THE KNIGHTBIRD'S TRACTOR BEAM!
WE NEED TO STOP THIS MONSTER, NOW!
ALL UNITS, ON ME!
O.K. TEAM,
IT'S TIME TO COMBINE!
AN EXTRAORDINARY METAMORPHOSIS TAKES PLACE AS MATTER IS TRANSFORMED INTO ENERGY...
...AND REFORMED BACK INTO MATTER!
THE PHOTON KNIGHTS, TOGETHER WITH THE KNIGHTBIRD, BECOME...
QUASAR ACE!
BOOM!

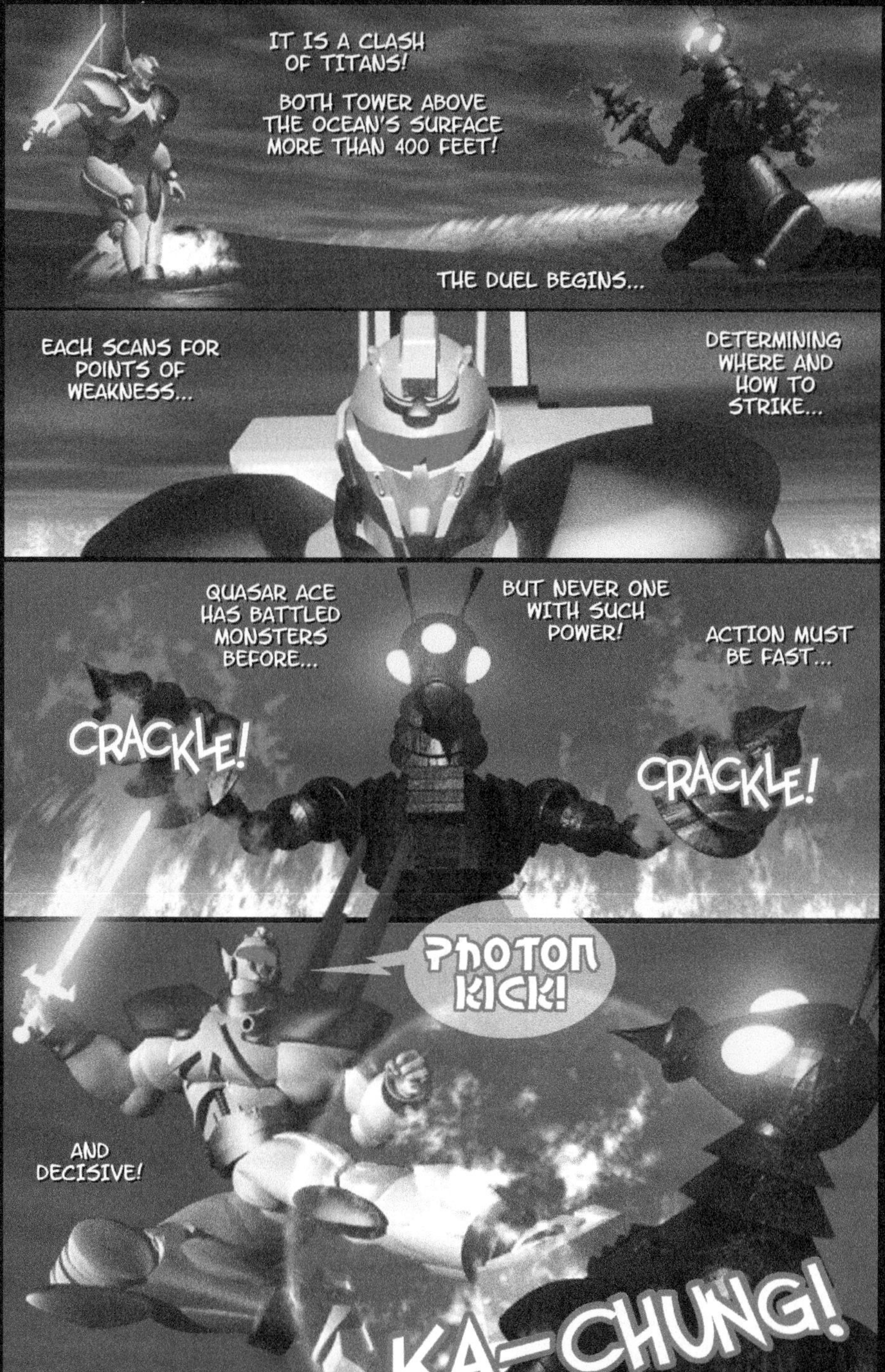
IT IS A CLASH OF TITANS!
BOTH TOWER ABOVE THE OCEAN'S SURFACE MORE THAN 400 FEET!
THE DUEL BEGINS...
EACH SCANS FOR POINTS OF WEAKNESS...
DETERMINING WHERE AND HOW TO STRIKE...
QUASAR ACE HAS BATTLED MONSTERS BEFORE...
BUT NEVER ONE WITH SUCH POWER!
ACTION MUST BE FAST...
CRACKLE!
CRACKLE!
PHOTON KICK!
AND DECISIVE!
KA-CHUNG!

THE MONSTER REELS FROM QUASAR ACE'S ATTACK.

IS IT DAMAGED?

—OR IN RETREAT?

SPLOOSH!

IT CAN'T BE THAT EASY!

QUASAR ACE SCANS BELOW THE WAVES FOR THE ROBOT.

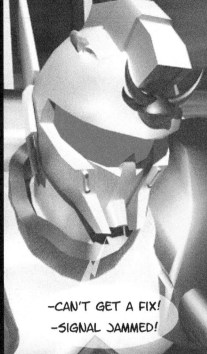

CHOOM!

—CAN'T GET A FIX!

—SIGNAL JAMMED!

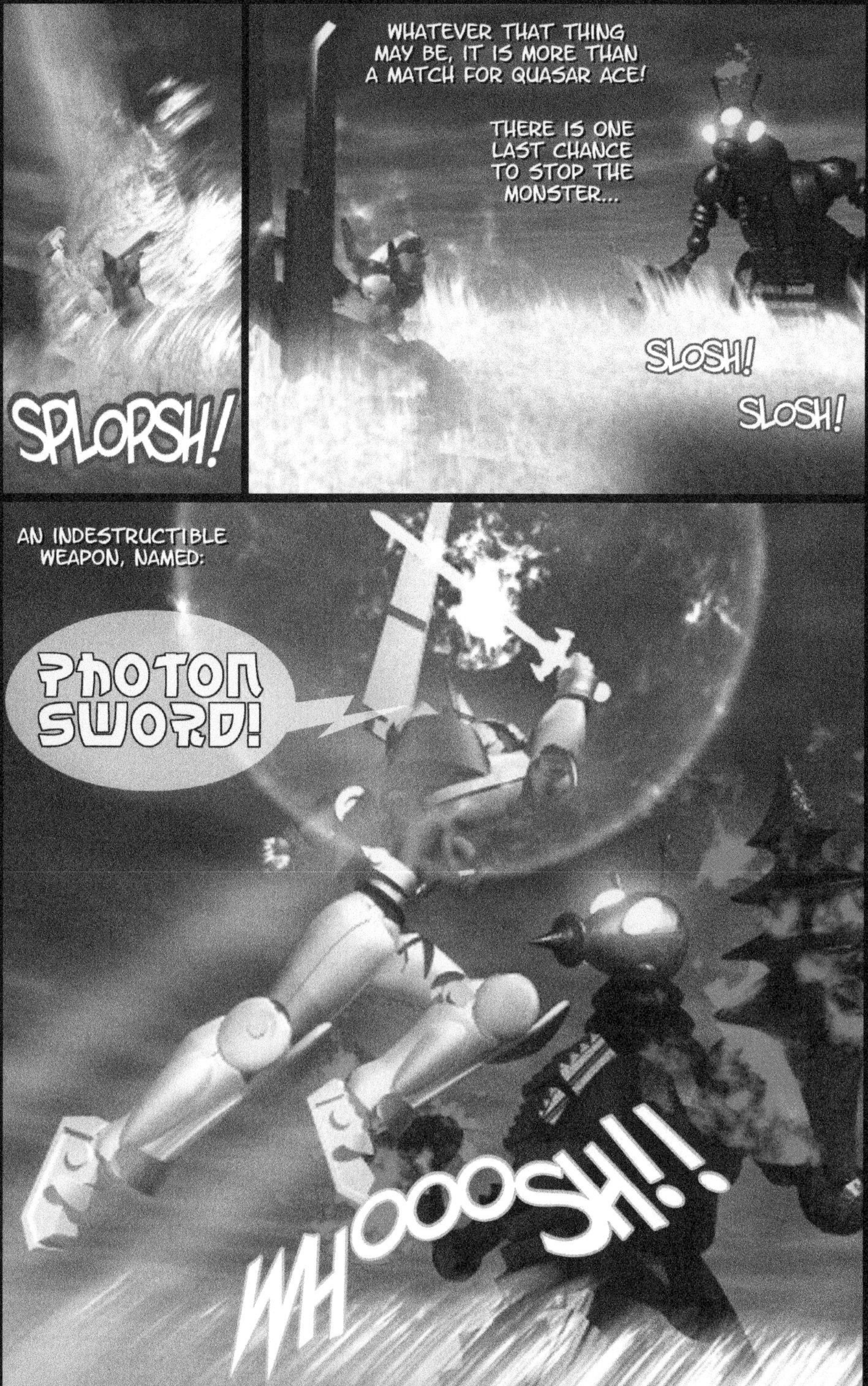
SPLORSH!
WHATEVER THAT THING MAY BE, IT IS MORE THAN A MATCH FOR QUASAR ACE!
THERE IS ONE LAST CHANCE TO STOP THE MONSTER...
SLOSH!
SLOSH!
AN INDESTRUCTIBLE WEAPON, NAMED:
PHOTON SWORD!
WHOOOSH!!!

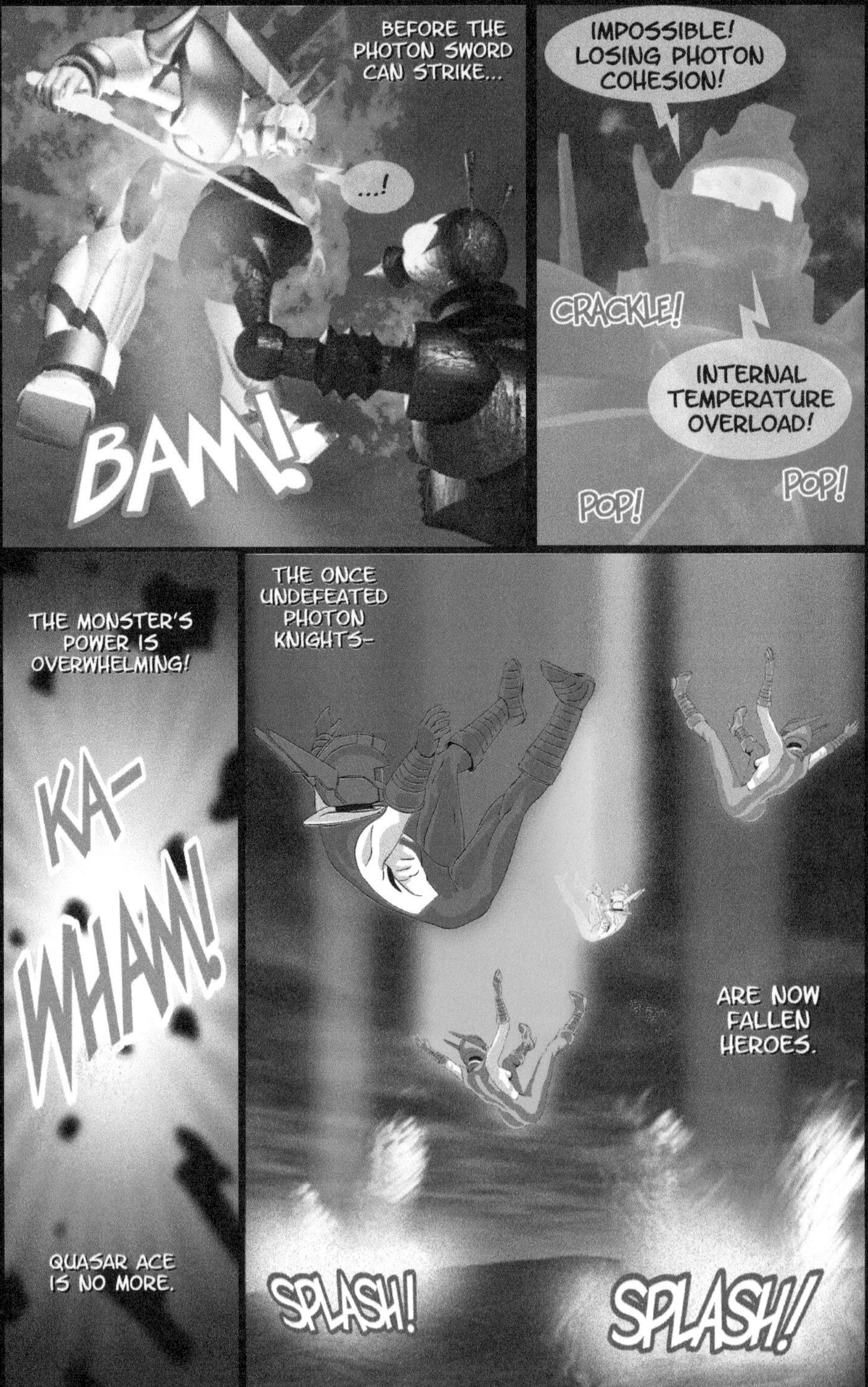
BEFORE THE PHOTON SWORD CAN STRIKE...
...!
BAM!
IMPOSSIBLE! LOSING PHOTON COHESION!
CRACKLE!
INTERNAL TEMPERATURE OVERLOAD!
POP!
POP!
THE MONSTER'S POWER IS OVERWHELMING!
KA-WHAM!
QUASAR ACE IS NO MORE.
THE ONCE UNDEFEATED PHOTON KNIGHTS-
ARE NOW FALLEN HEROES.
SPLASH!
SPLASH!

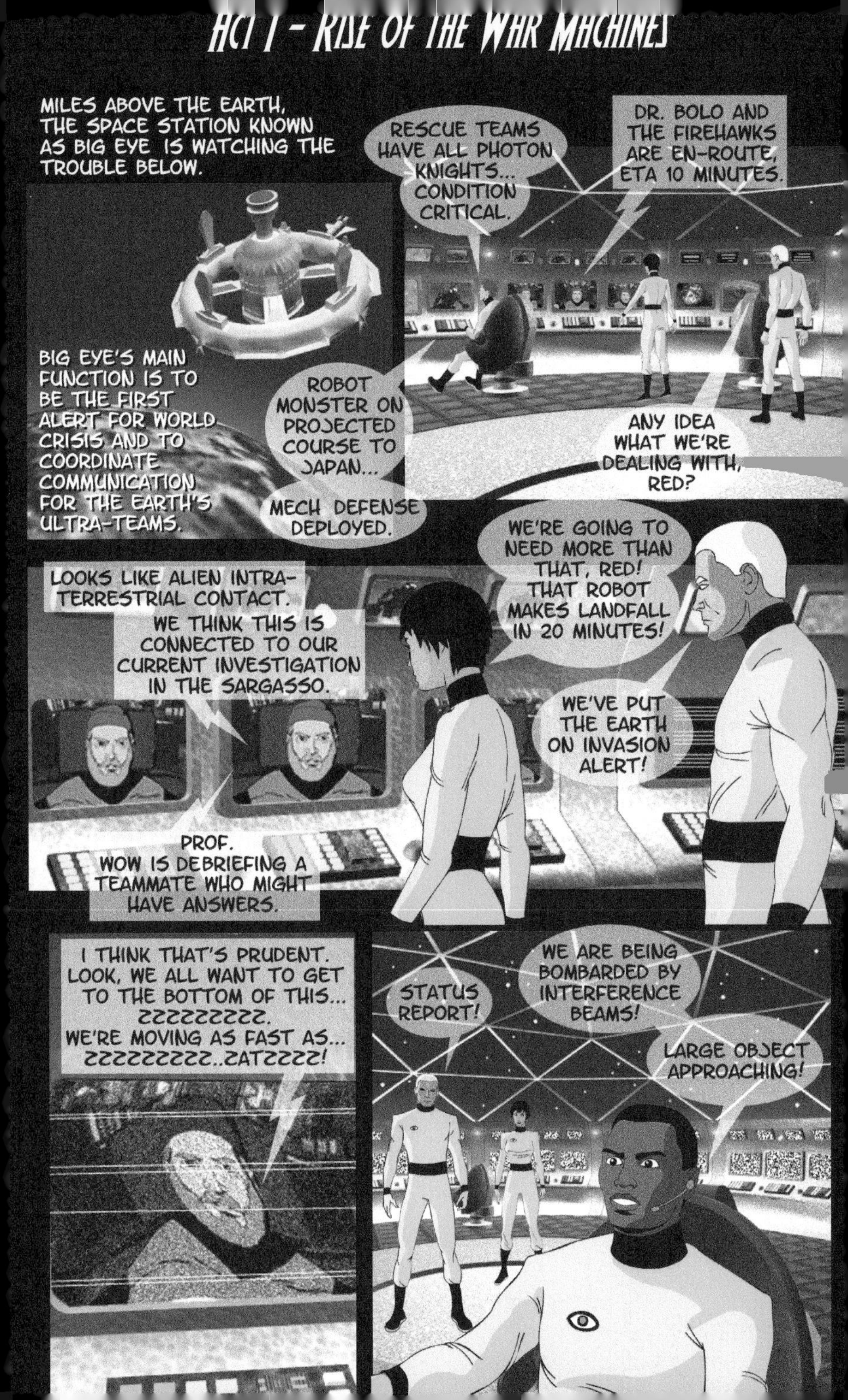
ACT 1 - RISE OF THE WAR MACHINES
MILES ABOVE THE EARTH, THE SPACE STATION KNOWN AS BIG EYE IS WATCHING THE TROUBLE BELOW.
BIG EYE'S MAIN FUNCTION IS TO BE THE FIRST ALERT FOR WORLD CRISIS AND TO COORDINATE COMMUNICATION FOR THE EARTH'S ULTRA-TEAMS.
RESCUE TEAMS HAVE ALL PHOTON KNIGHTS... CONDITION CRITICAL.
DR. BOLO AND THE FIREHAWKS ARE EN-ROUTE, ETA 10 MINUTES.
ROBOT MONSTER ON PROJECTED COURSE TO JAPAN...
MECH DEFENSE DEPLOYED.
ANY IDEA WHAT WE'RE DEALING WITH, RED?
LOOKS LIKE ALIEN INTRA-TERRESTRIAL CONTACT.
WE THINK THIS IS CONNECTED TO OUR CURRENT INVESTIGATION IN THE SARGASSO.
WE'RE GOING TO NEED MORE THAN THAT, RED! THAT ROBOT MAKES LANDFALL IN 20 MINUTES!
WE'VE PUT THE EARTH ON INVASION ALERT!
PROF. WOW IS DEBRIEFING A TEAMMATE WHO MIGHT HAVE ANSWERS.
I THINK THAT'S PRUDENT. LOOK, WE ALL WANT TO GET TO THE BOTTOM OF THIS... ZZZZZZZZZ. WE'RE MOVING AS FAST AS... ZZZZZZZZZ..ZATZZZZ!
STATUS REPORT!
WE ARE BEING BOMBARDED BY INTERFERENCE BEAMS!
LARGE OBJECT APPROACHING!

THE UNDERSEA ADVENTURES OF CAPT'N ELI

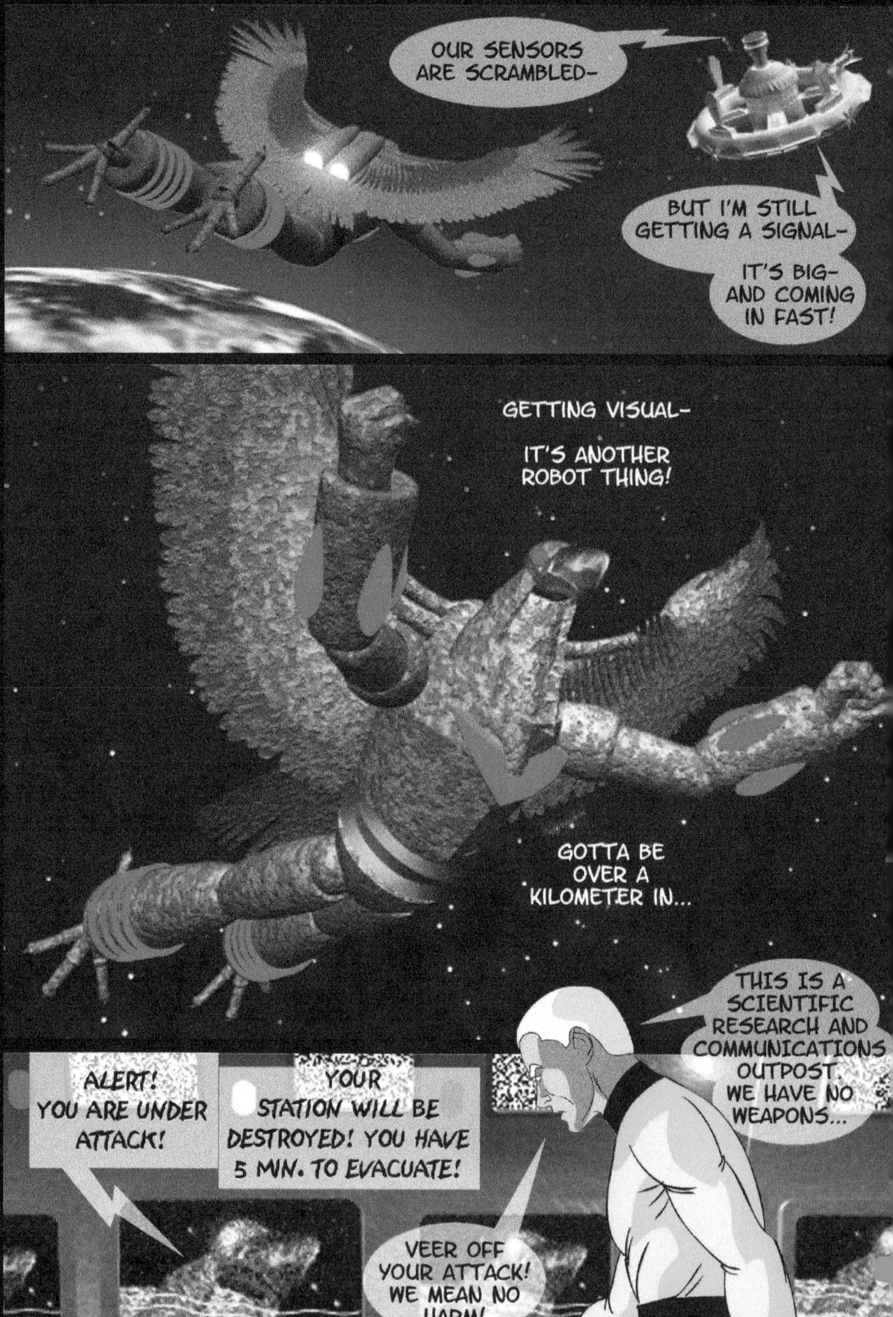

OUR SENSORS ARE SCRAMBLED-
BUT I'M STILL GETTING A SIGNAL-
IT'S BIG- AND COMING IN FAST!
GETTING VISUAL-
IT'S ANOTHER ROBOT THING!
GOTTA BE OVER A KILOMETER IN...
ALERT! YOU ARE UNDER ATTACK!
YOUR STATION WILL BE DESTROYED! YOU HAVE 5 MIN. TO EVACUATE!
THIS IS A SCIENTIFIC RESEARCH AND COMMUNICATIONS OUTPOST. WE HAVE NO WEAPONS...
VEER OFF YOUR ATTACK! WE MEAN NO HARM!

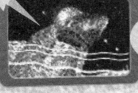

Act I - Rise of the War Machines

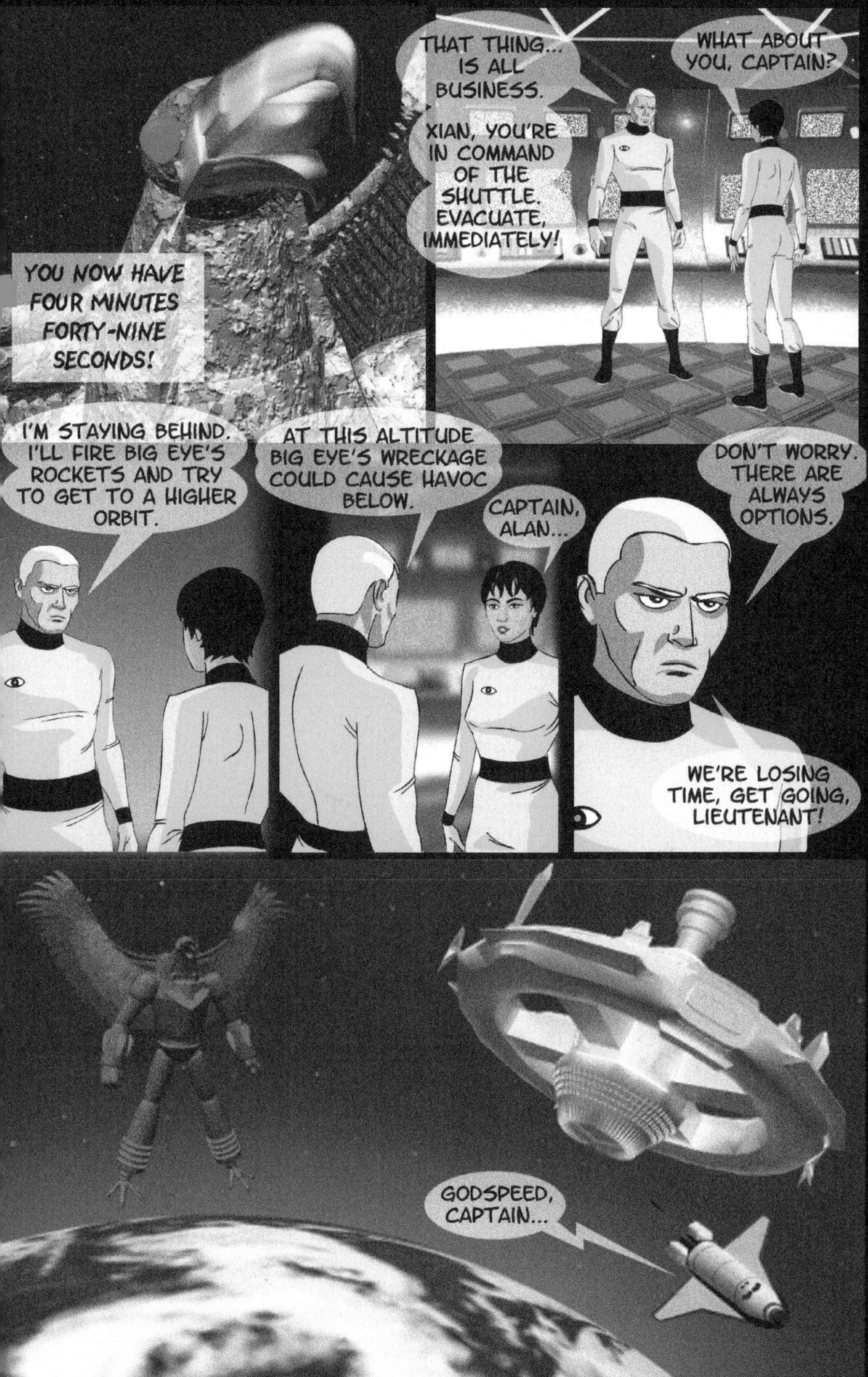

YOU NOW HAVE FOUR MINUTES FORTY-NINE SECONDS!
THAT THING... IS ALL BUSINESS.
XIAN, YOU'RE IN COMMAND OF THE SHUTTLE. EVACUATE, IMMEDIATELY!
WHAT ABOUT YOU, CAPTAIN?
I'M STAYING BEHIND. I'LL FIRE BIG EYE'S ROCKETS AND TRY TO GET TO A HIGHER ORBIT.
AT THIS ALTITUDE BIG EYE'S WRECKAGE COULD CAUSE HAVOC BELOW.
CAPTAIN, ALAN...
DON'T WORRY. THERE ARE ALWAYS OPTIONS.
WE'RE LOSING TIME, GET GOING, LIEUTENANT!
GODSPEED, CAPTAIN...

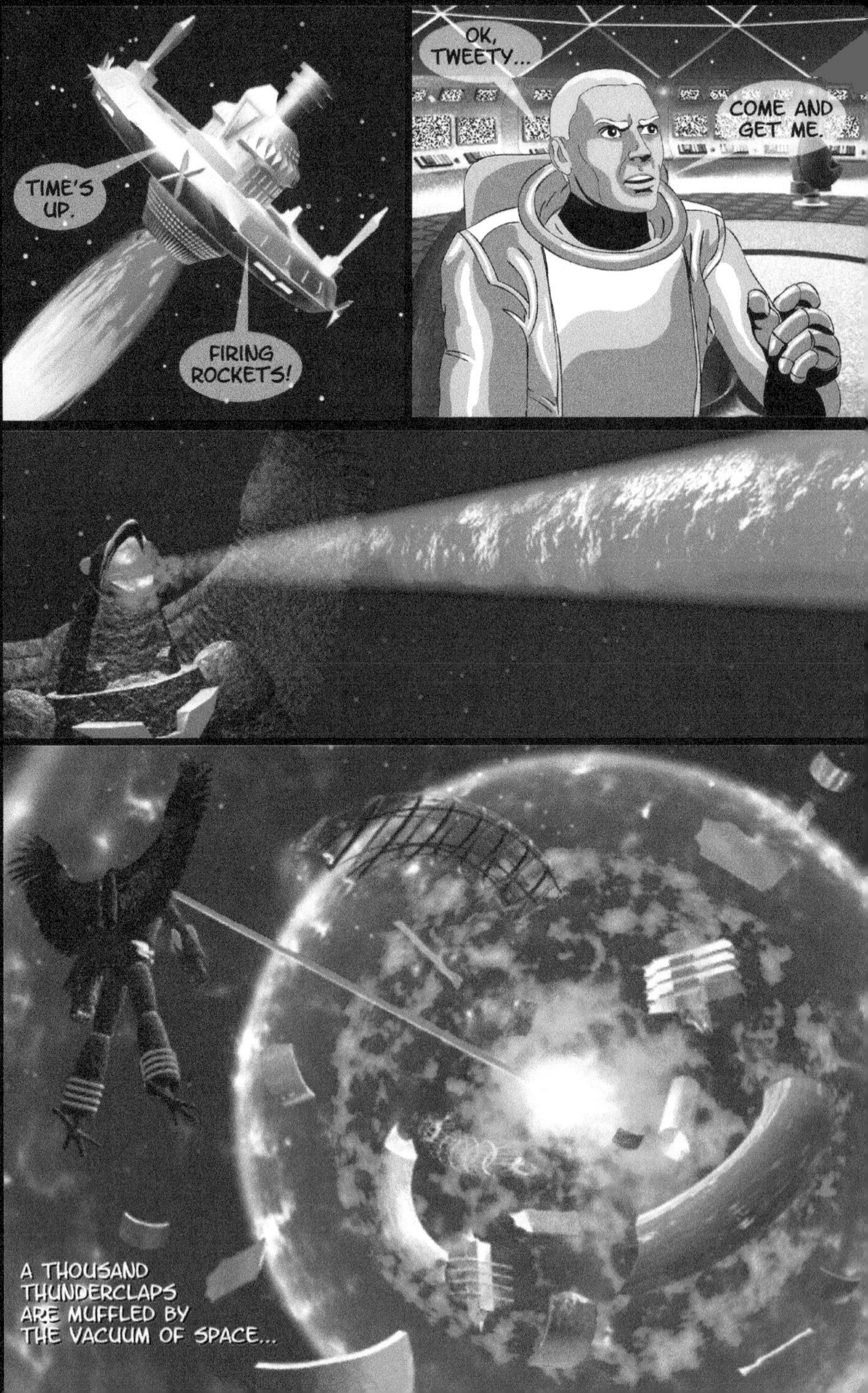
TIME'S UP.
FIRING ROCKETS!
OK, TWEETY...
COME AND GET ME.
A THOUSAND THUNDERCLAPS ARE MUFFLED BY THE VACUUM OF SPACE...

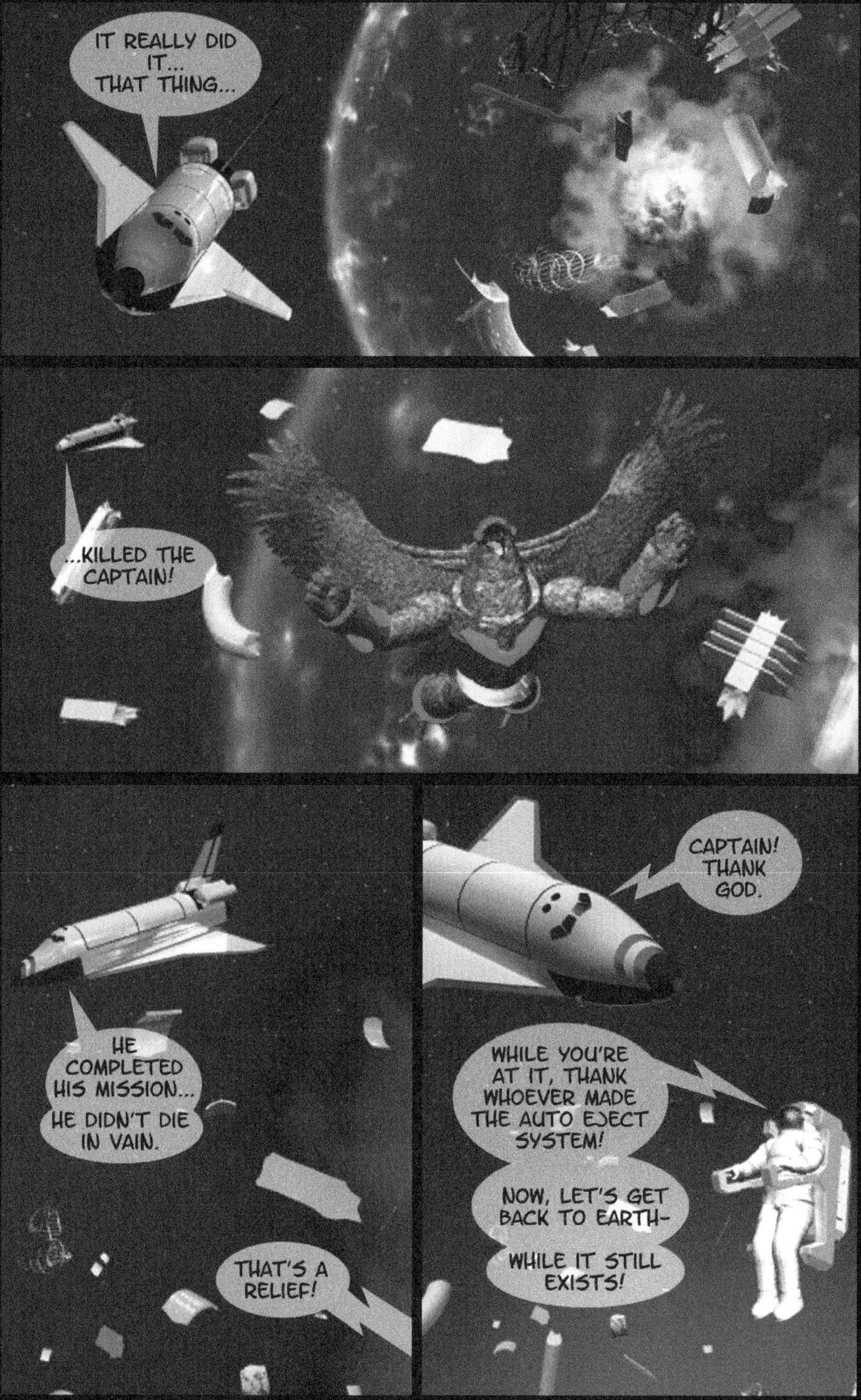
IT REALLY DID IT... THAT THING...
...KILLED THE CAPTAIN!
HE COMPLETED HIS MISSION...
HE DIDN'T DIE IN VAIN.
THAT'S A RELIEF!
CAPTAIN! THANK GOD.
WHILE YOU'RE AT IT, THANK WHOEVER MADE THE AUTO EJECT SYSTEM!
NOW, LET'S GET BACK TO EARTH-
WHILE IT STILL EXISTS!

NEWS OF THE DESTRUCTION TRAVELS QUICKLY.

AT THIS HOUR, WE APPEAR TO BE UNDER ATTACK...

MARTIAL LAW HAS BEEN DECLARED IN 10 COUNTRIES...

STAY IN YOUR HOMES. DEFENSE FORCES HAVE BEEN DEPLOYED...

I UNDERSTAND, SIR...

WE'VE RUN OUT OF TIME, RED. I NEED ANSWERS NOW!

GET ME PROF. WOW, IMMEDIA---

ZZZZZZZZ!

ZATZ!

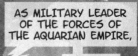

GREETINGS TO ALL SURFACE DWELLERS!

I REGRET WE MEET UNDER SUCH CIRCUMSTANCES...

I AM LORD HYDRO, LORD PROTECTOR OF AQUARIA.

AS MILITARY LEADER OF THE FORCES OF THE AQUARIAN EMPIRE,

HEED MY WORDS!

THIS IS A WARNING!

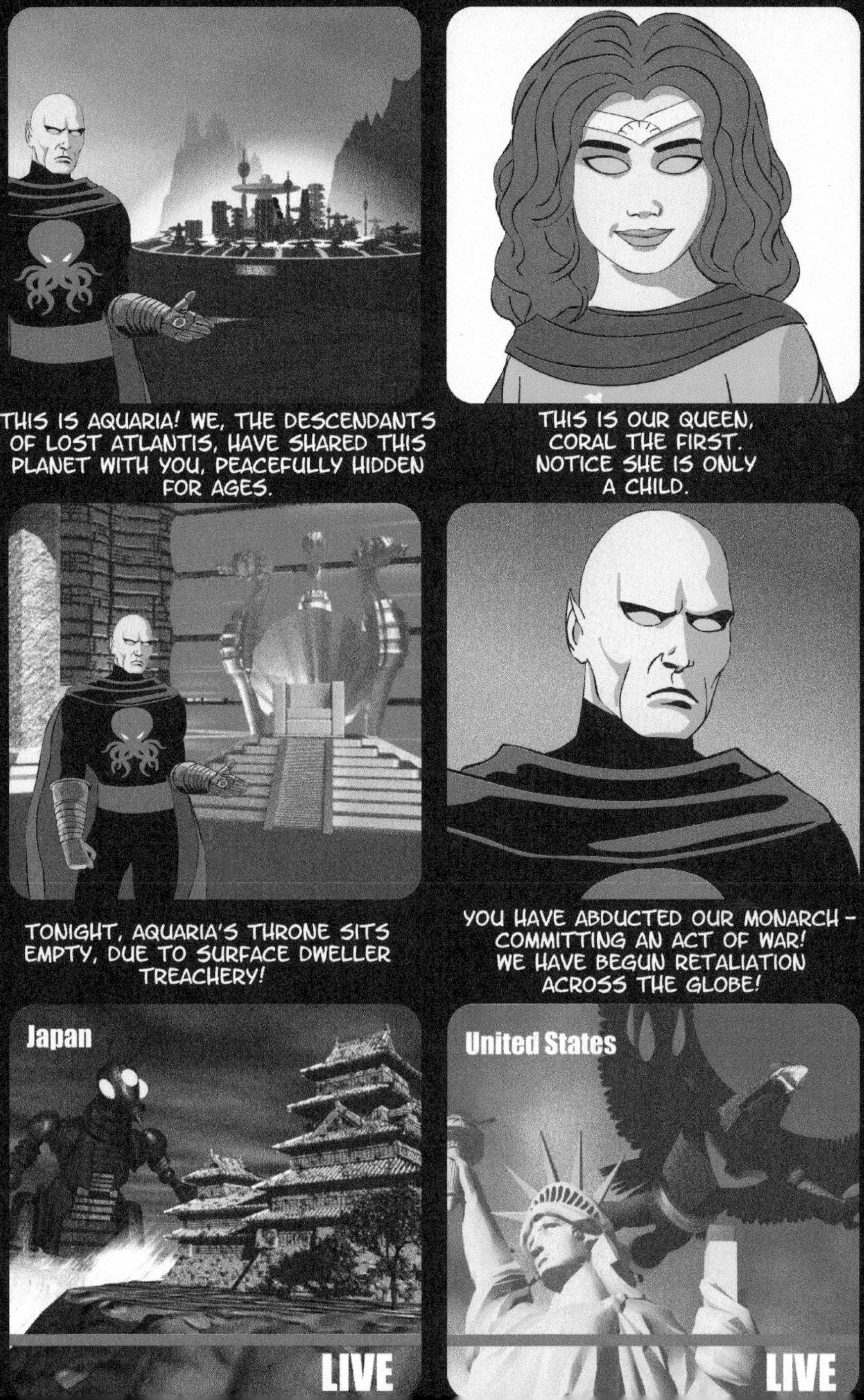
THIS IS AQUARIA! WE, THE DESCENDANTS OF LOST ATLANTIS, HAVE SHARED THIS PLANET WITH YOU, PEACEFULLY HIDDEN FOR AGES.
THIS IS OUR QUEEN, CORAL THE FIRST. NOTICE SHE IS ONLY A CHILD.
TONIGHT, AQUARIA'S THRONE SITS EMPTY, DUE TO SURFACE DWELLER TREACHERY!
YOU HAVE ABDUCTED OUR MONARCH - COMMITTING AN ACT OF WAR! WE HAVE BEGUN RETALIATION ACROSS THE GLOBE!
Japan
LIVE
United States
LIVE

THE UNDERSEA ADVENTURES OF CAPT'N ELI

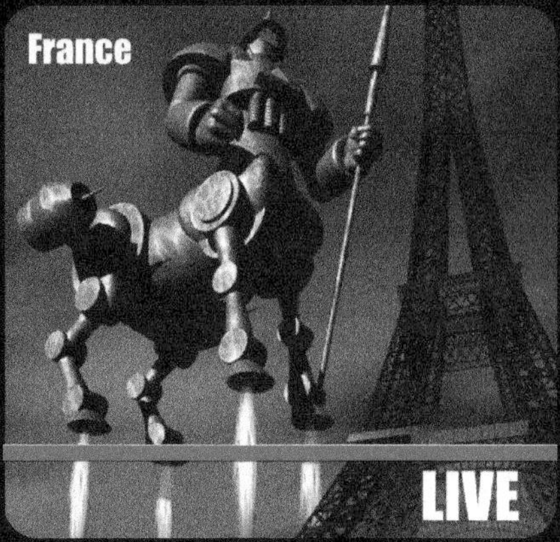
France
LIVE

YOU HAVE SEEN WHAT OUR WAR MACHINES CAN DO, IN THE SEA OF JAPAN AND IN SPACE.

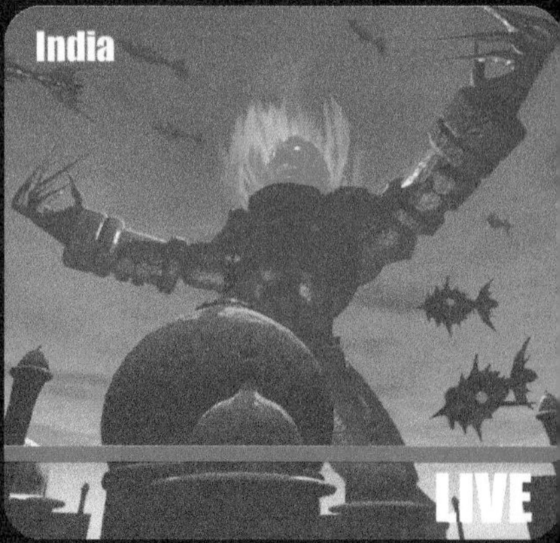
India
LIVE

THEY WERE BUILT TO INFLICT TOTAL DEVASTATION.

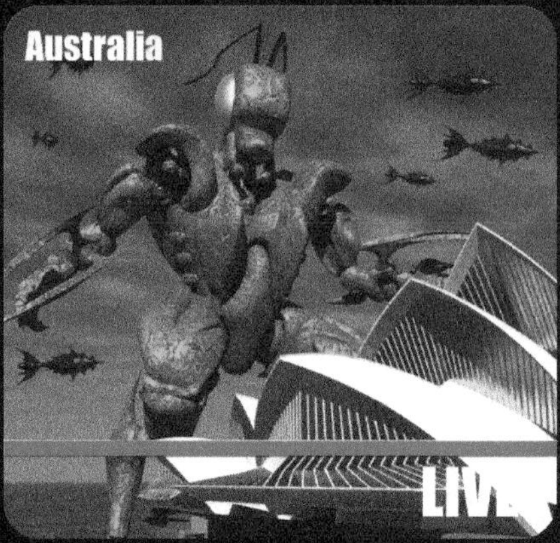
Australia
LIVE

THE WAR MACHINES WILL DECIMATE YOUR SURFACE WORLD...

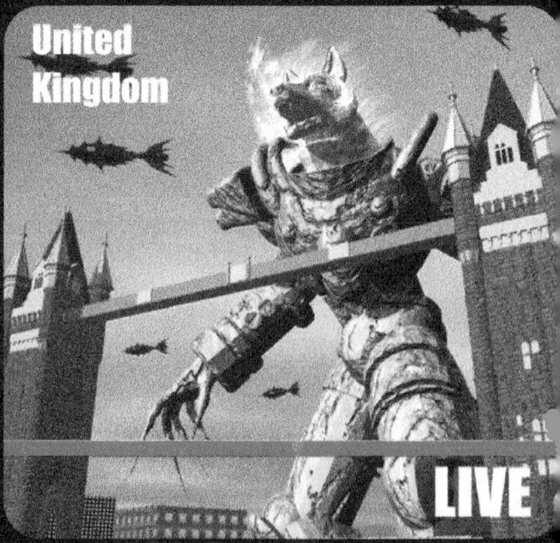
United Kingdom
LIVE

UNLESS...QUEEN CORAL IS SAFELY RETURNED TO HER HOMELAND!

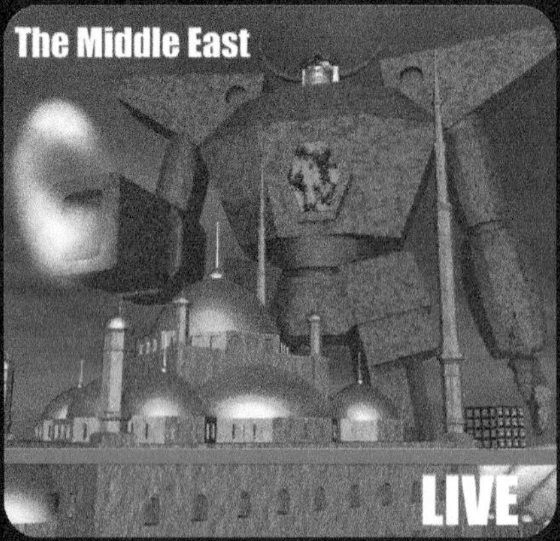
The Middle East
LIVE

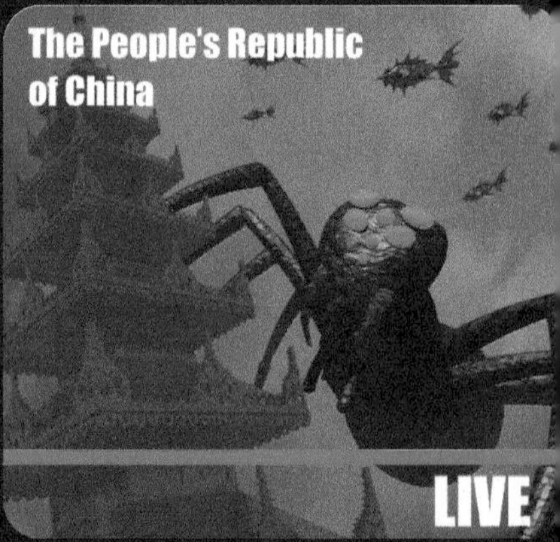
The People's Republic of China
LIVE

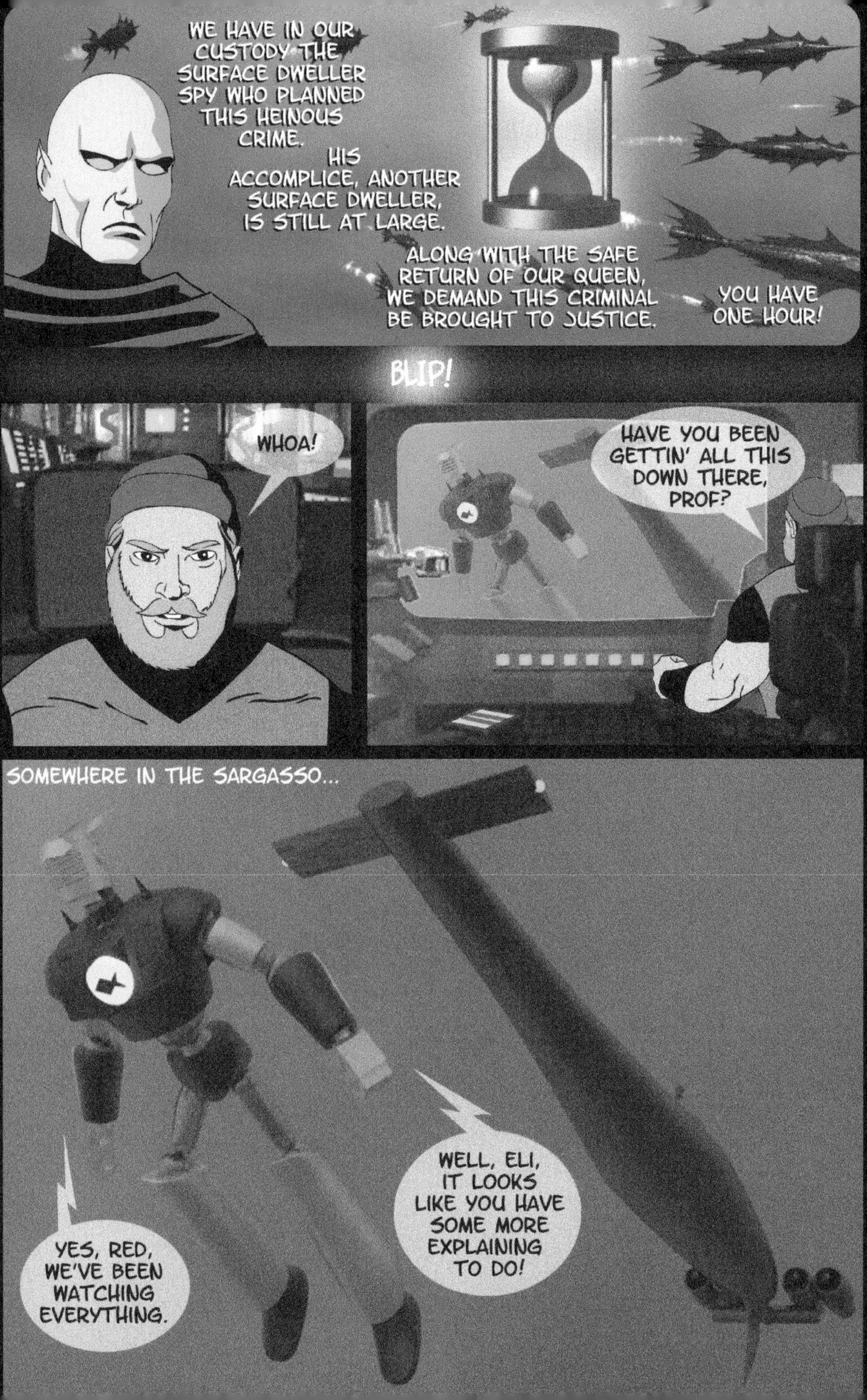
WE HAVE IN OUR CUSTODY THE SURFACE DWELLER SPY WHO PLANNED THIS HEINOUS CRIME.
HIS ACCOMPLICE, ANOTHER SURFACE DWELLER, IS STILL AT LARGE.
ALONG WITH THE SAFE RETURN OF OUR QUEEN, WE DEMAND THIS CRIMINAL BE BROUGHT TO JUSTICE.
YOU HAVE ONE HOUR!
BLIP!
WHOA!
HAVE YOU BEEN GETTIN' ALL THIS DOWN THERE, PROF?
SOMEWHERE IN THE SARGASSO...
WELL, ELI, IT LOOKS LIKE YOU HAVE SOME MORE EXPLAINING TO DO!
YES, RED, WE'VE BEEN WATCHING EVERYTHING.

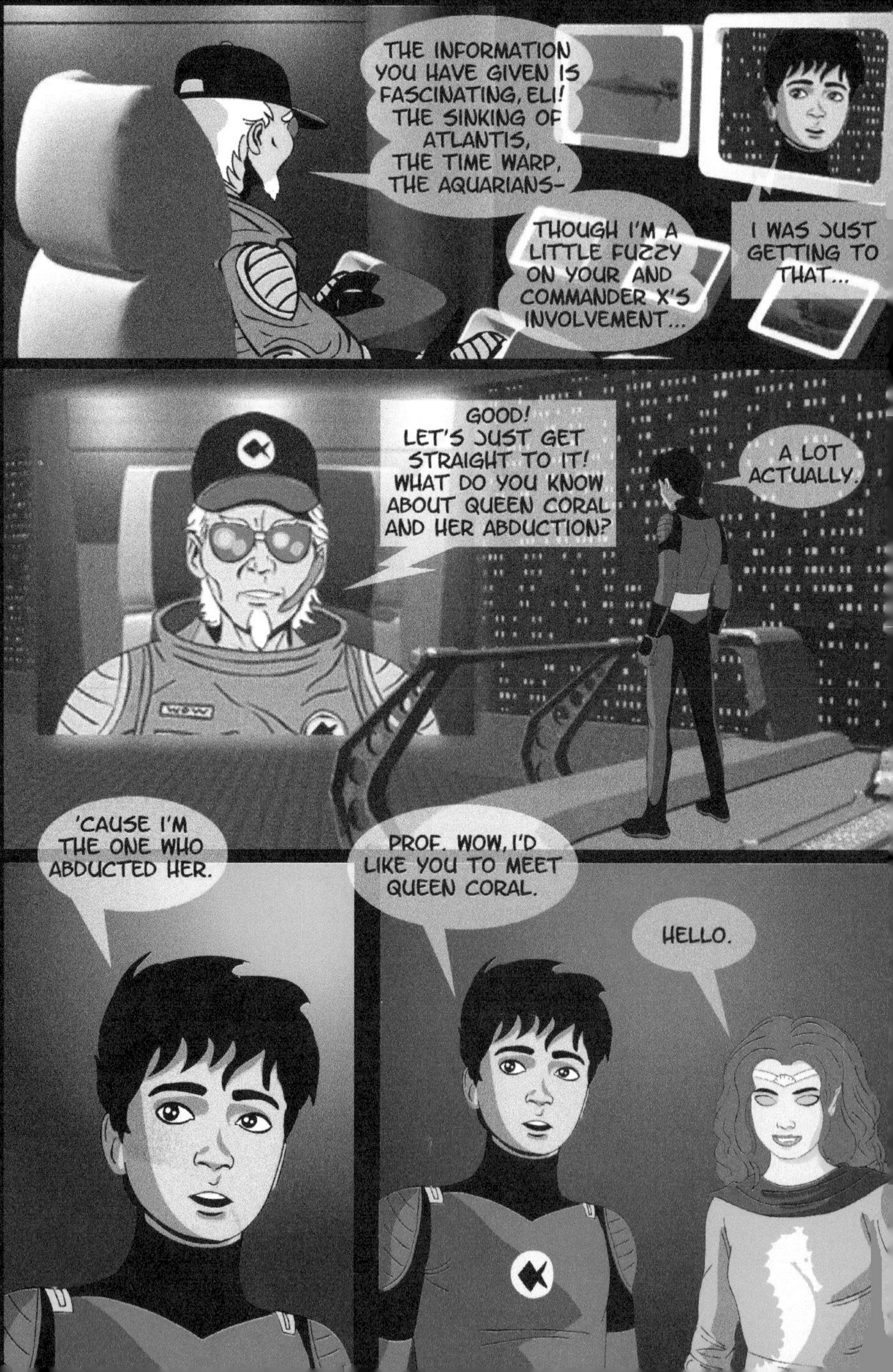
THE INFORMATION YOU HAVE GIVEN IS FASCINATING, ELI! THE SINKING OF ATLANTIS, THE TIME WARP, THE AQUARIANS-
THOUGH I'M A LITTLE FUZZY ON YOUR AND COMMANDER X'S INVOLVEMENT...
I WAS JUST GETTING TO THAT...
GOOD! LET'S JUST GET STRAIGHT TO IT! WHAT DO YOU KNOW ABOUT QUEEN CORAL AND HER ABDUCTION?
A LOT ACTUALLY.
'CAUSE I'M THE ONE WHO ABDUCTED HER.
PROF. WOW, I'D LIKE YOU TO MEET QUEEN CORAL.
HELLO.

ACT 2

CLASH OF HEROES

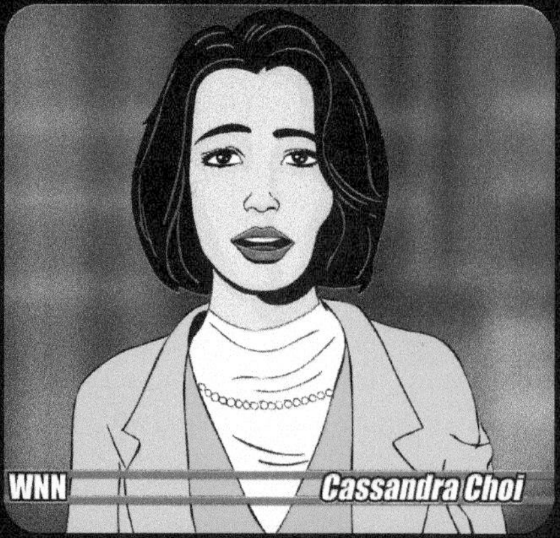
WNN
Cassandra Choi

... WE CONTINUE OUR COVERAGE OF THIS WORLD CRISIS, IT IS T-MINUS 39 MINUTES 'TIL THE AQUARIAN DEADLINE.

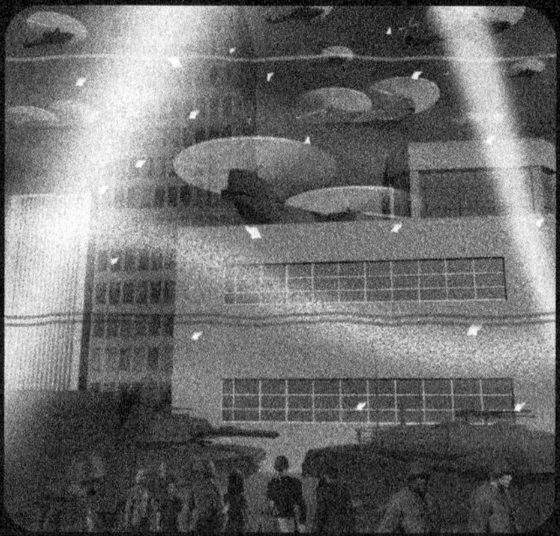

ALL EARTH IS A POTENTIAL BATTLEFIELD. CITIES AND CAPITALS IN OVER 10 COUNTRIES ARE EVACUATING, WHILE EMERGENCY FORCES MOVE IN.

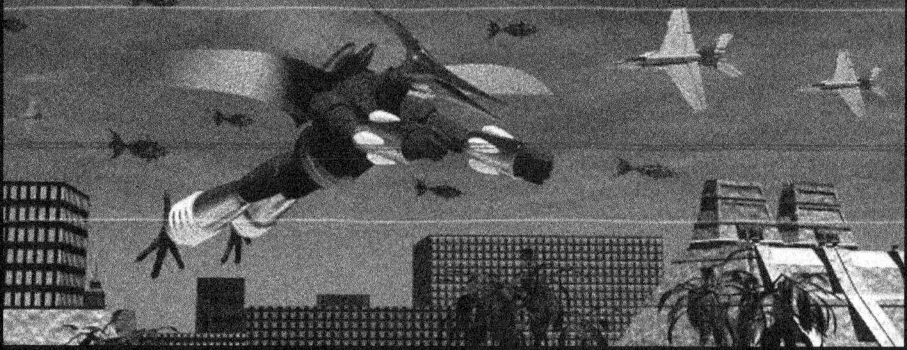

AS GLOBAL DEFENSE FORCES CONTINUE TO DEPLOY, SO DO THE AQUARIAN WAR MACHINES. THE SKIES OF MEXICO CITY NOW ARE FILLED WITH THE AQUARIAN INVADERS.

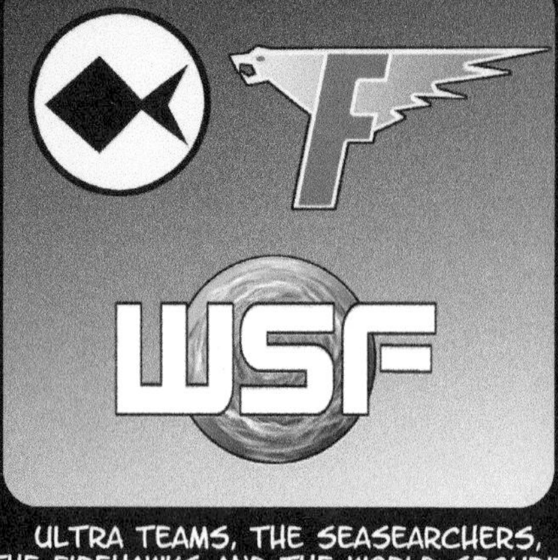
WSF

ULTRA TEAMS, THE SEASEARCHERS, THE FIREHAWKS AND THE WORLD SECURITY FORCE HAVE BEEN ENGAGED.

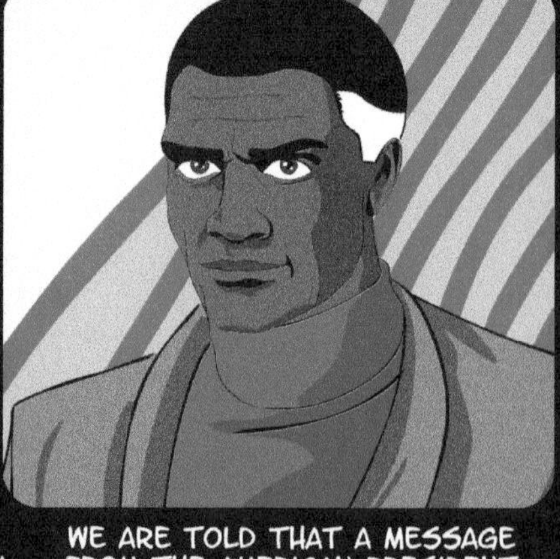

WE ARE TOLD THAT A MESSAGE FROM THE AMERICAN PRESIDENT IS JUST MOMENTS AWAY....

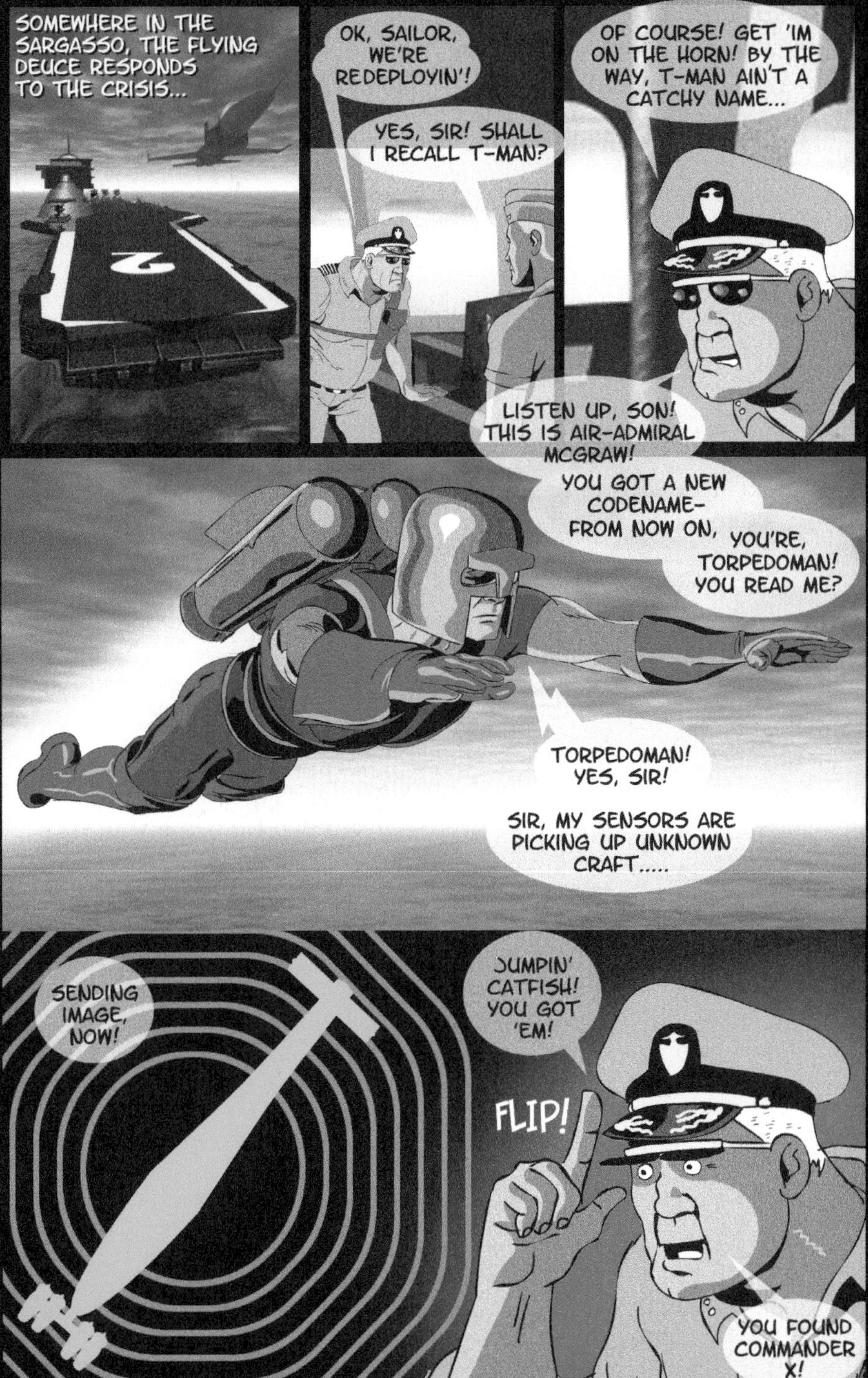
SOMEWHERE IN THE SARGASSO, THE FLYING DEUCE RESPONDS TO THE CRISIS...
OK, SAILOR, WE'RE REDEPLOYIN'!
YES, SIR! SHALL I RECALL T-MAN?
OF COURSE! GET 'IM ON THE HORN! BY THE WAY, T-MAN AIN'T A CATCHY NAME...
LISTEN UP, SON! THIS IS AIR-ADMIRAL MCGRAW!
YOU GOT A NEW CODENAME- FROM NOW ON,
YOU'RE, TORPEDOMAN! YOU READ ME?
TORPEDOMAN! YES, SIR!
SIR, MY SENSORS ARE PICKING UP UNKNOWN CRAFT.....
SENDING IMAGE, NOW!
JUMPIN' CATFISH! YOU GOT 'EM!
FLIP!
YOU FOUND COMMANDER X!

SOMEWHERE BELOW THE SURFACE OF THE SARGASSO....

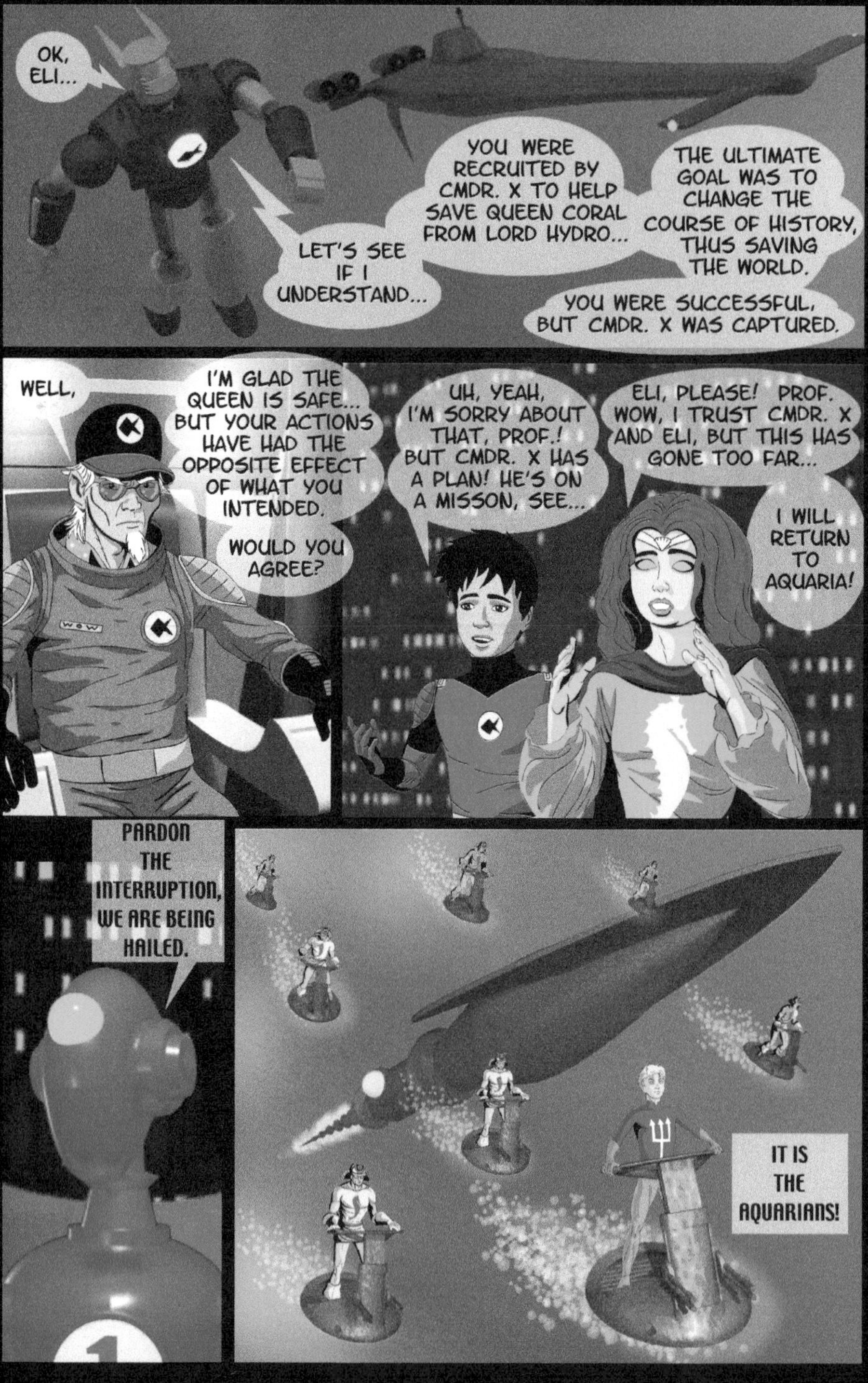
OK, ELI...
LET'S SEE IF I UNDERSTAND...
YOU WERE RECRUITED BY CMDR. X TO HELP SAVE QUEEN CORAL FROM LORD HYDRO...
THE ULTIMATE GOAL WAS TO CHANGE THE COURSE OF HISTORY, THUS SAVING THE WORLD.
YOU WERE SUCCESSFUL, BUT CMDR. X WAS CAPTURED.
WELL,
I'M GLAD THE QUEEN IS SAFE... BUT YOUR ACTIONS HAVE HAD THE OPPOSITE EFFECT OF WHAT YOU INTENDED.
WOULD YOU AGREE?
UH, YEAH, I'M SORRY ABOUT THAT, PROF.! BUT CMDR. X HAS A PLAN! HE'S ON A MISSON, SEE...
ELI, PLEASE! PROF. WOW, I TRUST CMDR. X AND ELI, BUT THIS HAS GONE TOO FAR...
I WILL RETURN TO AQUARIA!
PARDON THE INTERRUPTION, WE ARE BEING HAILED.
IT IS THE AQUARIANS!

Act 2 - Clash of Heroes

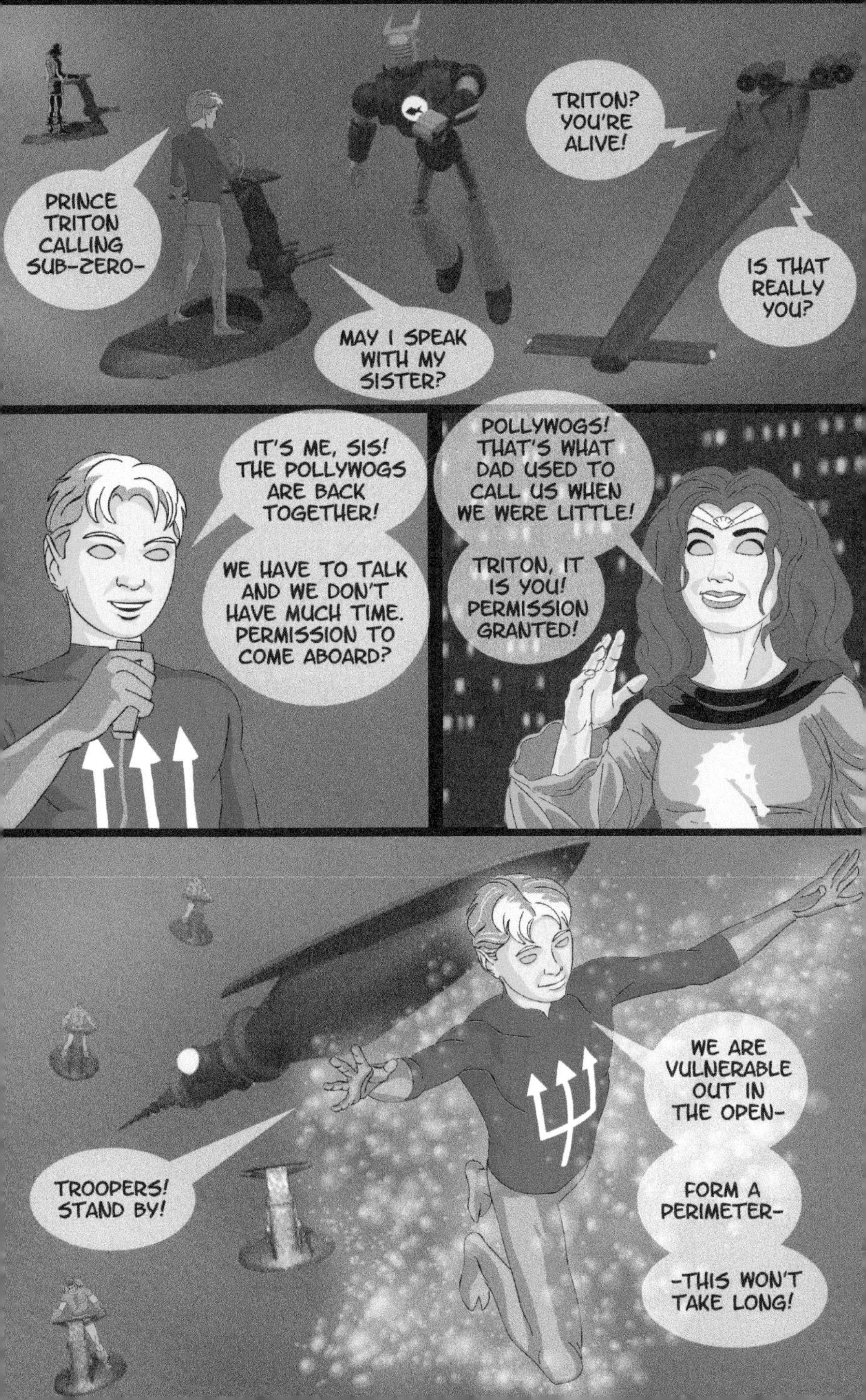
PRINCE TRITON CALLING SUB-ZERO-
TRITON? YOU'RE ALIVE!
IS THAT REALLY YOU?
MAY I SPEAK WITH MY SISTER?
IT'S ME, SIS! THE POLLYWOGS ARE BACK TOGETHER!
WE HAVE TO TALK AND WE DON'T HAVE MUCH TIME. PERMISSION TO COME ABOARD?
POLLYWOGS! THAT'S WHAT DAD USED TO CALL US WHEN WE WERE LITTLE!
TRITON, IT IS YOU! PERMISSION GRANTED!
WE ARE VULNERABLE OUT IN THE OPEN-
FORM A PERIMETER-
-THIS WON'T TAKE LONG!
TROOPERS! STAND BY!

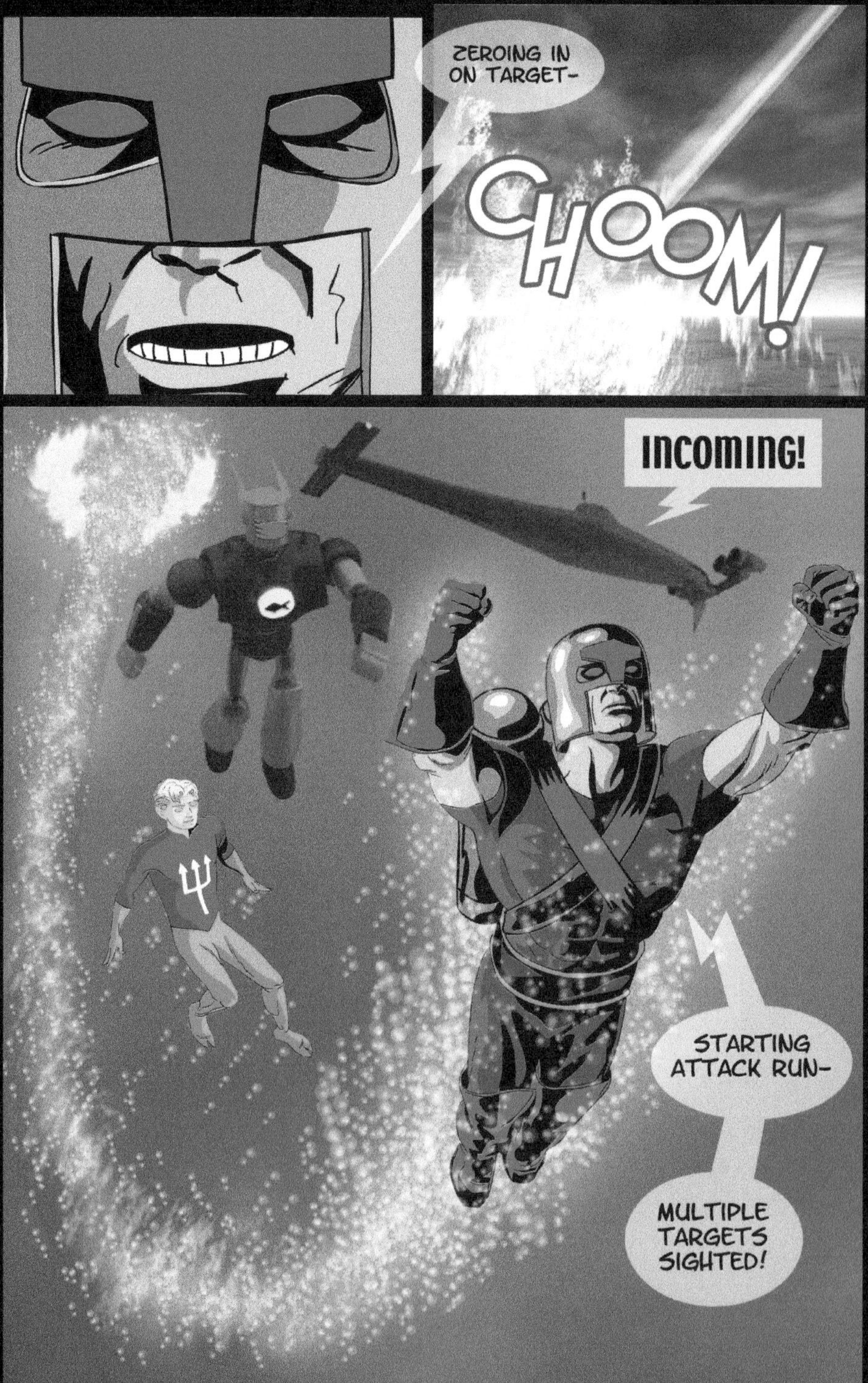
ZEROING IN ON TARGET-
CHOOM!
INCOMING!
STARTING ATTACK RUN-
MULTIPLE TARGETS SIGHTED!

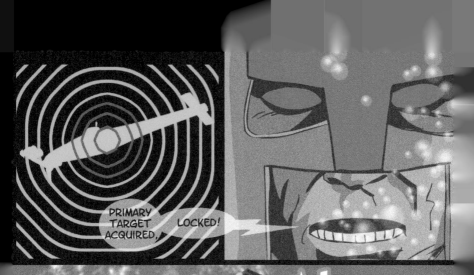

PRIMARY TARGET ACQUIRED, LOCKED!

BA-CHOOM!

RUNNING HOT, STRAIGHT AND NORMAL!

WE'RE OK, TRITON! JUST SHAKEN.

THAT GUY KNOWS HOW TO MAKE AN ENTRANCE!

DAMAGE REPORT!

SHIELDS ARE DOWN! SHE CAN'T TAKE ANOTHER BLOW, CAPT'N!

CORAL!

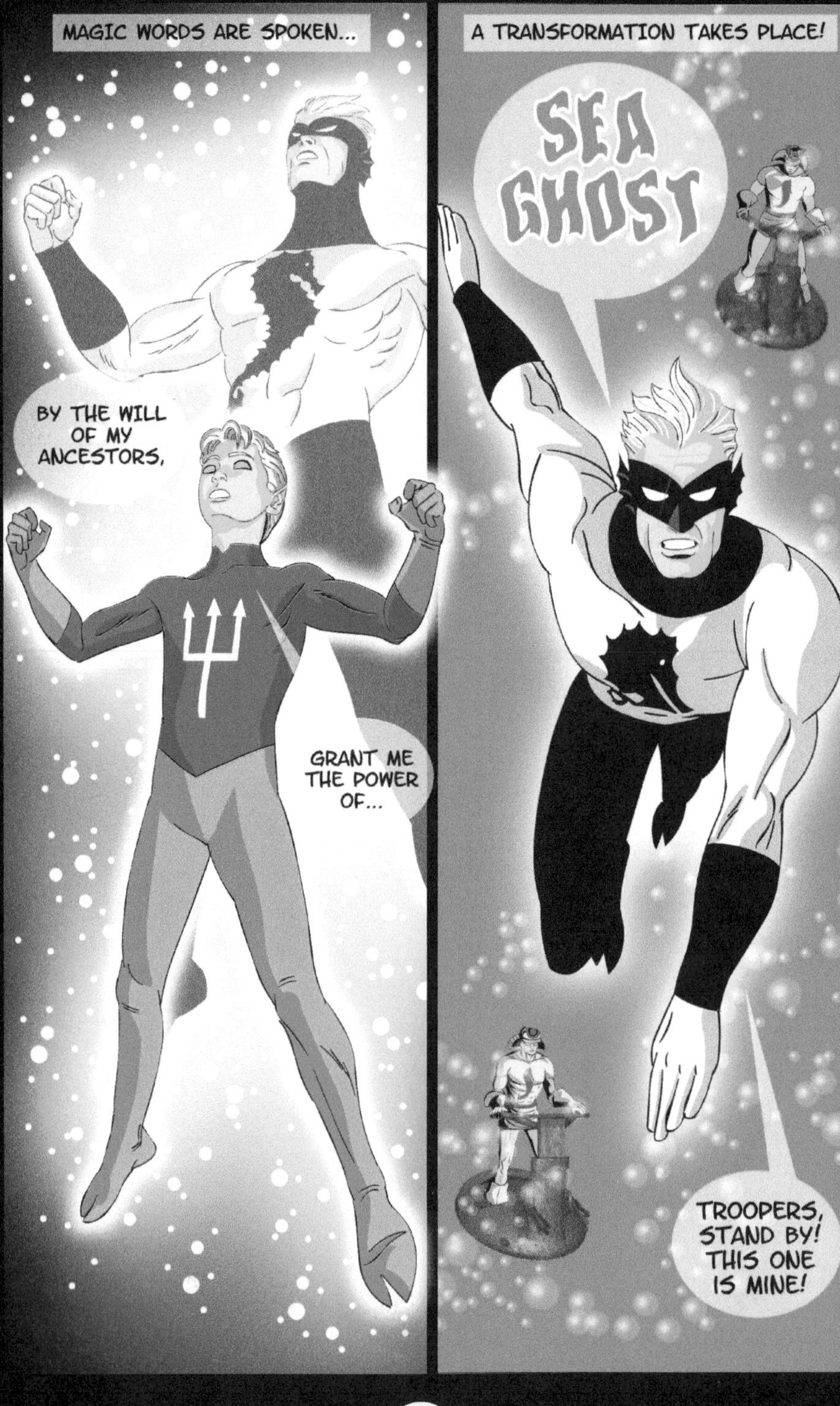
MAGIC WORDS ARE SPOKEN...
BY THE WILL OF MY ANCESTORS,
GRANT ME THE POWER OF...
A TRANSFORMATION TAKES PLACE!
SEA GHOST
TROOPERS, STAND BY! THIS ONE IS MINE!

Act 2 - Clash of Heroes

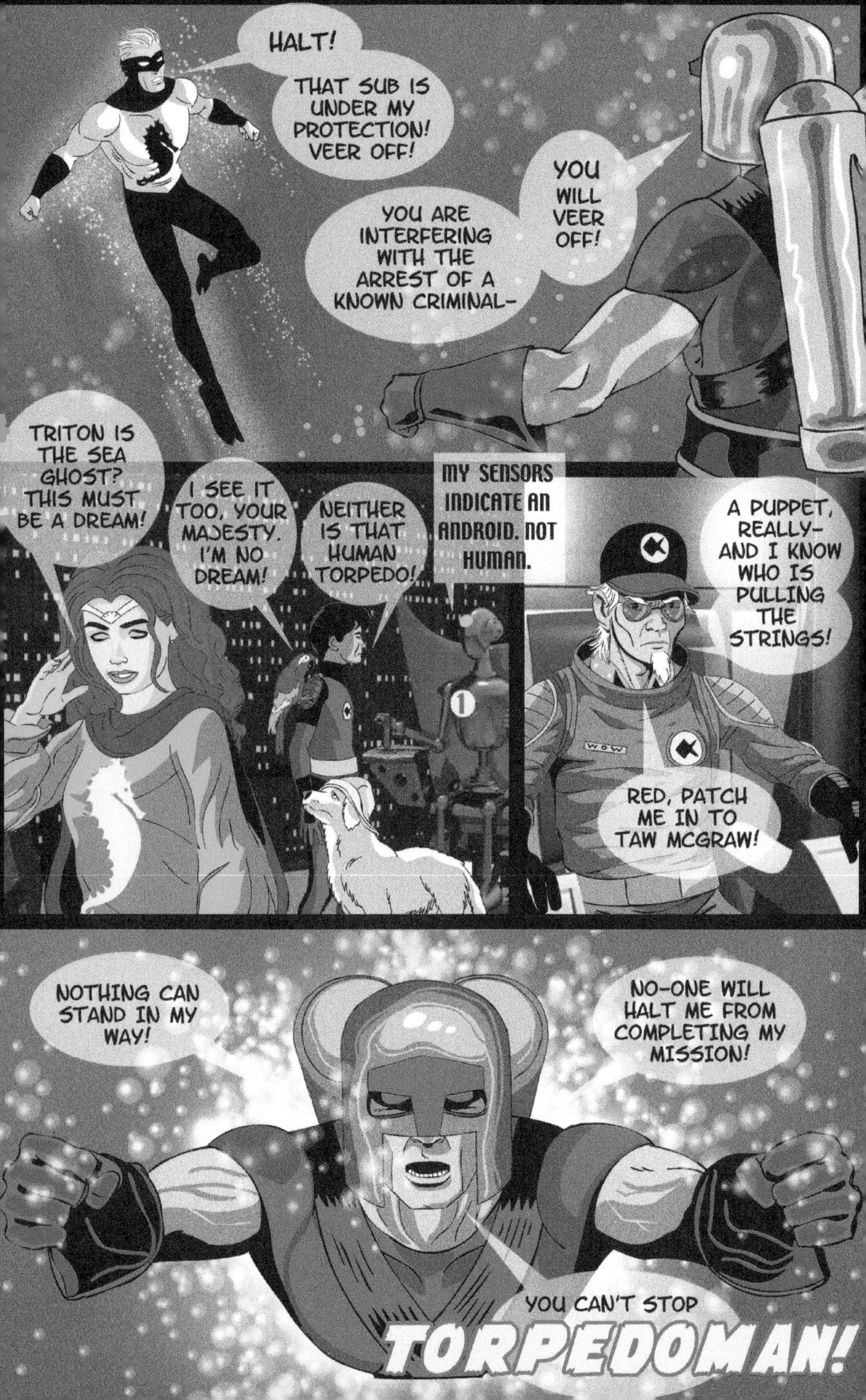
HALT!
THAT SUB IS UNDER MY PROTECTION! VEER OFF!
YOU WILL VEER OFF!
YOU ARE INTERFERING WITH THE ARREST OF A KNOWN CRIMINAL-
TRITON IS THE SEA GHOST? THIS MUST BE A DREAM!
I SEE IT TOO, YOUR MAJESTY. I'M NO DREAM!
NEITHER IS THAT HUMAN TORPEDO!
MY SENSORS INDICATE AN ANDROID. NOT HUMAN.
A PUPPET, REALLY- AND I KNOW WHO IS PULLING THE STRINGS!
RED, PATCH ME IN TO TAW MCGRAW!
NOTHING CAN STAND IN MY WAY!
NO-ONE WILL HALT ME FROM COMPLETING MY MISSION!
YOU CAN'T STOP TORPEDOMAN!

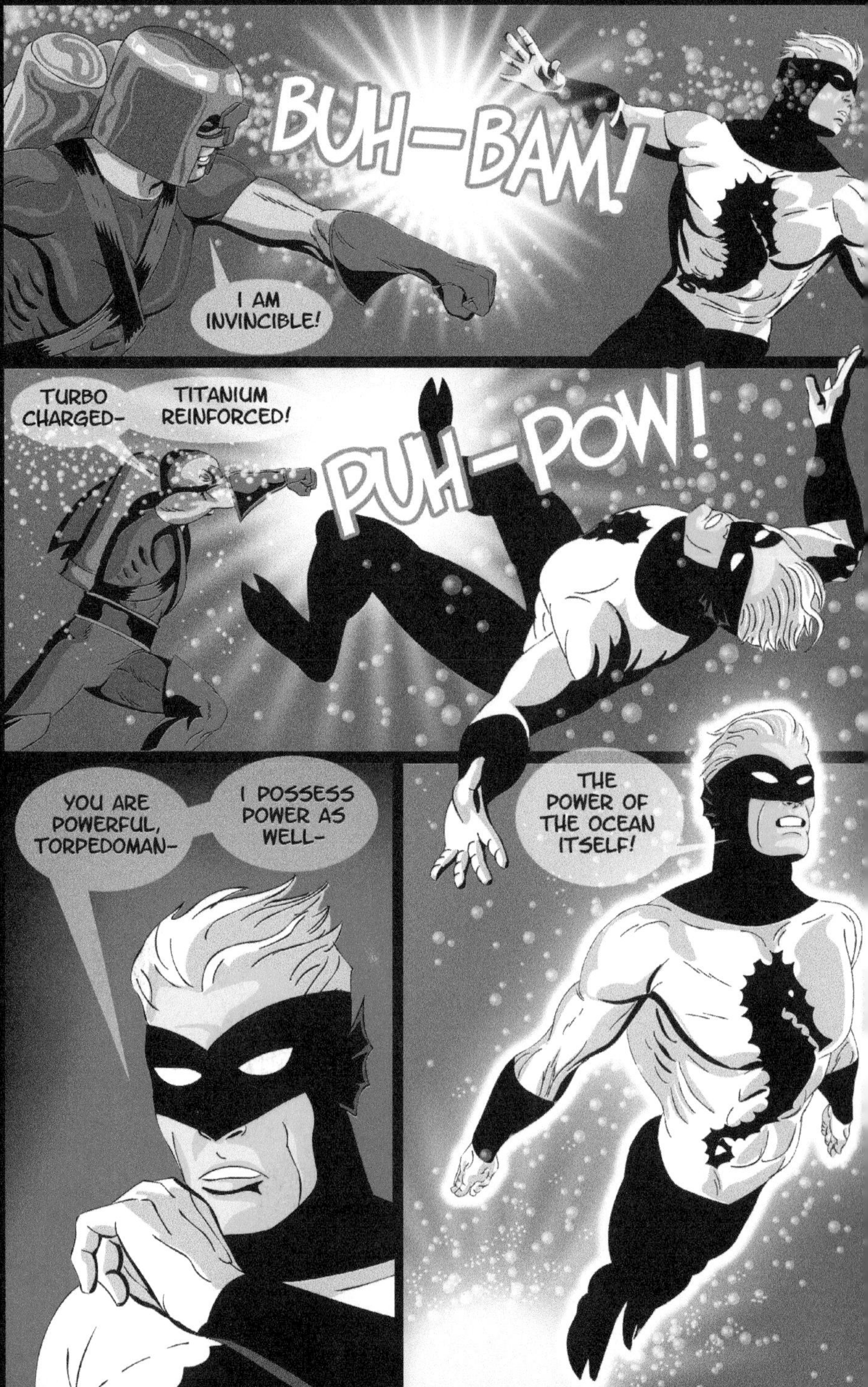
BUH-BAM!
I AM INVINCIBLE!
TURBO CHARGED-
TITANIUM REINFORCED!
PUH-POW!
YOU ARE POWERFUL, TORPEDOMAN-
I POSSESS POWER AS WELL-
THE POWER OF THE OCEAN ITSELF!

THE POWER OF LIGHTNING!
THE FORCE OF A HURRICANE!
ZA-BLAM!
UNBELIEVABLE! YOU ARE RELENTLESS!
UNSTOPPABLE, REALLY!
BUH-BAFF!
SSHHOOOOWW!

KA-CHOOM!

THAT'S ENOUGH!

YOU'RE BOTH SUPPOSED TO BE ULTRA-HEROES...

START ACTING LIKE IT!

TORPEDOMAN, STAND BY FOR A MESSAGE!

MCGRAW!

UH, IT'S ME, SON! STAND DOWN, YOU'RE ENGAGING "FRIENDLIES". COMMANDER X IS NOT ABOARD THAT CRAFT.

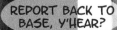
REPORT BACK TO BASE, Y'HEAR?

OK, WOW. IT'S YOUR SHOW.

Act 2 - Clash of Heroes

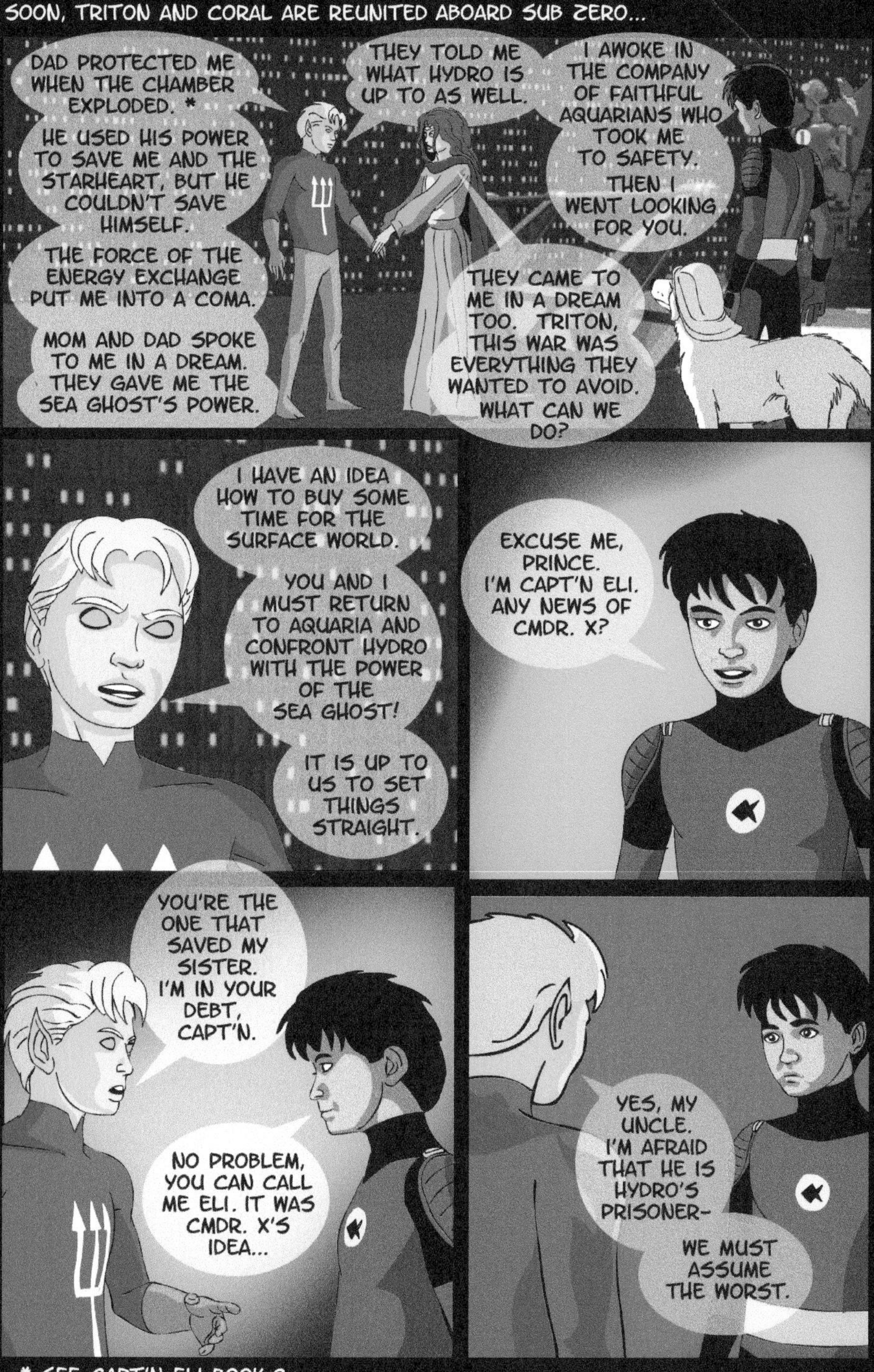
SOON, TRITON AND CORAL ARE REUNITED ABOARD SUB ZERO...
DAD PROTECTED ME WHEN THE CHAMBER EXPLODED. *
HE USED HIS POWER TO SAVE ME AND THE STARHEART, BUT HE COULDN'T SAVE HIMSELF.
THE FORCE OF THE ENERGY EXCHANGE PUT ME INTO A COMA.
MOM AND DAD SPOKE TO ME IN A DREAM. THEY GAVE ME THE SEA GHOST'S POWER.
THEY TOLD ME WHAT HYDRO IS UP TO AS WELL.
I AWOKE IN THE COMPANY OF FAITHFUL AQUARIANS WHO TOOK ME TO SAFETY.
THEN I WENT LOOKING FOR YOU.
THEY CAME TO ME IN A DREAM TOO. TRITON, THIS WAR WAS EVERYTHING THEY WANTED TO AVOID. WHAT CAN WE DO?
I HAVE AN IDEA HOW TO BUY SOME TIME FOR THE SURFACE WORLD.
YOU AND I MUST RETURN TO AQUARIA AND CONFRONT HYDRO WITH THE POWER OF THE SEA GHOST!
IT IS UP TO US TO SET THINGS STRAIGHT.
EXCUSE ME, PRINCE. I'M CAPT'N ELI. ANY NEWS OF CMDR. X?
YOU'RE THE ONE THAT SAVED MY SISTER. I'M IN YOUR DEBT, CAPT'N.
NO PROBLEM, YOU CAN CALL ME ELI. IT WAS CMDR. X'S IDEA...
YES, MY UNCLE. I'M AFRAID THAT HE IS HYDRO'S PRISONER-
WE MUST ASSUME THE WORST.

* SEE CAPT'N ELI BOOK 2

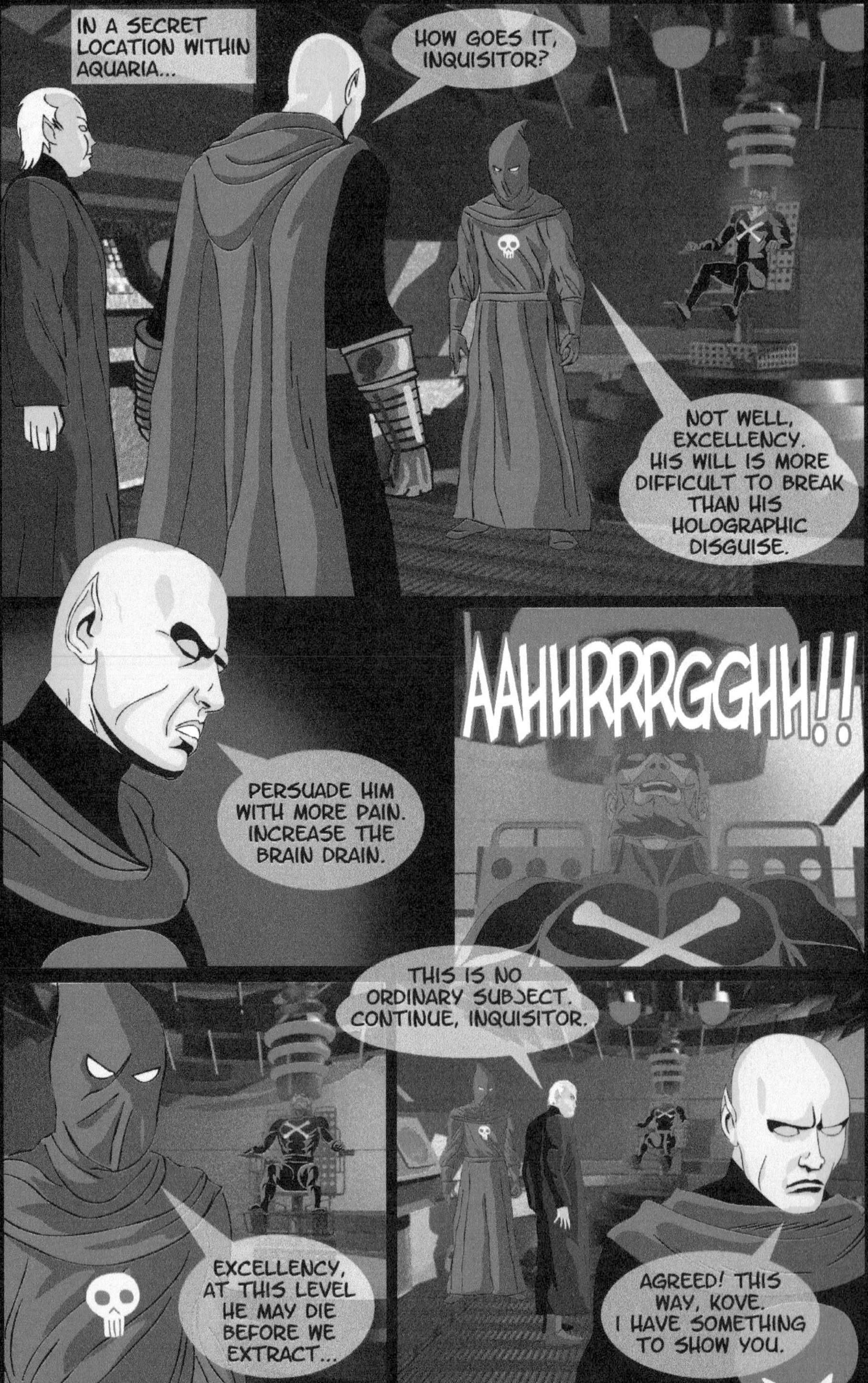
IN A SECRET LOCATION WITHIN AQUARIA...
HOW GOES IT, INQUISITOR?
NOT WELL, EXCELLENCY. HIS WILL IS MORE DIFFICULT TO BREAK THAN HIS HOLOGRAPHIC DISGUISE.
PERSUADE HIM WITH MORE PAIN. INCREASE THE BRAIN DRAIN.
AAHHRRRGGHH!!
EXCELLENCY, AT THIS LEVEL HE MAY DIE BEFORE WE EXTRACT...
THIS IS NO ORDINARY SUBJECT. CONTINUE, INQUISITOR.
AGREED! THIS WAY, KOVE. I HAVE SOMETHING TO SHOW YOU.

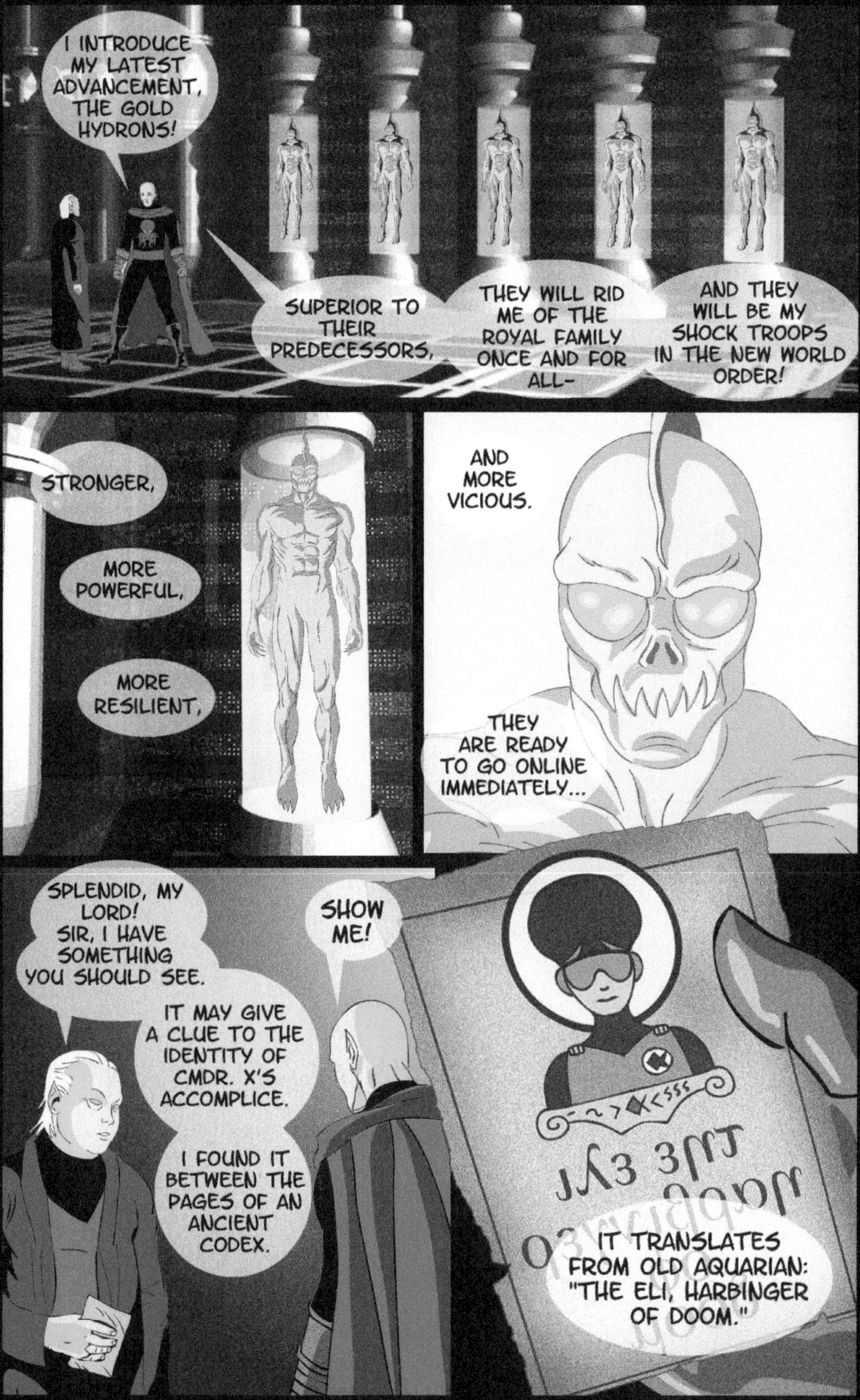
I INTRODUCE MY LATEST ADVANCEMENT, THE GOLD HYDRONS!
SUPERIOR TO THEIR PREDECESSORS,
THEY WILL RID ME OF THE ROYAL FAMILY ONCE AND FOR ALL-
AND THEY WILL BE MY SHOCK TROOPS IN THE NEW WORLD ORDER!
STRONGER,
MORE POWERFUL,
MORE RESILIENT,
AND MORE VICIOUS.
THEY ARE READY TO GO ONLINE IMMEDIATELY...
SPLENDID, MY LORD! SIR, I HAVE SOMETHING YOU SHOULD SEE.
SHOW ME!
IT MAY GIVE A CLUE TO THE IDENTITY OF CMDR. X'S ACCOMPLICE.
I FOUND IT BETWEEN THE PAGES OF AN ANCIENT CODEX.
IT TRANSLATES FROM OLD AQUARIAN: "THE ELI, HARBINGER OF DOOM."

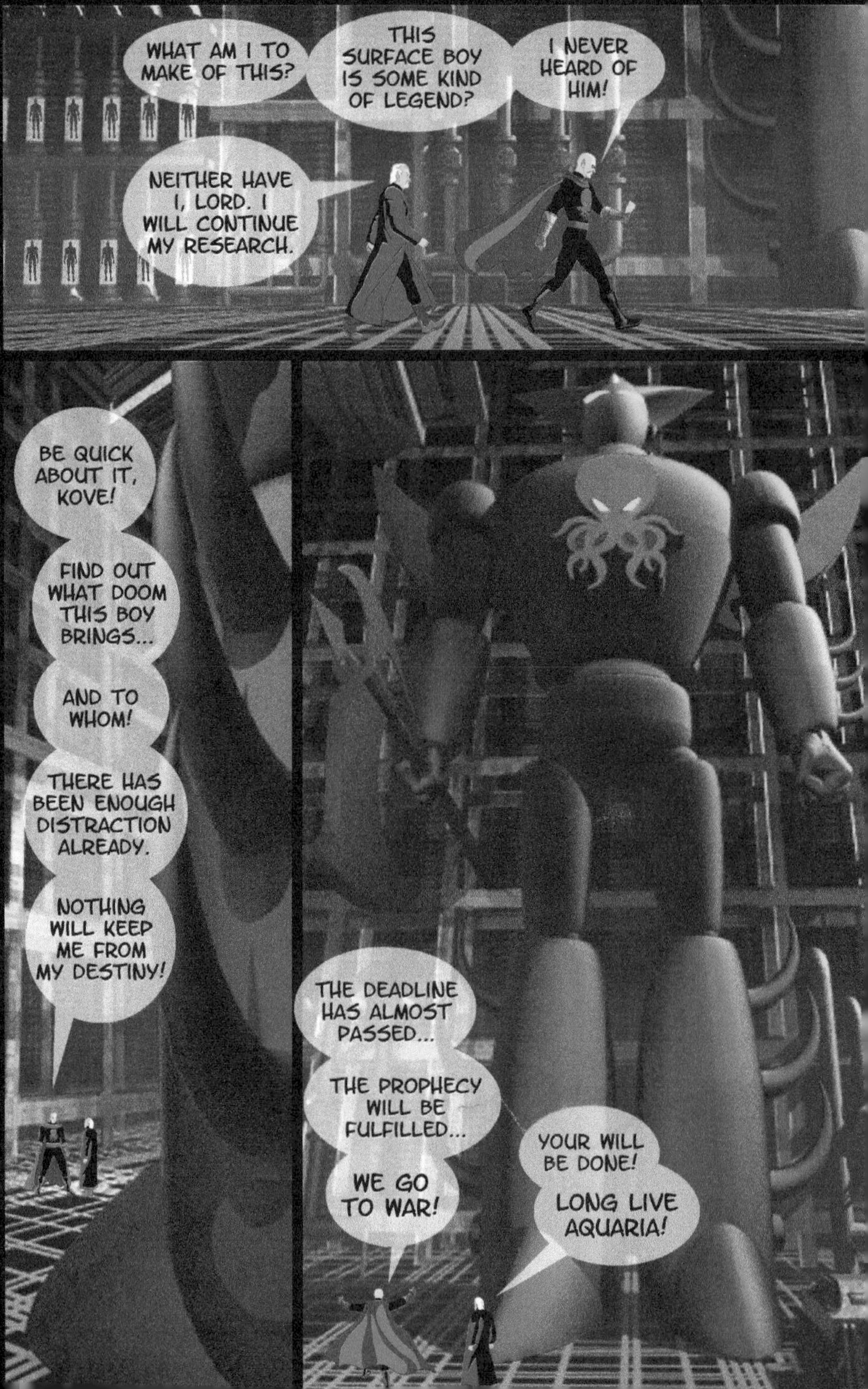
WHAT AM I TO MAKE OF THIS?
THIS SURFACE BOY IS SOME KIND OF LEGEND?
I NEVER HEARD OF HIM!
NEITHER HAVE I, LORD. I WILL CONTINUE MY RESEARCH.
BE QUICK ABOUT IT, KOVE!
FIND OUT WHAT DOOM THIS BOY BRINGS...
AND TO WHOM!
THERE HAS BEEN ENOUGH DISTRACTION ALREADY.
NOTHING WILL KEEP ME FROM MY DESTINY!
THE DEADLINE HAS ALMOST PASSED...
THE PROPHECY WILL BE FULFILLED...
WE GO TO WAR!
YOUR WILL BE DONE!
LONG LIVE AQUARIA!

ACT 2 - CLASH OF HEROES

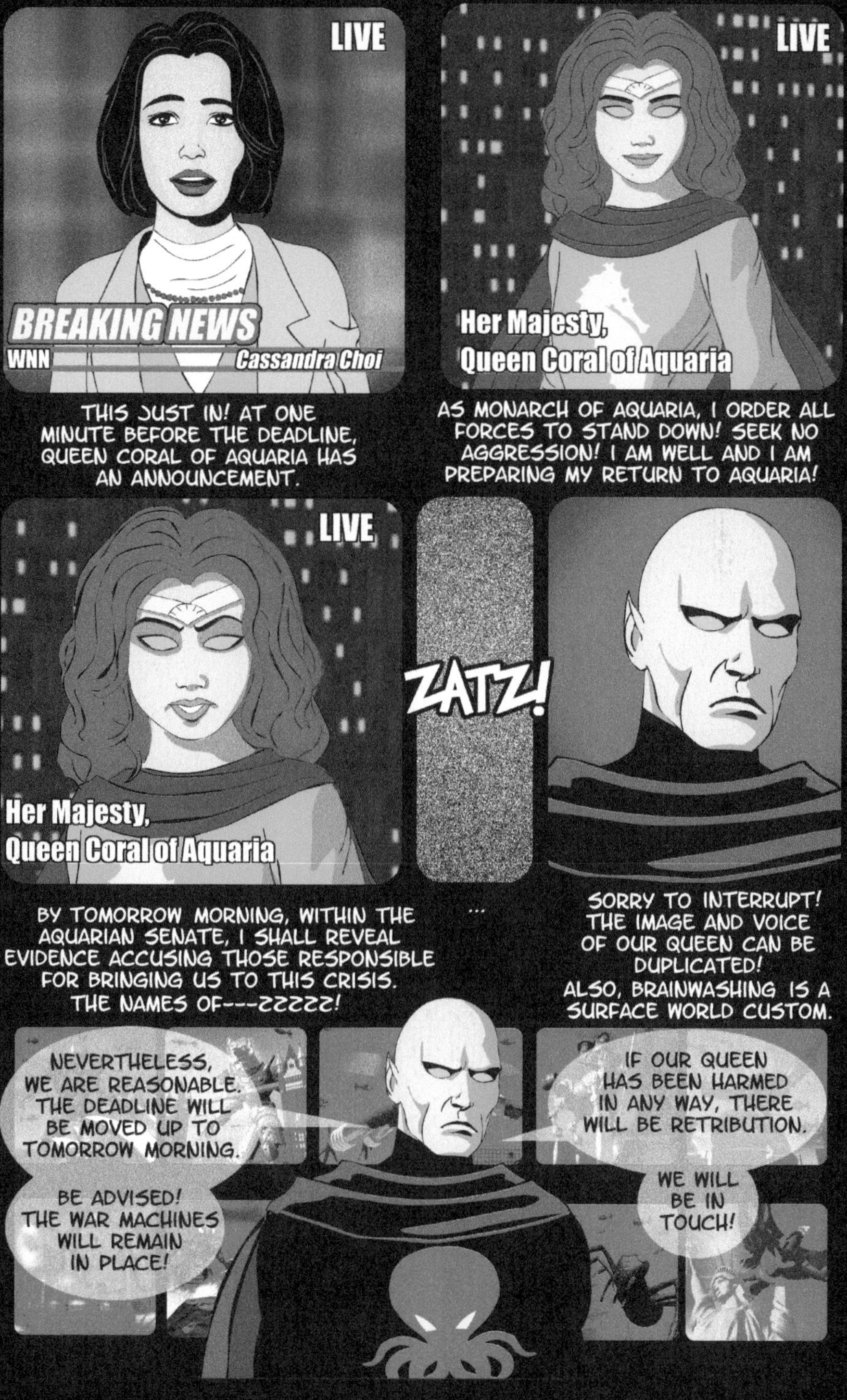
LIVE
BREAKING NEWS
WNN
Cassandra Choi
THIS JUST IN! AT ONE MINUTE BEFORE THE DEADLINE, QUEEN CORAL OF AQUARIA HAS AN ANNOUNCEMENT.
LIVE
Her Majesty, Queen Coral of Aquaria
AS MONARCH OF AQUARIA, I ORDER ALL FORCES TO STAND DOWN! SEEK NO AGGRESSION! I AM WELL AND I AM PREPARING MY RETURN TO AQUARIA!
LIVE
Her Majesty, Queen Coral of Aquaria
BY TOMORROW MORNING, WITHIN THE AQUARIAN SENATE, I SHALL REVEAL EVIDENCE ACCUSING THOSE RESPONSIBLE FOR BRINGING US TO THIS CRISIS. THE NAMES OF---ZZZZZ!
ZATZ!
...
SORRY TO INTERRUPT! THE IMAGE AND VOICE OF OUR QUEEN CAN BE DUPLICATED! ALSO, BRAINWASHING IS A SURFACE WORLD CUSTOM.
NEVERTHELESS, WE ARE REASONABLE. THE DEADLINE WILL BE MOVED UP TO TOMORROW MORNING.
BE ADVISED! THE WAR MACHINES WILL REMAIN IN PLACE!
IF OUR QUEEN HAS BEEN HARMED IN ANY WAY, THERE WILL BE RETRIBUTION.
WE WILL BE IN TOUCH!

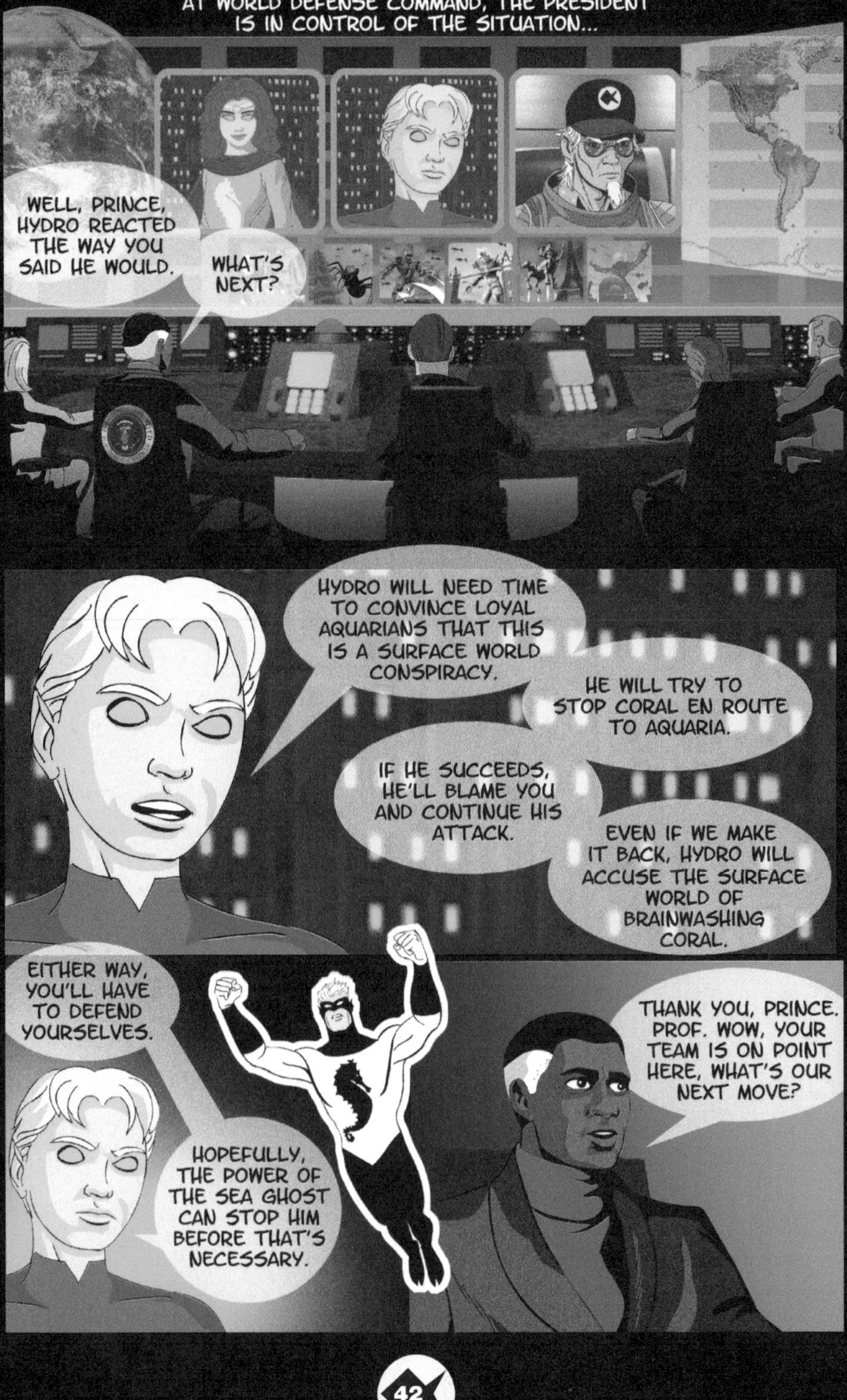
AT WORLD DEFENSE COMMAND, THE PRESIDENT IS IN CONTROL OF THE SITUATION...
WELL, PRINCE, HYDRO REACTED THE WAY YOU SAID HE WOULD.
WHAT'S NEXT?
HYDRO WILL NEED TIME TO CONVINCE LOYAL AQUARIANS THAT THIS IS A SURFACE WORLD CONSPIRACY.
HE WILL TRY TO STOP CORAL EN ROUTE TO AQUARIA.
IF HE SUCCEEDS, HE'LL BLAME YOU AND CONTINUE HIS ATTACK.
EVEN IF WE MAKE IT BACK, HYDRO WILL ACCUSE THE SURFACE WORLD OF BRAINWASHING CORAL.
EITHER WAY, YOU'LL HAVE TO DEFEND YOURSELVES.
HOPEFULLY, THE POWER OF THE SEA GHOST CAN STOP HIM BEFORE THAT'S NECESSARY.
THANK YOU, PRINCE. PROF. WOW, YOUR TEAM IS ON POINT HERE, WHAT'S OUR NEXT MOVE?

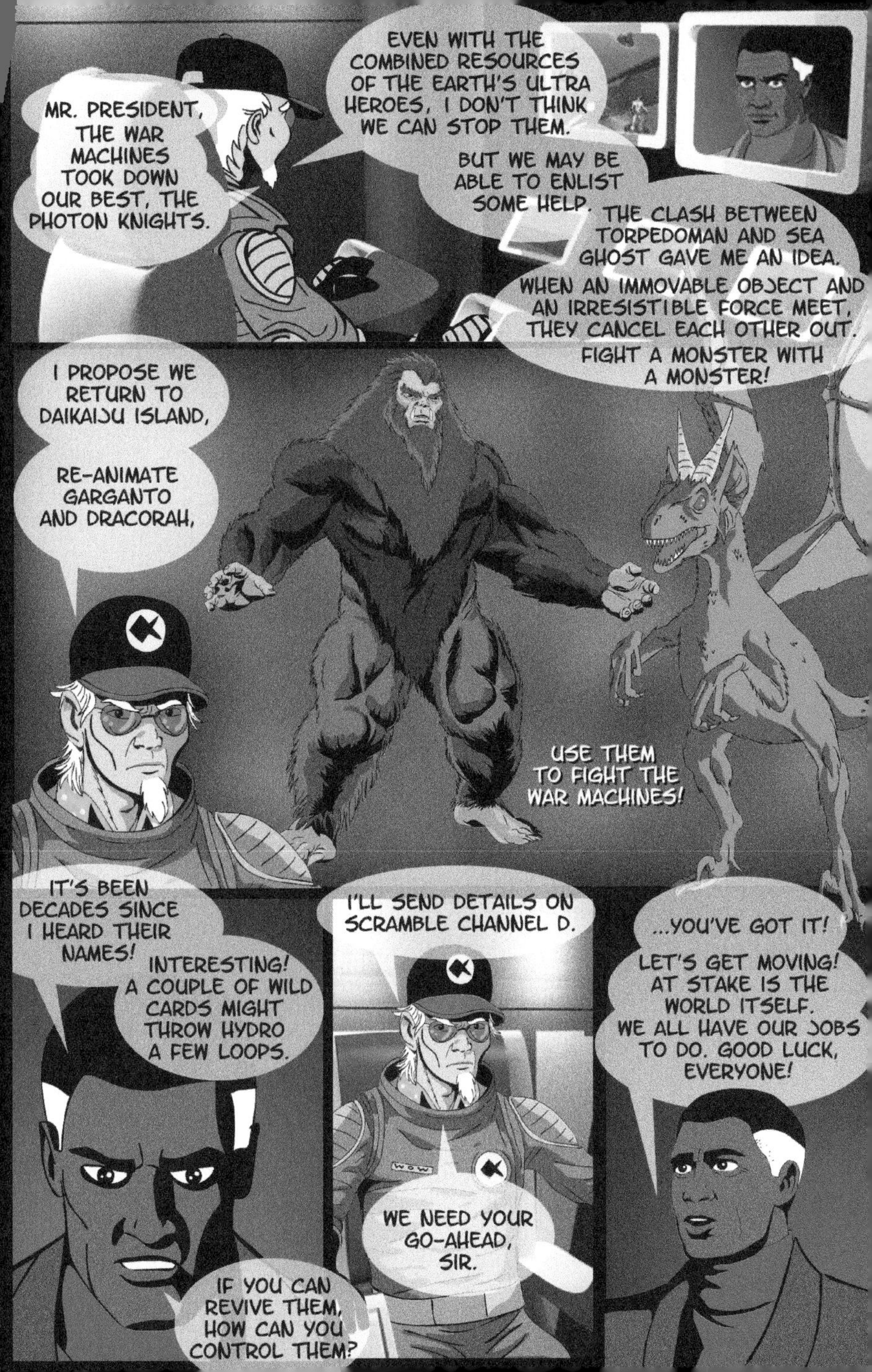
MR. PRESIDENT, THE WAR MACHINES TOOK DOWN OUR BEST, THE PHOTON KNIGHTS.
EVEN WITH THE COMBINED RESOURCES OF THE EARTH'S ULTRA HEROES, I DON'T THINK WE CAN STOP THEM.
BUT WE MAY BE ABLE TO ENLIST SOME HELP.
THE CLASH BETWEEN TORPEDOMAN AND SEA GHOST GAVE ME AN IDEA.
WHEN AN IMMOVABLE OBJECT AND AN IRRESISTIBLE FORCE MEET, THEY CANCEL EACH OTHER OUT.
FIGHT A MONSTER WITH A MONSTER!
I PROPOSE WE RETURN TO DAIKAIJU ISLAND,
RE-ANIMATE GARGANTO AND DRACORAH,
USE THEM TO FIGHT THE WAR MACHINES!
IT'S BEEN DECADES SINCE I HEARD THEIR NAMES!
INTERESTING! A COUPLE OF WILD CARDS MIGHT THROW HYDRO A FEW LOOPS.
IF YOU CAN REVIVE THEM, HOW CAN YOU CONTROL THEM?
I'LL SEND DETAILS ON SCRAMBLE CHANNEL D.
WOW
WE NEED YOUR GO-AHEAD, SIR.
...YOU'VE GOT IT!
LET'S GET MOVING! AT STAKE IS THE WORLD ITSELF. WE ALL HAVE OUR JOBS TO DO. GOOD LUCK, EVERYONE!

THE UNDERSEA ADVENTURES OF CAPT'N ELI

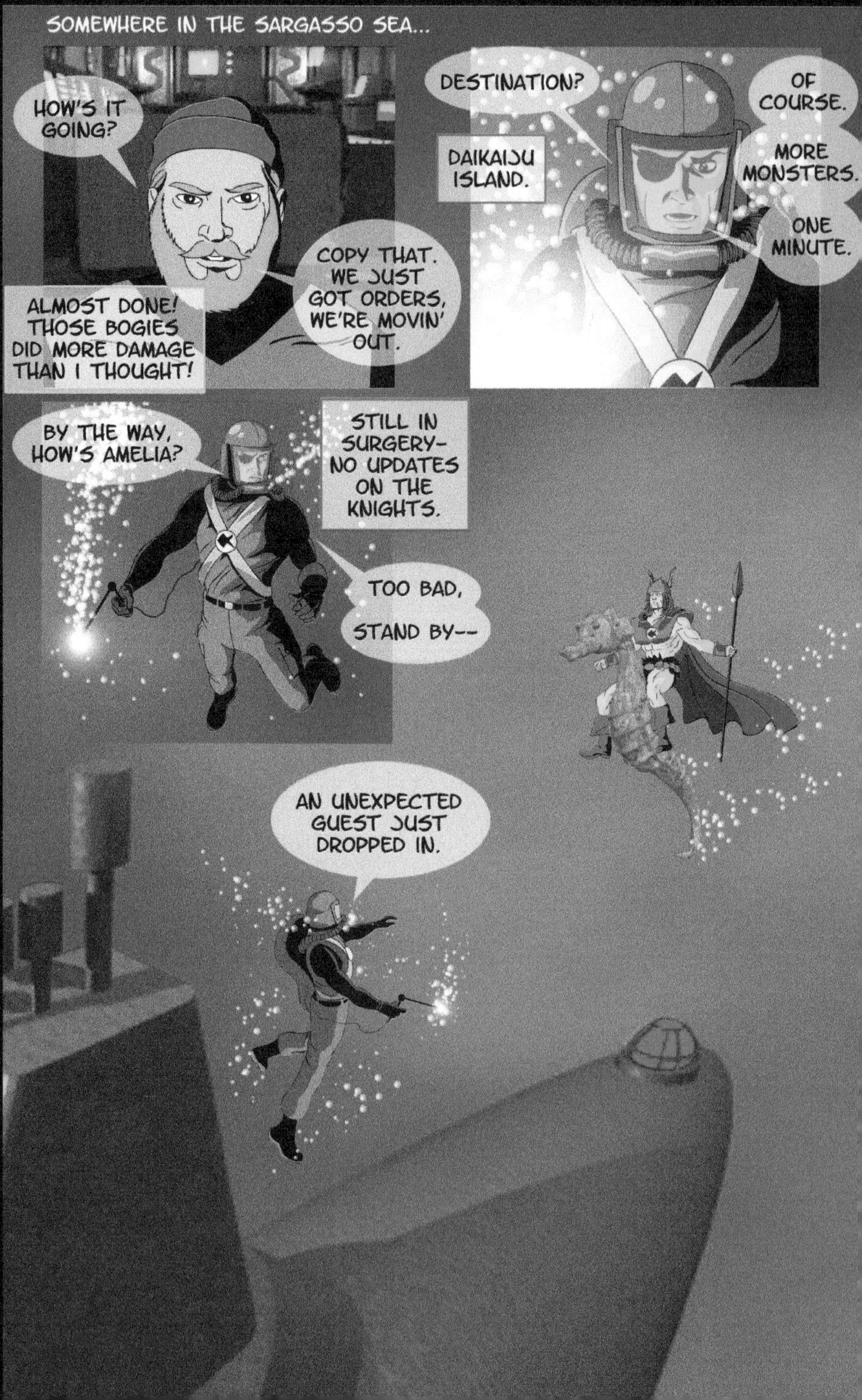
SOMEWHERE IN THE SARGASSO SEA...
HOW'S IT GOING?
ALMOST DONE! THOSE BOGIES DID MORE DAMAGE THAN I THOUGHT!
COPY THAT. WE JUST GOT ORDERS, WE'RE MOVIN' OUT.
DESTINATION?
DAIKAIJU ISLAND.
OF COURSE.
MORE MONSTERS.
ONE MINUTE.
BY THE WAY, HOW'S AMELIA?
STILL IN SURGERY- NO UPDATES ON THE KNIGHTS.
TOO BAD,
STAND BY--
AN UNEXPECTED GUEST JUST DROPPED IN.

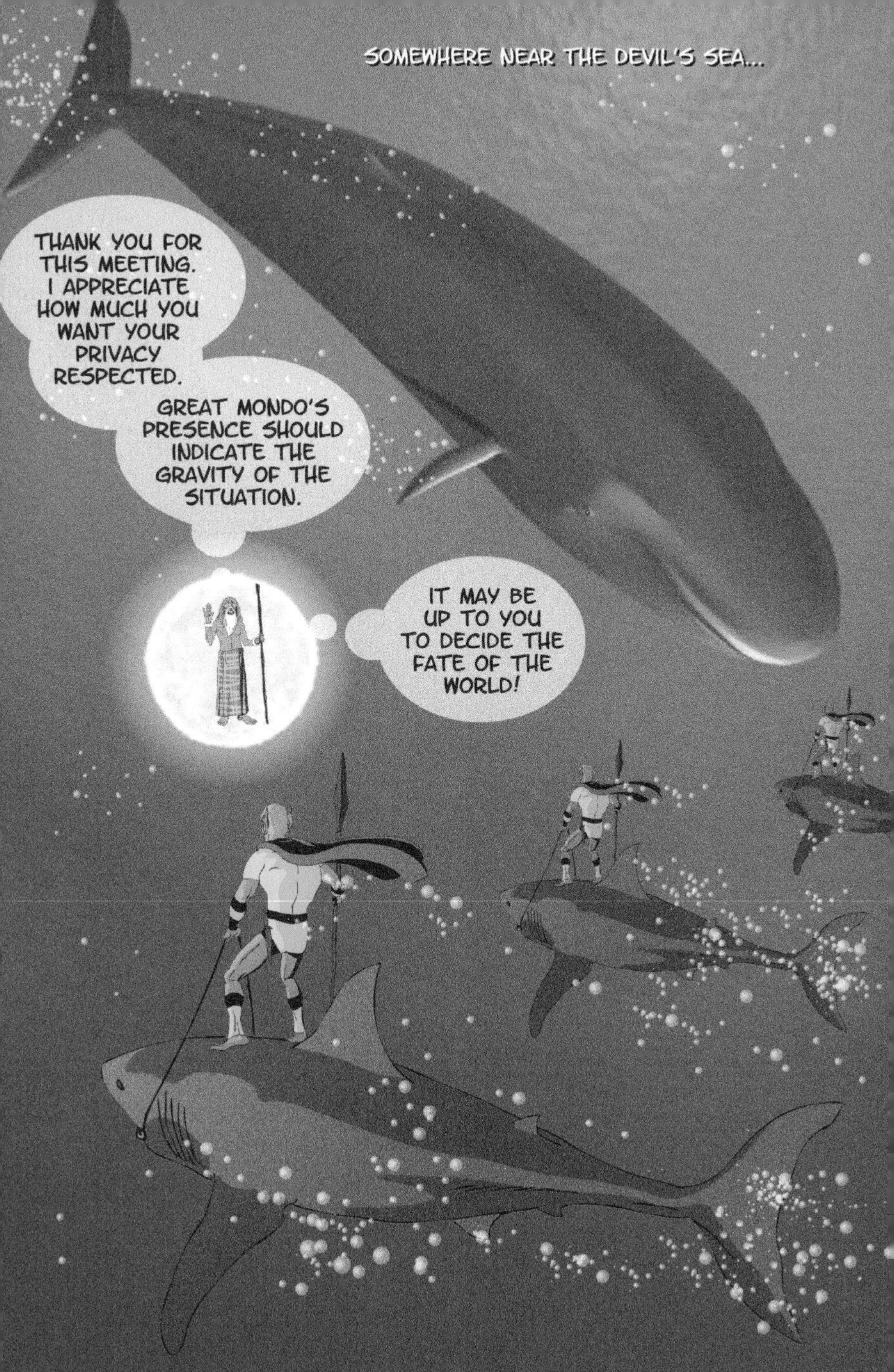
SOMEWHERE NEAR THE DEVIL'S SEA...
THANK YOU FOR THIS MEETING. I APPRECIATE HOW MUCH YOU WANT YOUR PRIVACY RESPECTED.
GREAT MONDO'S PRESENCE SHOULD INDICATE THE GRAVITY OF THE SITUATION.
IT MAY BE UP TO YOU TO DECIDE THE FATE OF THE WORLD!

END OF ACT TWO

Act 3

The Island of Monsters

TOKYO, JAPAN
CYBERNETIC DEFENSE HEADQUARTERS
THE PHOTON KNIGHTS HAVE BEEN CRITICALLY WOUNDED. DR. AMELIA BOLO, AN EXPERT IN CYBERNETIC SURGERY HAS BEEN CALLED IN TO HELP.
THAT SHOULD DO IT, JIRO.
THE ALIEN RADIATION HAS BEEN DRAINED FROM ALL OF THEM.
AMAZING WORK DOCTOR!
WE NEVER ENCOUNTERED THIS KIND OF ENERGY BEFORE. THANK YOU!
GLAD TO BE OF SERVICE! I LEFT A REPORT AT MY WORKSTATION.
SOON...
ALL SET HERE, PROF.!
YOU WERE RIGHT, THE ALIEN ENERGY HAS THE SAME FREQUENCY OF WHAT WE ENCOUNTERED IN THE SARGASSO.
GOOD WORK, AMELIA! WE'LL SEE YOU AT RENDEZVOUS ALPHA!

The Undersea Adventures of Capt'n Eli

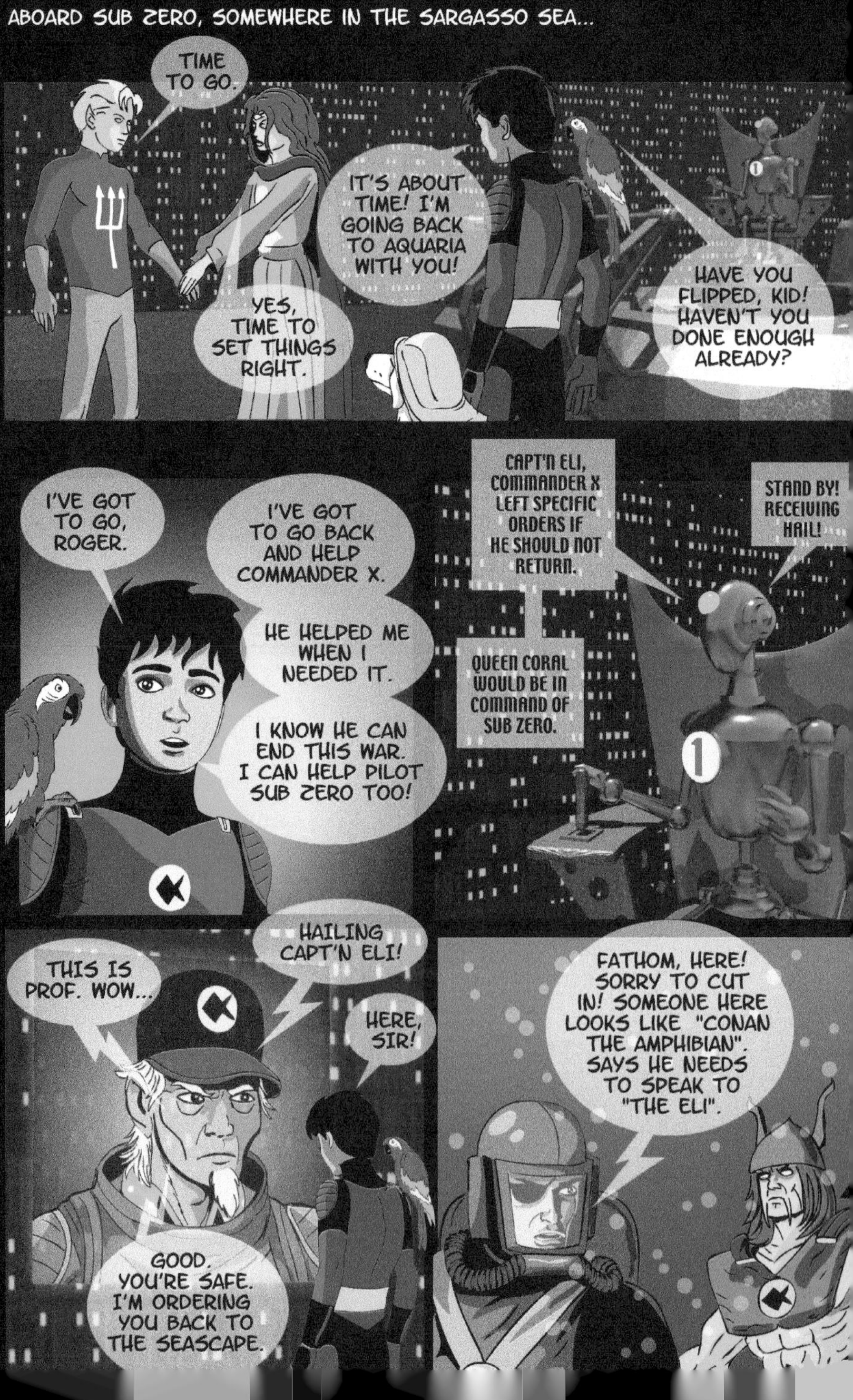
ABOARD SUB ZERO, SOMEWHERE IN THE SARGASSO SEA...
TIME TO GO.
IT'S ABOUT TIME! I'M GOING BACK TO AQUARIA WITH YOU!
YES, TIME TO SET THINGS RIGHT.
HAVE YOU FLIPPED, KID! HAVEN'T YOU DONE ENOUGH ALREADY?
I'VE GOT TO GO, ROGER.
I'VE GOT TO GO BACK AND HELP COMMANDER X.
HE HELPED ME WHEN I NEEDED IT.
I KNOW HE CAN END THIS WAR. I CAN HELP PILOT SUB ZERO TOO!
CAPT'N ELI, COMMANDER X LEFT SPECIFIC ORDERS IF HE SHOULD NOT RETURN.
QUEEN CORAL WOULD BE IN COMMAND OF SUB ZERO.
STAND BY! RECEIVING HAIL!
HAILING CAPT'N ELI!
THIS IS PROF. WOW...
HERE, SIR!
GOOD. YOU'RE SAFE. I'M ORDERING YOU BACK TO THE SEASCAPE.
FATHOM, HERE! SORRY TO CUT IN! SOMEONE HERE LOOKS LIKE "CONAN THE AMPHIBIAN". SAYS HE NEEDS TO SPEAK TO "THE ELI".

Act 3 - The Island Of Monsters

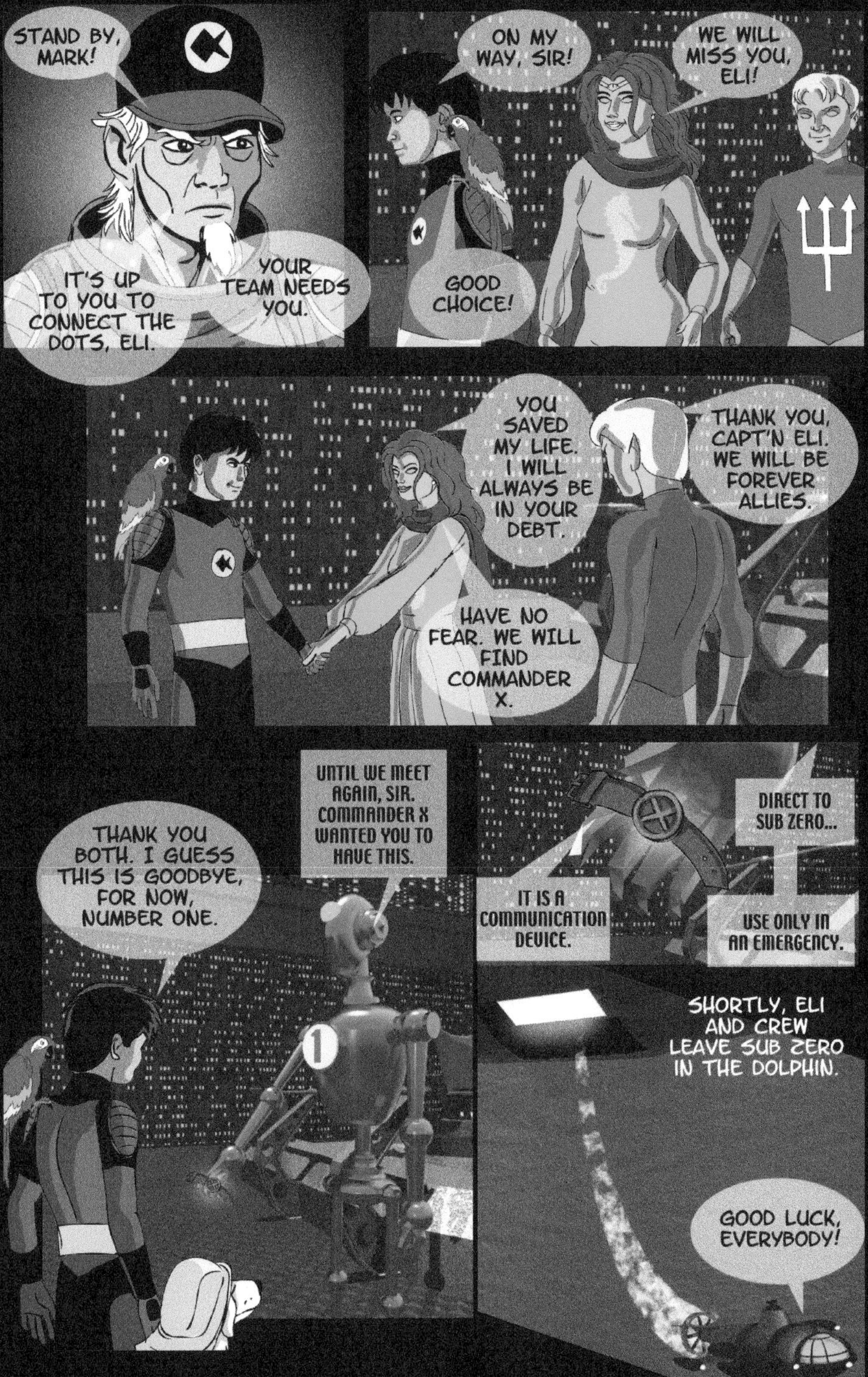
STAND BY, MARK!
IT'S UP TO YOU TO CONNECT THE DOTS, ELI.
YOUR TEAM NEEDS YOU.
ON MY WAY, SIR!
GOOD CHOICE!
WE WILL MISS YOU, ELI!
YOU SAVED MY LIFE. I WILL ALWAYS BE IN YOUR DEBT.
HAVE NO FEAR. WE WILL FIND COMMANDER X.
THANK YOU, CAPT'N ELI. WE WILL BE FOREVER ALLIES.
THANK YOU BOTH. I GUESS THIS IS GOODBYE, FOR NOW, NUMBER ONE.
UNTIL WE MEET AGAIN, SIR. COMMANDER X WANTED YOU TO HAVE THIS.
IT IS A COMMUNICATION DEVICE.
DIRECT TO SUB ZERO...
USE ONLY IN AN EMERGENCY.
SHORTLY, ELI AND CREW LEAVE SUB ZERO IN THE DOLPHIN.
GOOD LUCK, EVERYBODY!

THE UNDERSEA ADVENTURES OF CAPT'N ELI

THE SEASCAPE, SOMEWHERE IN THE SARGASSO SEA...

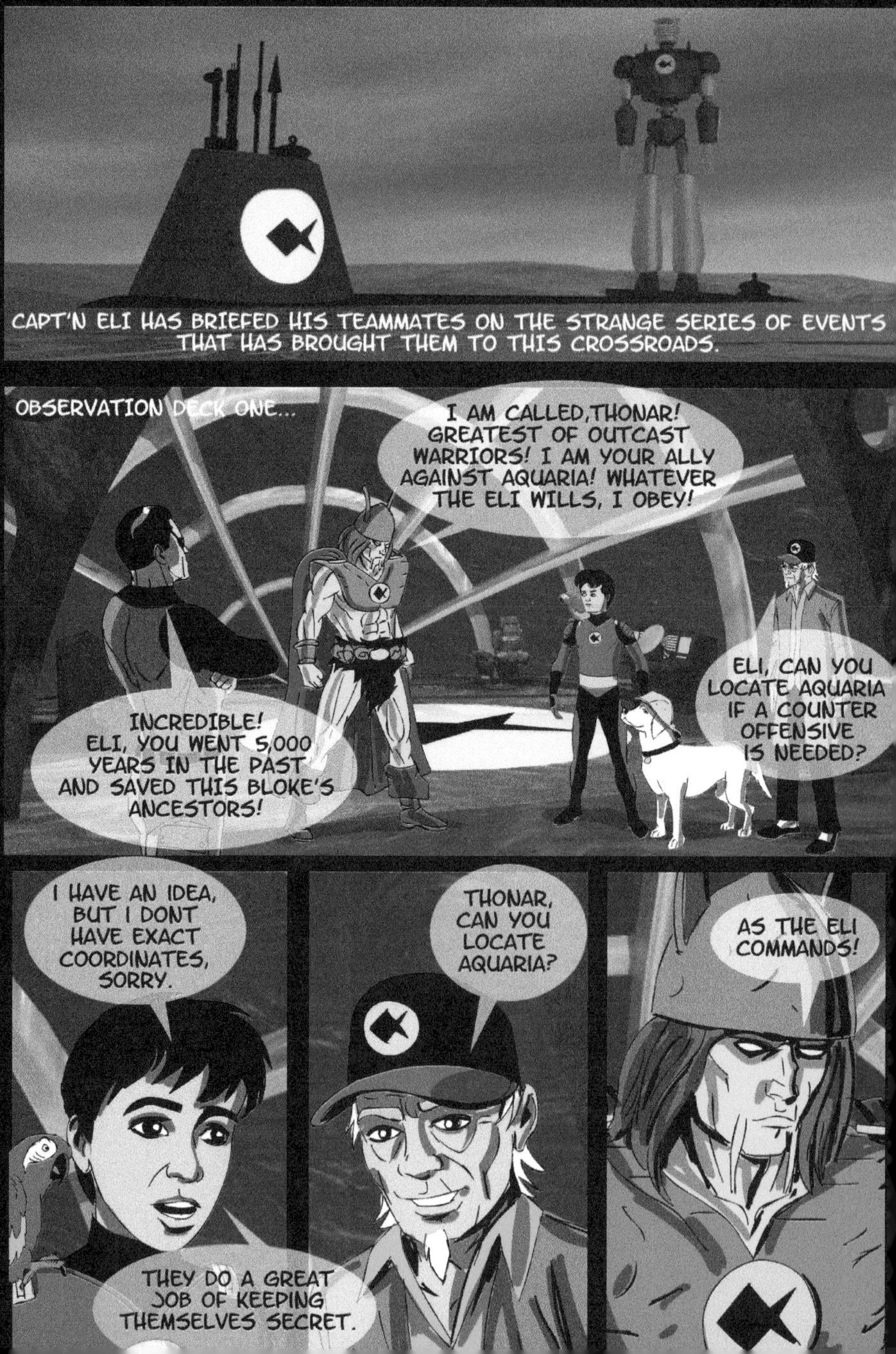
CAPT'N ELI HAS BRIEFED HIS TEAMMATES ON THE STRANGE SERIES OF EVENTS THAT HAS BROUGHT THEM TO THIS CROSSROADS.
OBSERVATION DECK ONE...
I AM CALLED,THONAR! GREATEST OF OUTCAST WARRIORS! I AM YOUR ALLY AGAINST AQUARIA! WHATEVER THE ELI WILLS, I OBEY!
INCREDIBLE! ELI, YOU WENT 5,000 YEARS IN THE PAST AND SAVED THIS BLOKE'S ANCESTORS!
ELI, CAN YOU LOCATE AQUARIA IF A COUNTER OFFENSIVE IS NEEDED?
I HAVE AN IDEA, BUT I DONT HAVE EXACT COORDINATES, SORRY.
THEY DO A GREAT JOB OF KEEPING THEMSELVES SECRET.
THONAR, CAN YOU LOCATE AQUARIA?
AS THE ELI COMMANDS!

Act 3 - The Island Of Monsters

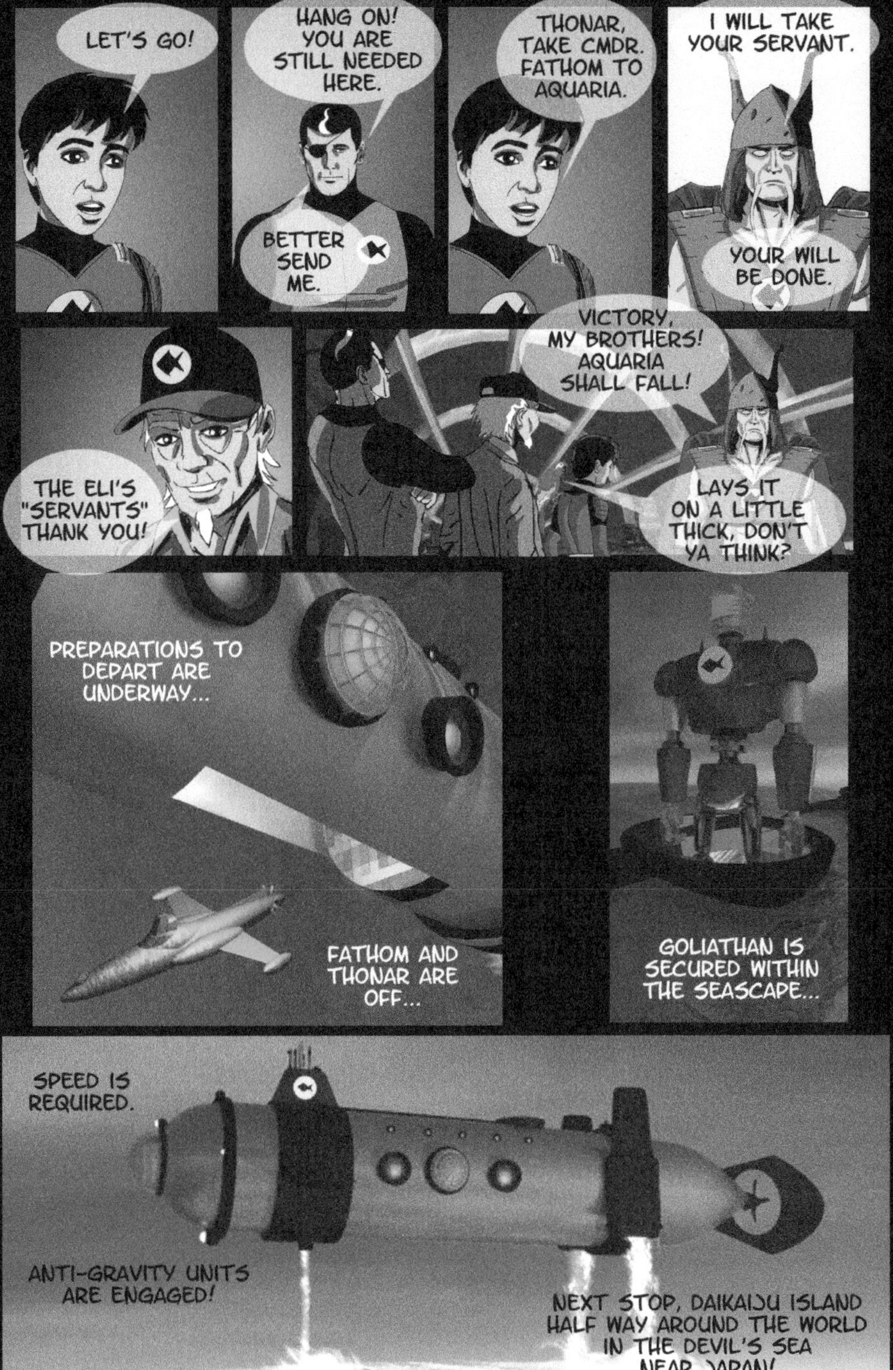
LET'S GO!
HANG ON! YOU ARE STILL NEEDED HERE.
BETTER SEND ME.
THONAR, TAKE CMDR. FATHOM TO AQUARIA.
I WILL TAKE YOUR SERVANT.
YOUR WILL BE DONE.
THE ELI'S "SERVANTS" THANK YOU!
VICTORY, MY BROTHERS! AQUARIA SHALL FALL!
LAYS IT ON A LITTLE THICK, DON'T YA THINK?
PREPARATIONS TO DEPART ARE UNDERWAY...
FATHOM AND THONAR ARE OFF...
GOLIATHAN IS SECURED WITHIN THE SEASCAPE...
SPEED IS REQUIRED.
ANTI-GRAVITY UNITS ARE ENGAGED!
NEXT STOP, DAIKAIJU ISLAND HALF WAY AROUND THE WORLD IN THE DEVIL'S SEA NEAR JAPAN!

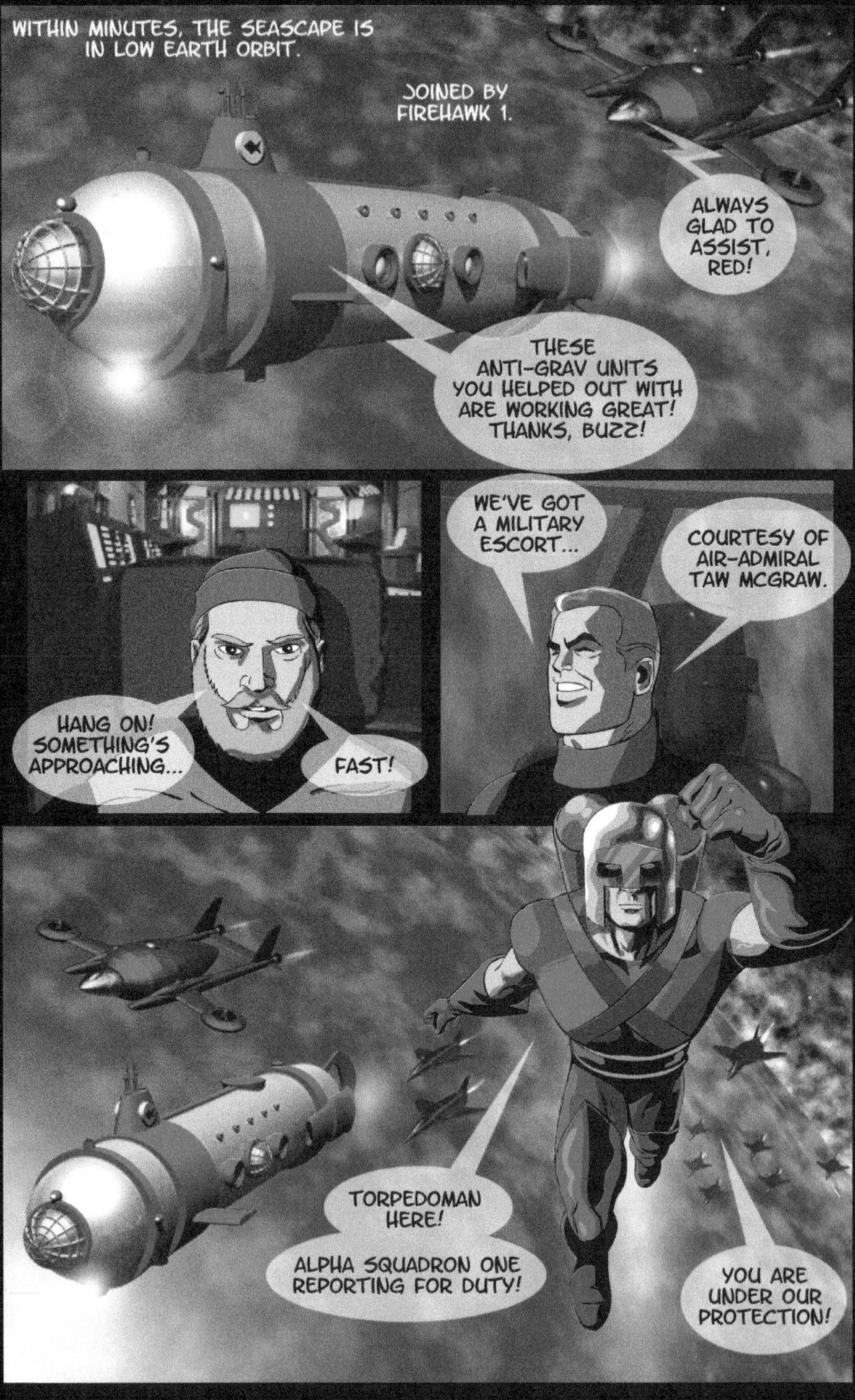
WITHIN MINUTES, THE SEASCAPE IS IN LOW EARTH ORBIT.
JOINED BY FIREHAWK 1.
THESE ANTI-GRAV UNITS YOU HELPED OUT WITH ARE WORKING GREAT! THANKS, BUZZ!
ALWAYS GLAD TO ASSIST, RED!
HANG ON! SOMETHING'S APPROACHING...
FAST!
WE'VE GOT A MILITARY ESCORT...
COURTESY OF AIR-ADMIRAL TAW MCGRAW.
TORPEDOMAN HERE!
ALPHA SQUADRON ONE REPORTING FOR DUTY!
YOU ARE UNDER OUR PROTECTION!

ACT 3 - THE ISLAND OF MONSTERS

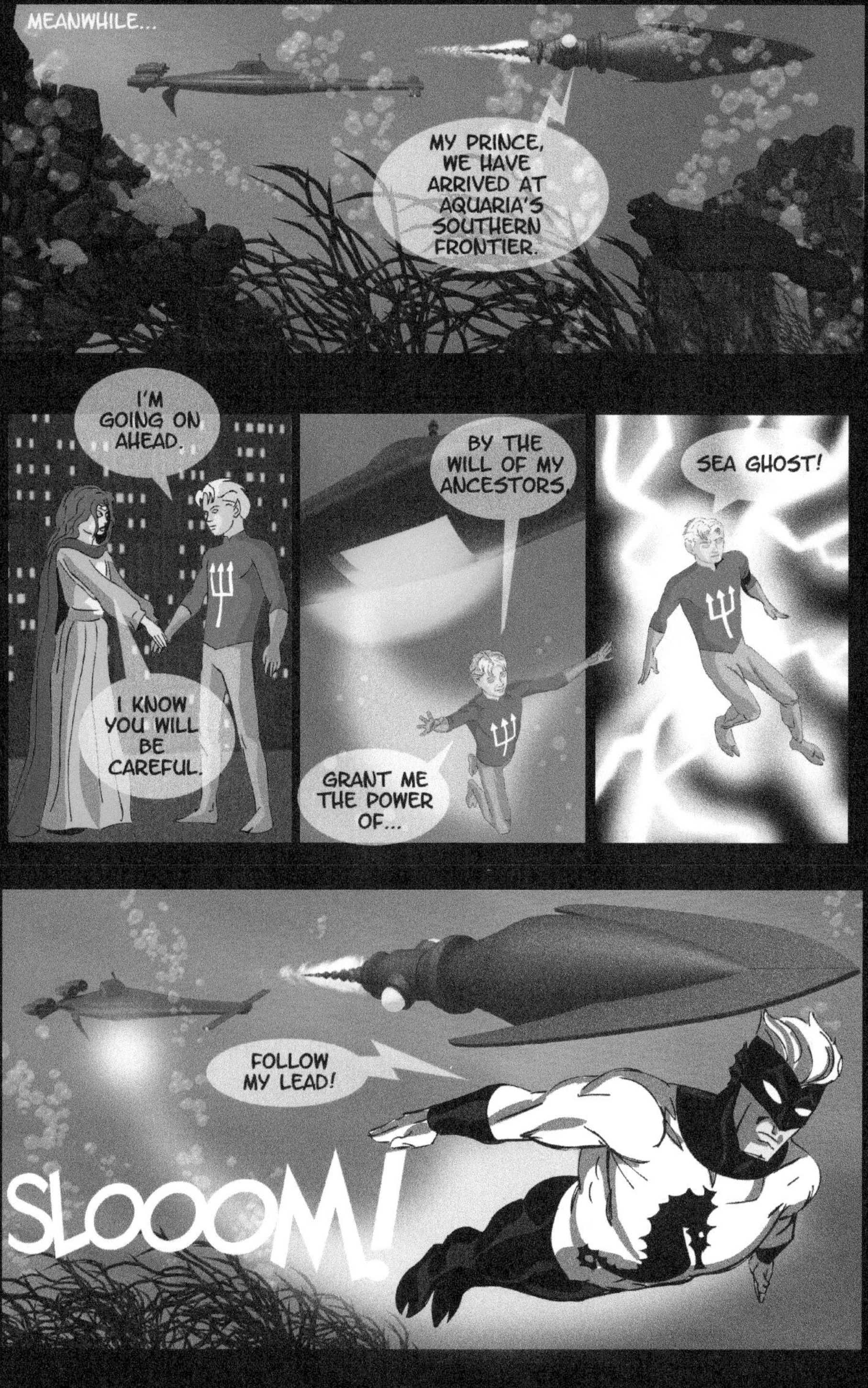
MEANWHILE...
MY PRINCE, WE HAVE ARRIVED AT AQUARIA'S SOUTHERN FRONTIER.
I'M GOING ON AHEAD.
I KNOW YOU WILL BE CAREFUL.
BY THE WILL OF MY ANCESTORS.
GRANT ME THE POWER OF...
SEA GHOST!
FOLLOW MY LEAD!
SLOOOM!

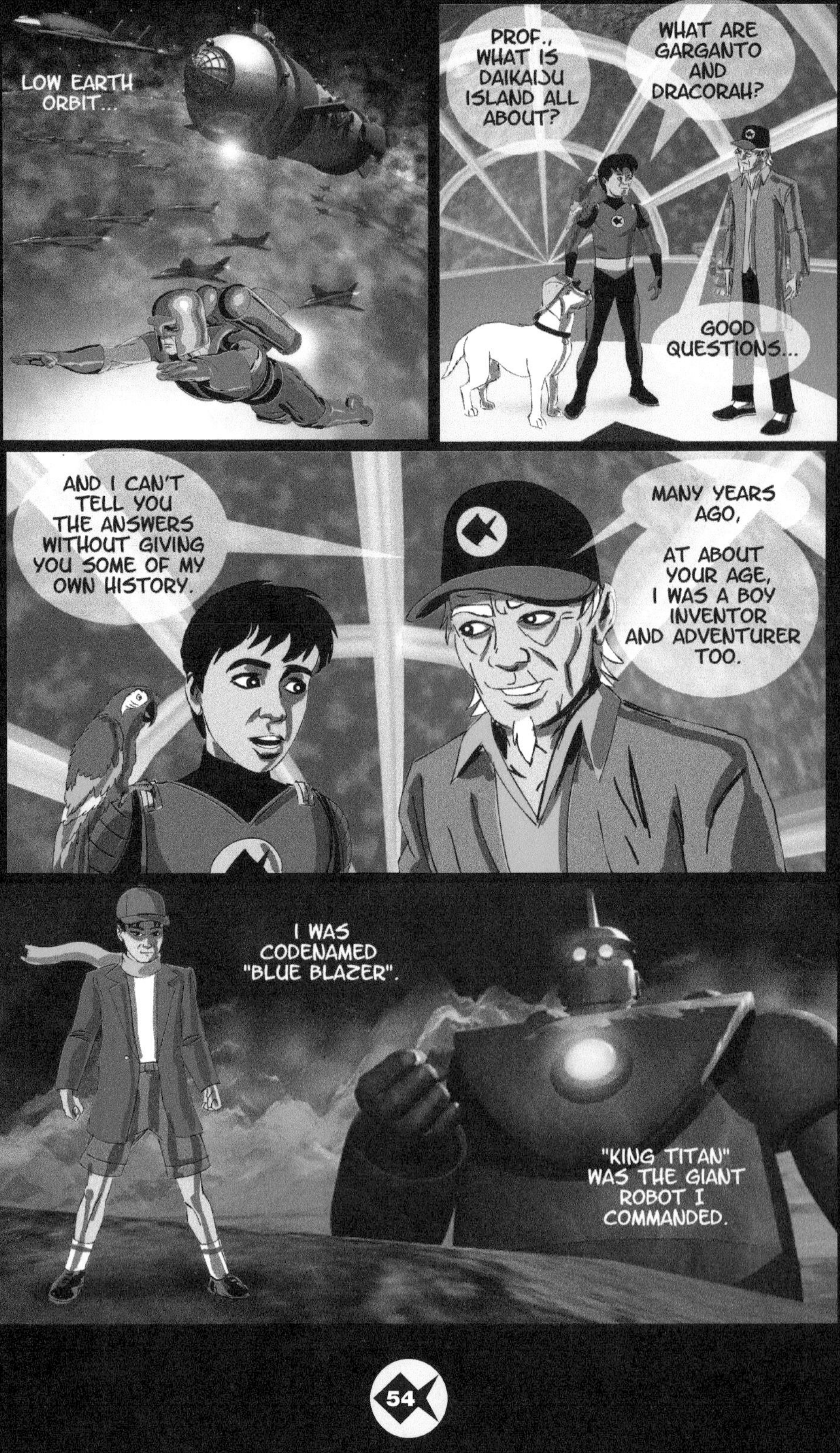
LOW EARTH ORBIT...
PROF., WHAT IS DAIKAIJU ISLAND ALL ABOUT?
WHAT ARE GARGANTO AND DRACORAH?
GOOD QUESTIONS...
AND I CAN'T TELL YOU THE ANSWERS WITHOUT GIVING YOU SOME OF MY OWN HISTORY.
MANY YEARS AGO,
AT ABOUT YOUR AGE, I WAS A BOY INVENTOR AND ADVENTURER TOO.
I WAS CODENAMED "BLUE BLAZER".
"KING TITAN" WAS THE GIANT ROBOT I COMMANDED.

Act 3 - The Island Of Monsters

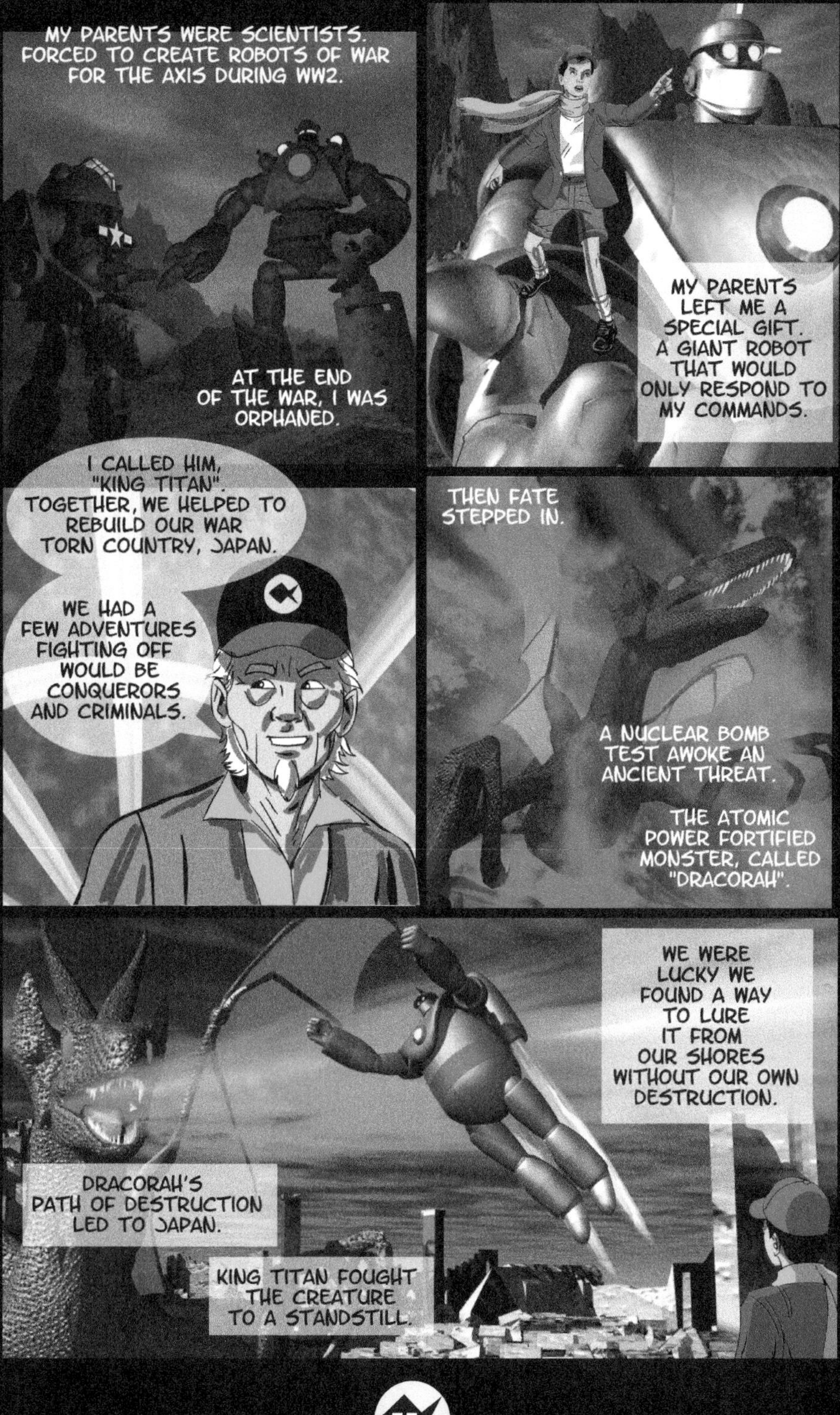

MY PARENTS WERE SCIENTISTS. FORCED TO CREATE ROBOTS OF WAR FOR THE AXIS DURING WW2.
AT THE END OF THE WAR, I WAS ORPHANED.
MY PARENTS LEFT ME A SPECIAL GIFT. A GIANT ROBOT THAT WOULD ONLY RESPOND TO MY COMMANDS.
I CALLED HIM, "KING TITAN". TOGETHER, WE HELPED TO REBUILD OUR WAR TORN COUNTRY, JAPAN.
WE HAD A FEW ADVENTURES FIGHTING OFF WOULD BE CONQUERORS AND CRIMINALS.
THEN FATE STEPPED IN.
A NUCLEAR BOMB TEST AWOKE AN ANCIENT THREAT.
THE ATOMIC POWER FORTIFIED MONSTER, CALLED "DRACORAH".
DRACORAH'S PATH OF DESTRUCTION LED TO JAPAN.
KING TITAN FOUGHT THE CREATURE TO A STANDSTILL.
WE WERE LUCKY WE FOUND A WAY TO LURE IT FROM OUR SHORES WITHOUT OUR OWN DESTRUCTION.

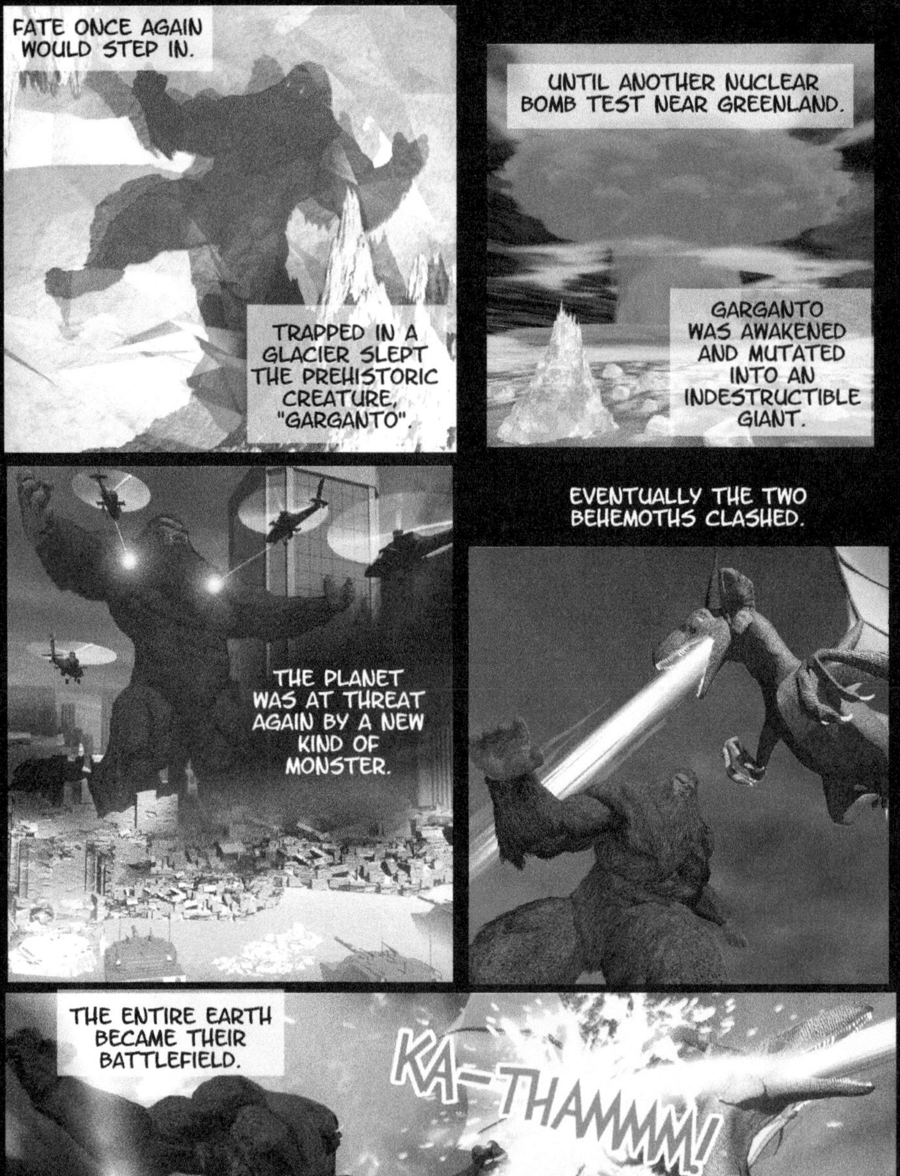
FATE ONCE AGAIN WOULD STEP IN.
TRAPPED IN A GLACIER SLEPT THE PREHISTORIC CREATURE, "GARGANTO".
UNTIL ANOTHER NUCLEAR BOMB TEST NEAR GREENLAND.
GARGANTO WAS AWAKENED AND MUTATED INTO AN INDESTRUCTIBLE GIANT.
THE PLANET WAS AT THREAT AGAIN BY A NEW KIND OF MONSTER.
EVENTUALLY THE TWO BEHEMOTHS CLASHED.
THE ENTIRE EARTH BECAME THEIR BATTLEFIELD.
KA-THAMMM!
THE DESTRUCTION WAS ENORMOUS. NOTHING COULD STOP THEM. ATOMIC WEAPONS MADE THEM STRONGER. SOMETHING HAD TO BE DONE

ACT 3 - THE ISLAND OF MONSTERS

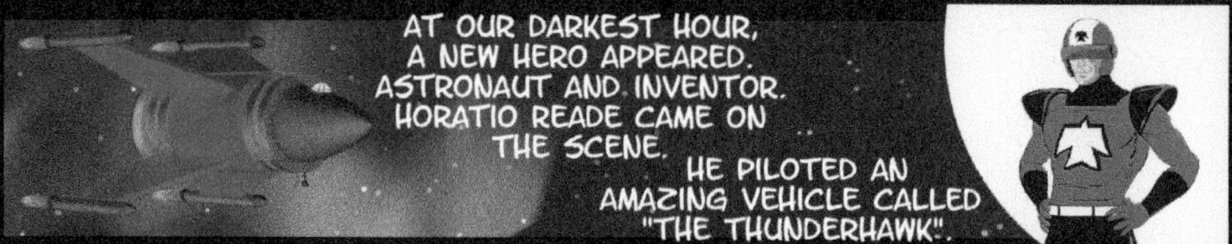
AT OUR DARKEST HOUR, A NEW HERO APPEARED. ASTRONAUT AND INVENTOR. HORATIO READE CAME ON THE SCENE.
HE PILOTED AN AMAZING VEHICLE CALLED "THE THUNDERHAWK".

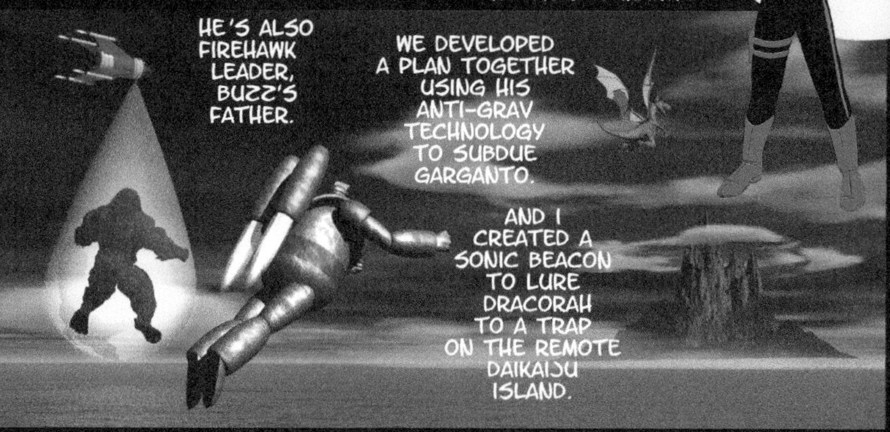
HE'S ALSO FIREHAWK LEADER, BUZZ'S FATHER.
WE DEVELOPED A PLAN TOGETHER USING HIS ANTI-GRAV TECHNOLOGY TO SUBDUE GARGANTO.
AND I CREATED A SONIC BEACON TO LURE DRACORAH TO A TRAP ON THE REMOTE DAIKAIJU ISLAND.

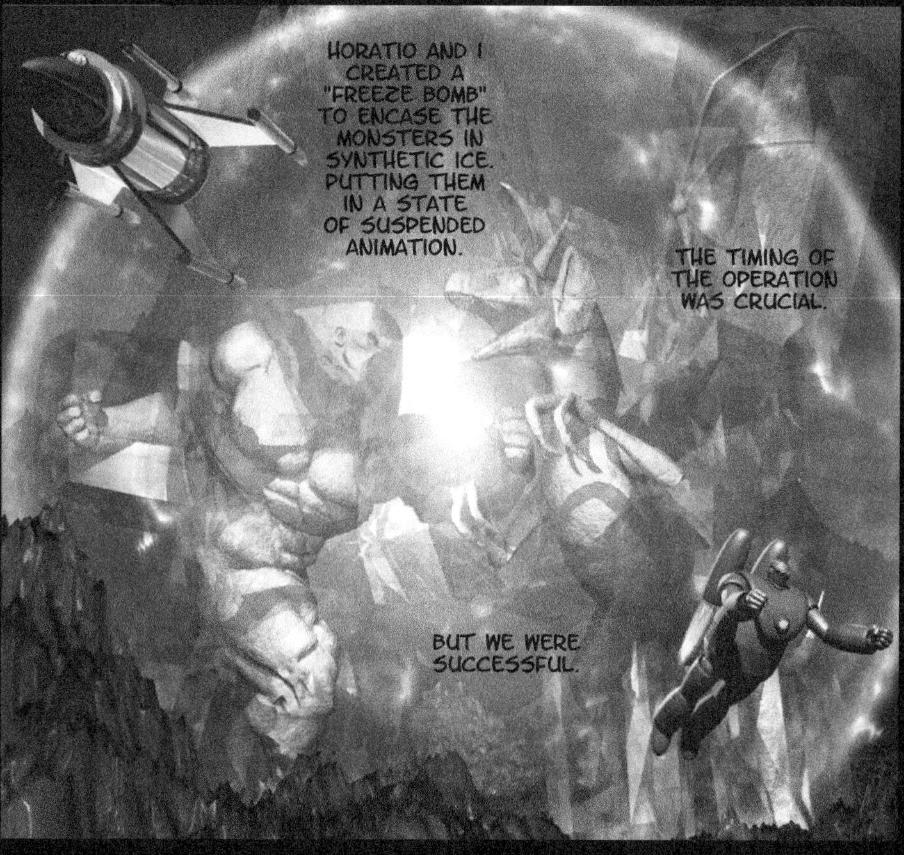
HORATIO AND I CREATED A "FREEZE BOMB" TO ENCASE THE MONSTERS IN SYNTHETIC ICE. PUTTING THEM IN A STATE OF SUSPENDED ANIMATION.
THE TIMING OF THE OPERATION WAS CRUCIAL.
BUT WE WERE SUCCESSFUL.

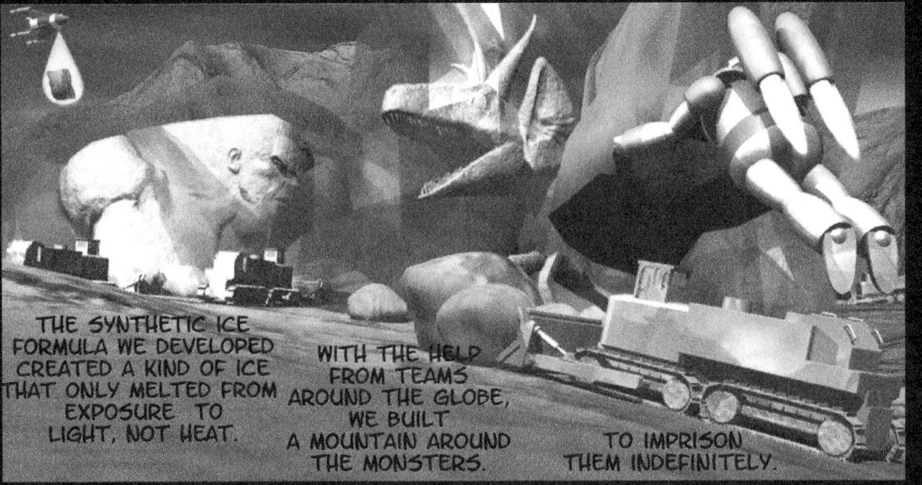
THE SYNTHETIC ICE FORMULA WE DEVELOPED CREATED A KIND OF ICE THAT ONLY MELTED FROM EXPOSURE TO LIGHT, NOT HEAT.
WITH THE HELP FROM TEAMS AROUND THE GLOBE, WE BUILT A MOUNTAIN AROUND THE MONSTERS.
TO IMPRISON THEM INDEFINITELY.

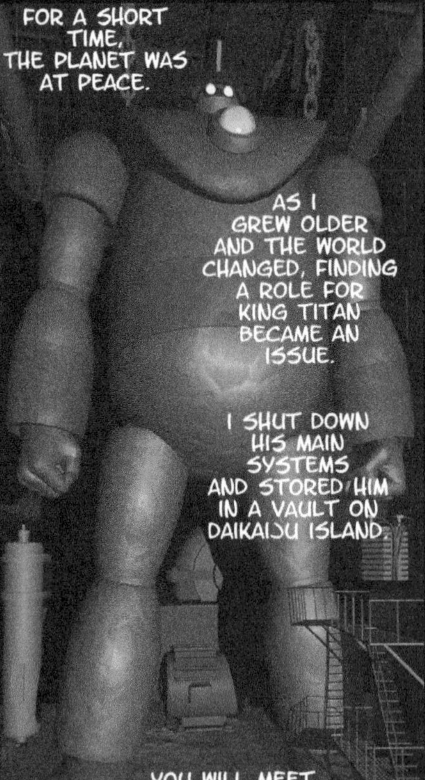
FOR A SHORT TIME, THE PLANET WAS AT PEACE.
AS I GREW OLDER AND THE WORLD CHANGED, FINDING A ROLE FOR KING TITAN BECAME AN ISSUE.
I SHUT DOWN HIS MAIN SYSTEMS AND STORED HIM IN A VAULT ON DAIKAIJU ISLAND.
YOU WILL MEET HIM AFTER WE ARRIVE, ELI.

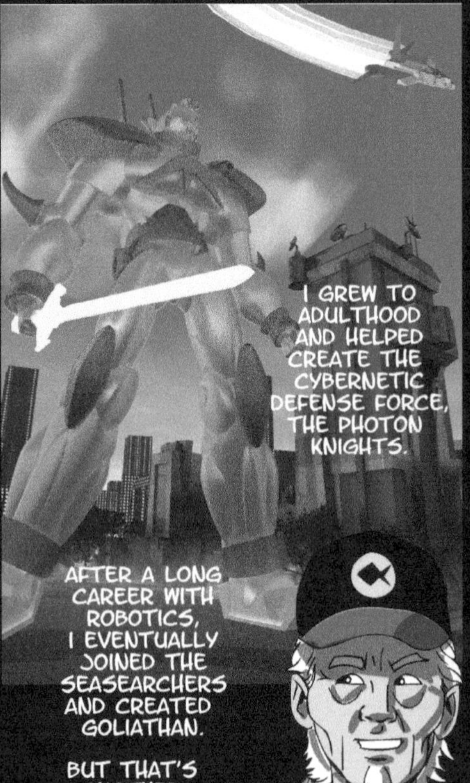
I GREW TO ADULTHOOD AND HELPED CREATE THE CYBERNETIC DEFENSE FORCE, THE PHOTON KNIGHTS.
AFTER A LONG CAREER WITH ROBOTICS, I EVENTUALLY JOINED THE SEASEARCHERS AND CREATED GOLIATHAN.
BUT THAT'S ANOTHER STORY.

Act 3 - The Island Of Monsters

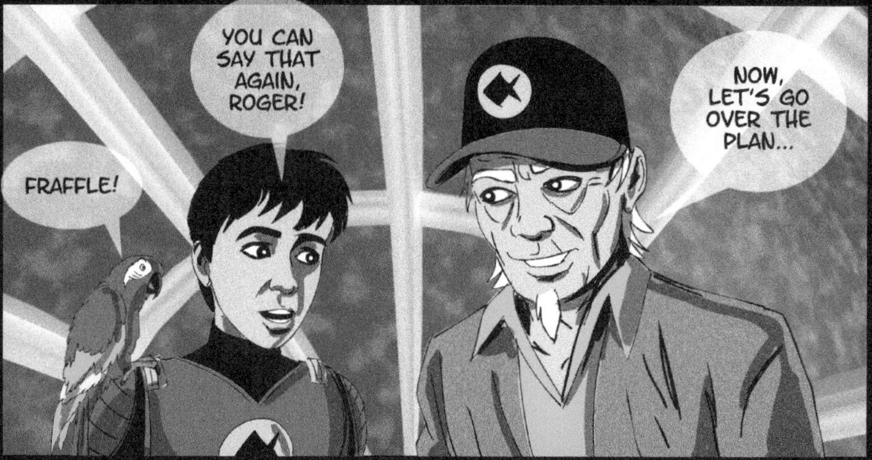
FRAFFLE!
YOU CAN SAY THAT AGAIN, ROGER!
NOW, LET'S GO OVER THE PLAN...

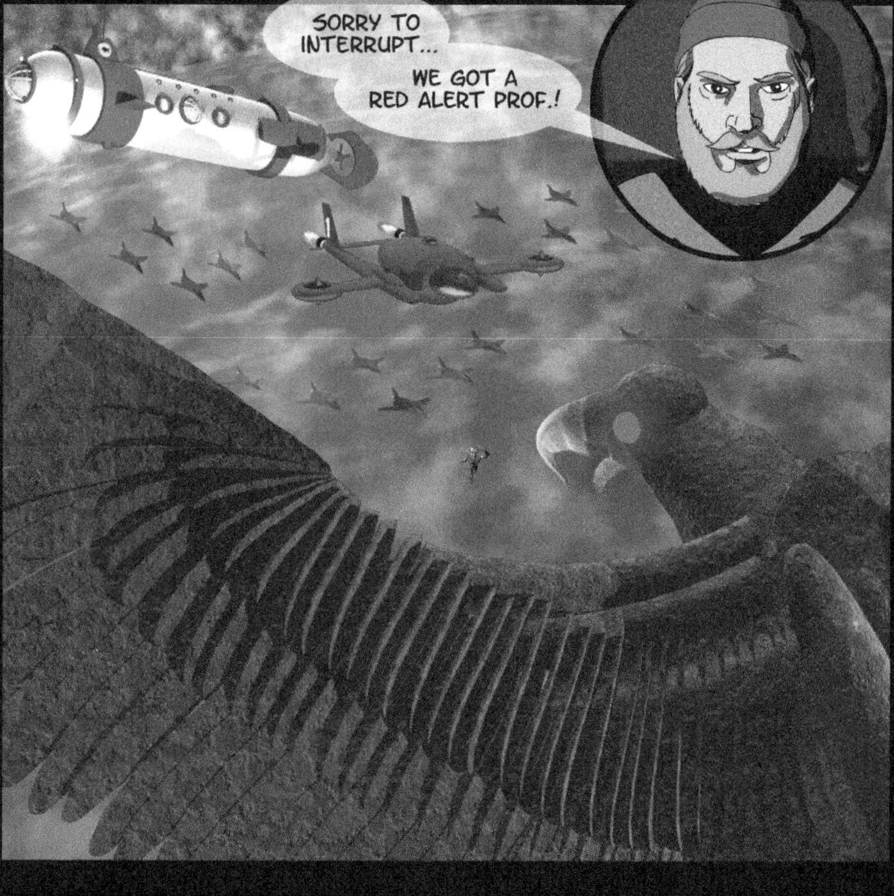
SORRY TO INTERRUPT...
WE GOT A RED ALERT PROF.!

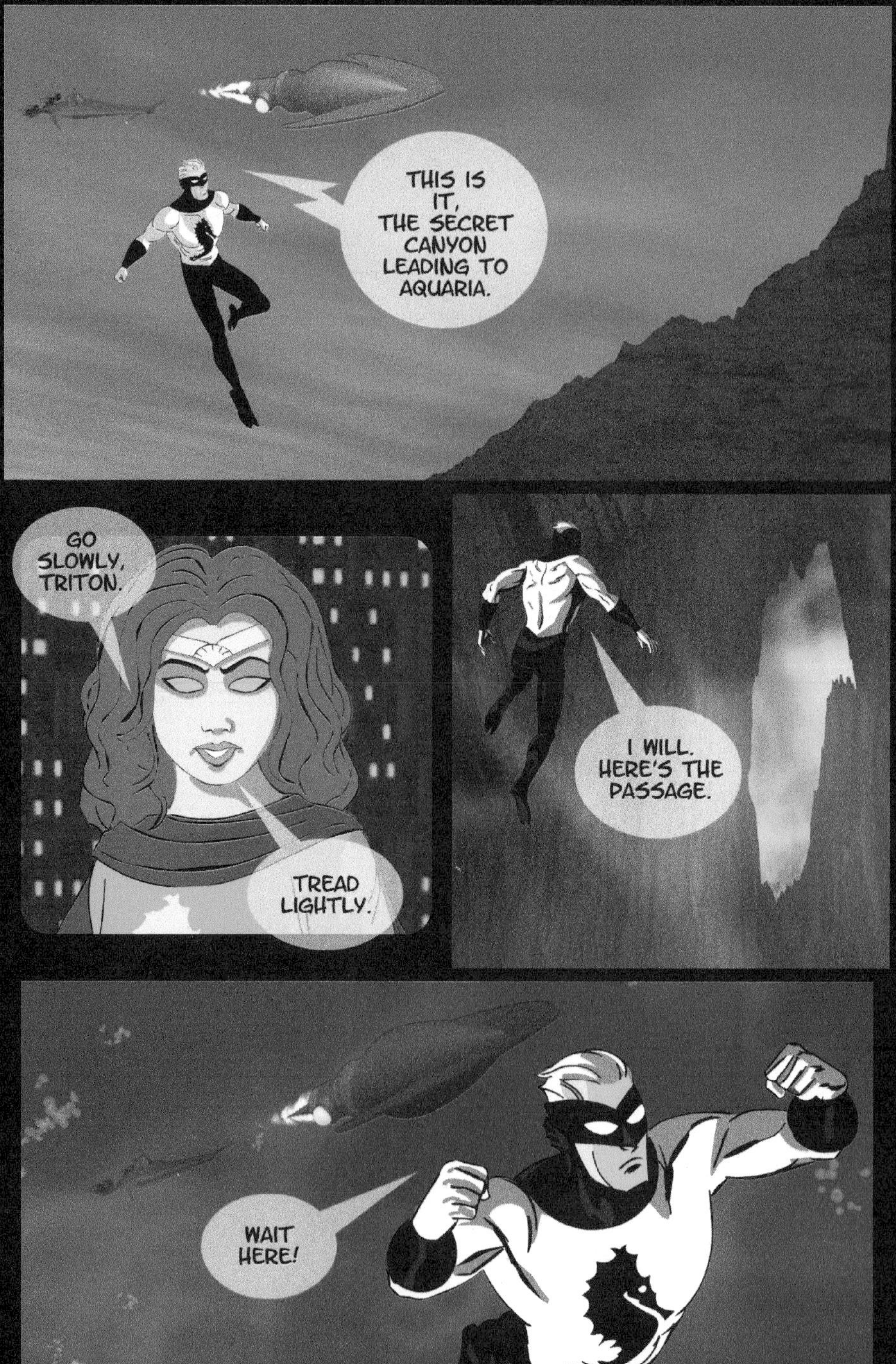
THIS IS IT, THE SECRET CANYON LEADING TO AQUARIA.
GO SLOWLY, TRITON.
TREAD LIGHTLY.
I WILL. HERE'S THE PASSAGE.
WAIT HERE!

Act 3 - The Island Of Monsters

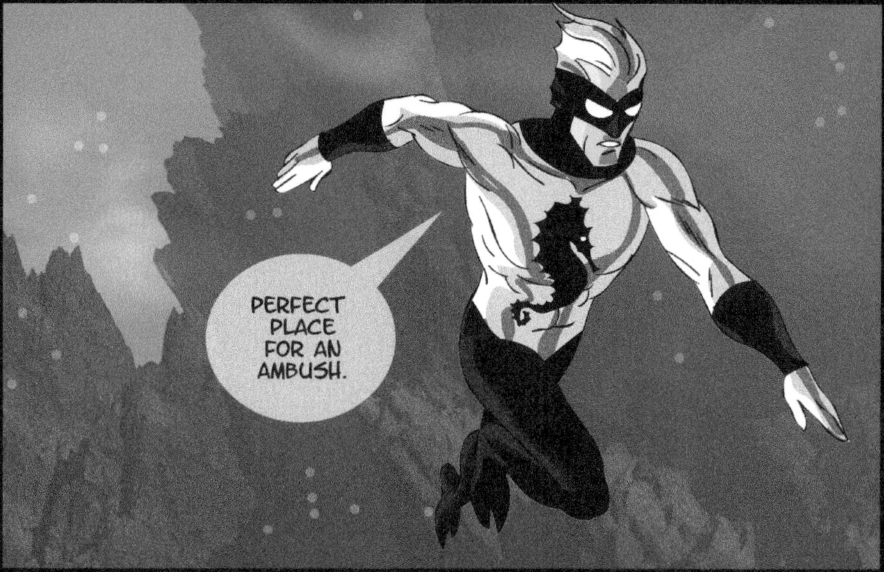
PERFECT PLACE FOR AN AMBUSH.

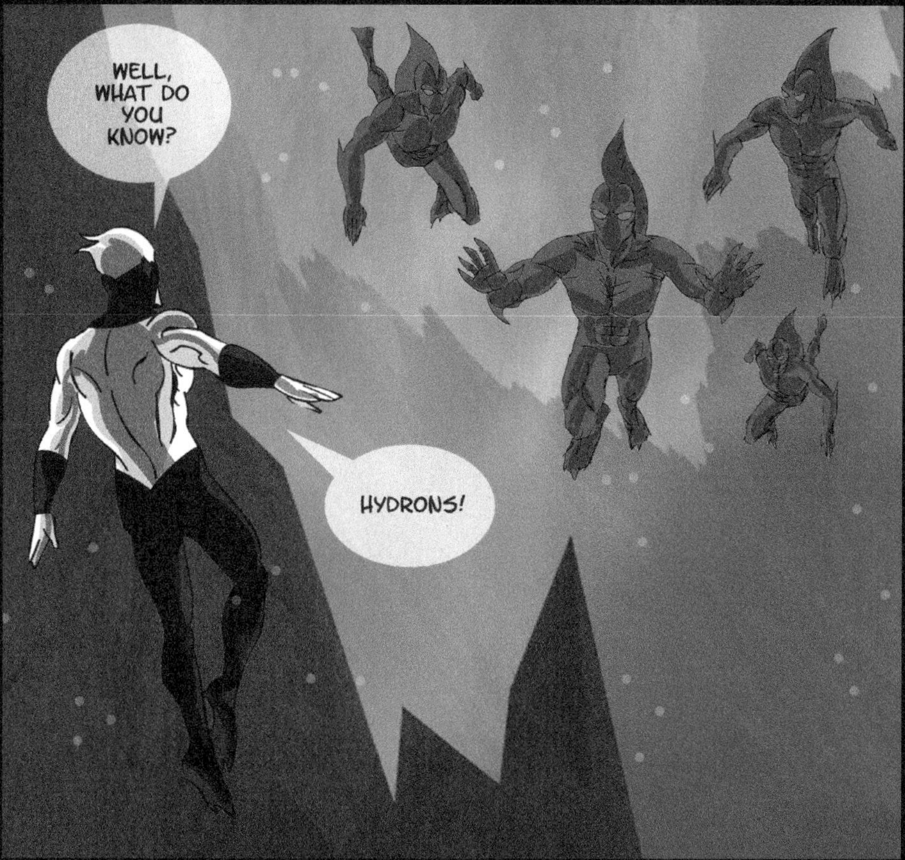
WELL, WHAT DO YOU KNOW?
HYDRONS!

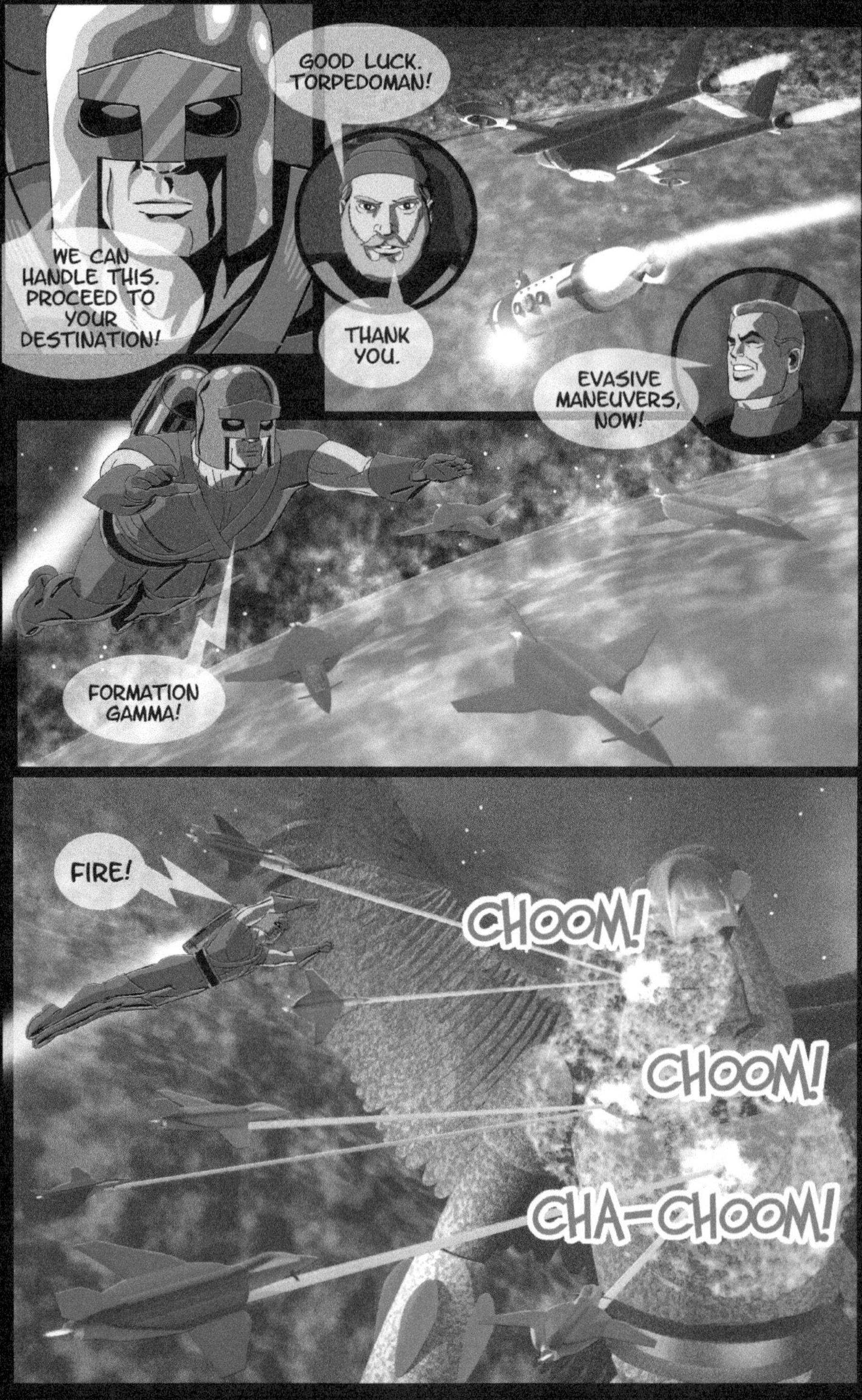
GOOD LUCK. TORPEDOMAN!
WE CAN HANDLE THIS. PROCEED TO YOUR DESTINATION!
THANK YOU.
EVASIVE MANEUVERS, NOW!
FORMATION GAMMA!
FIRE!
CHOOM!
CHOOM!
CHA-CHOOM!

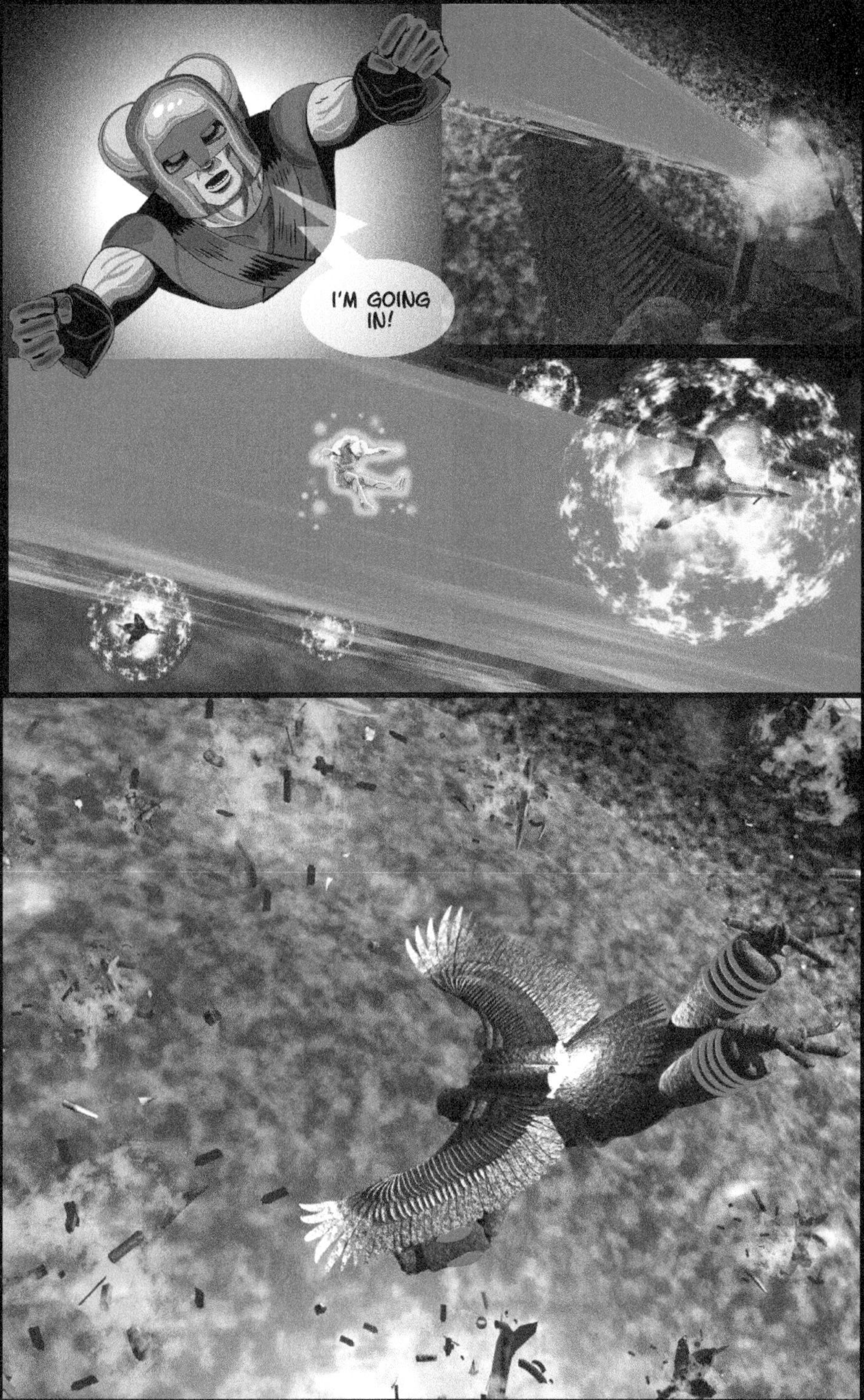
I'M GOING IN!

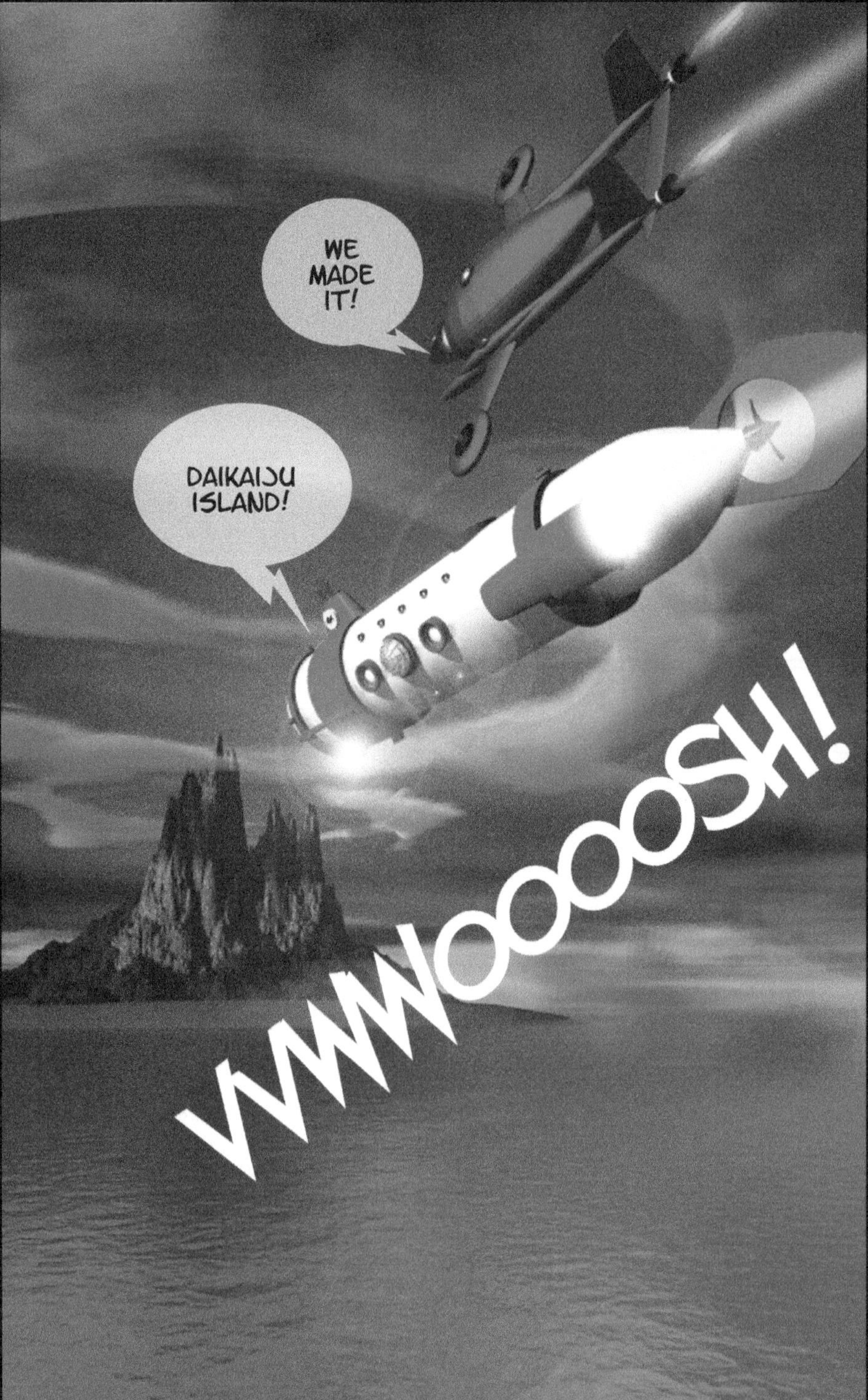
WE MADE IT!
DAIKAIJU ISLAND!
VVVWOOOOOSH!

Act 3 - The Island Of Monsters

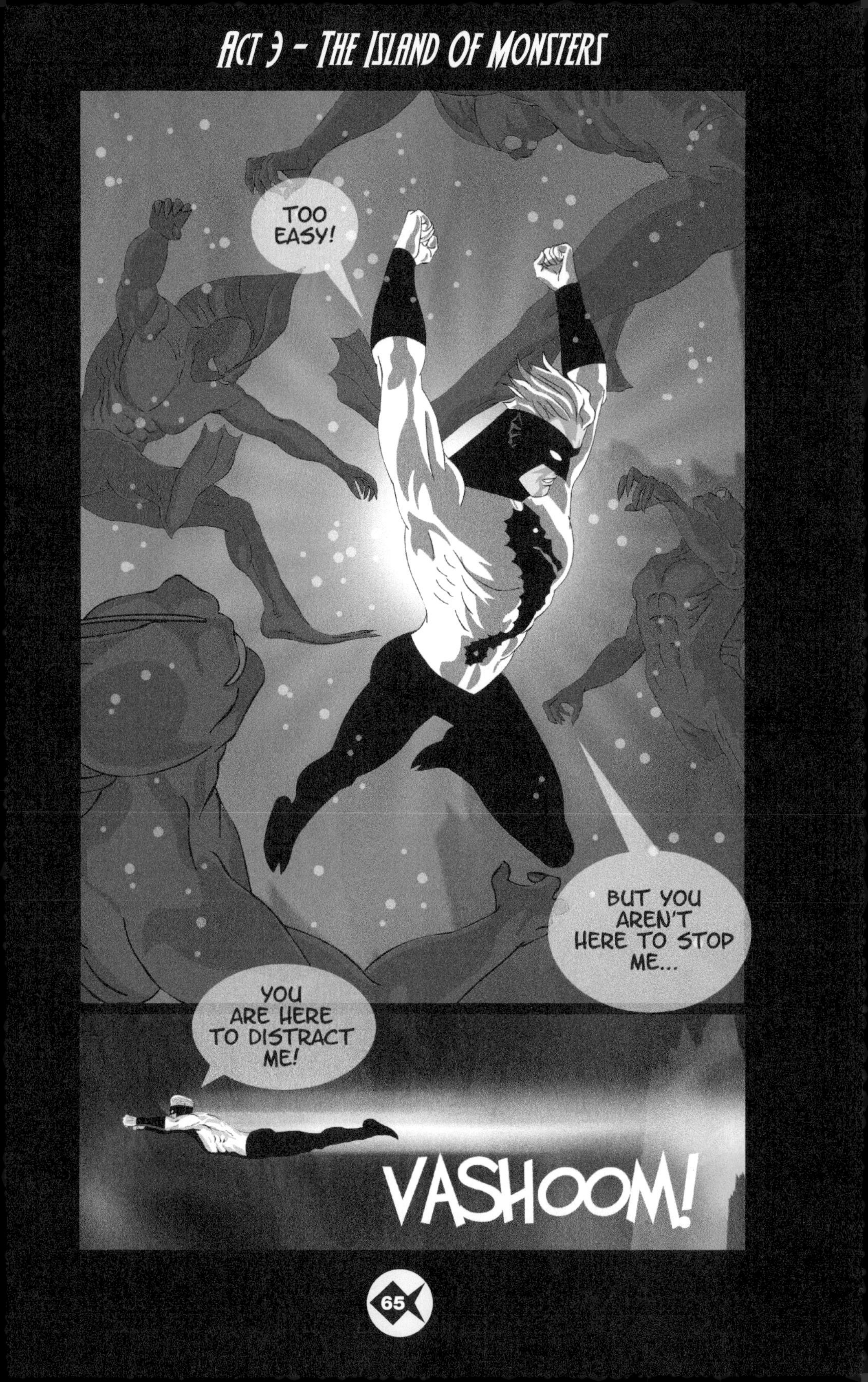
TOO EASY!
BUT YOU AREN'T HERE TO STOP ME...
YOU ARE HERE TO DISTRACT ME!
VASHOOM!

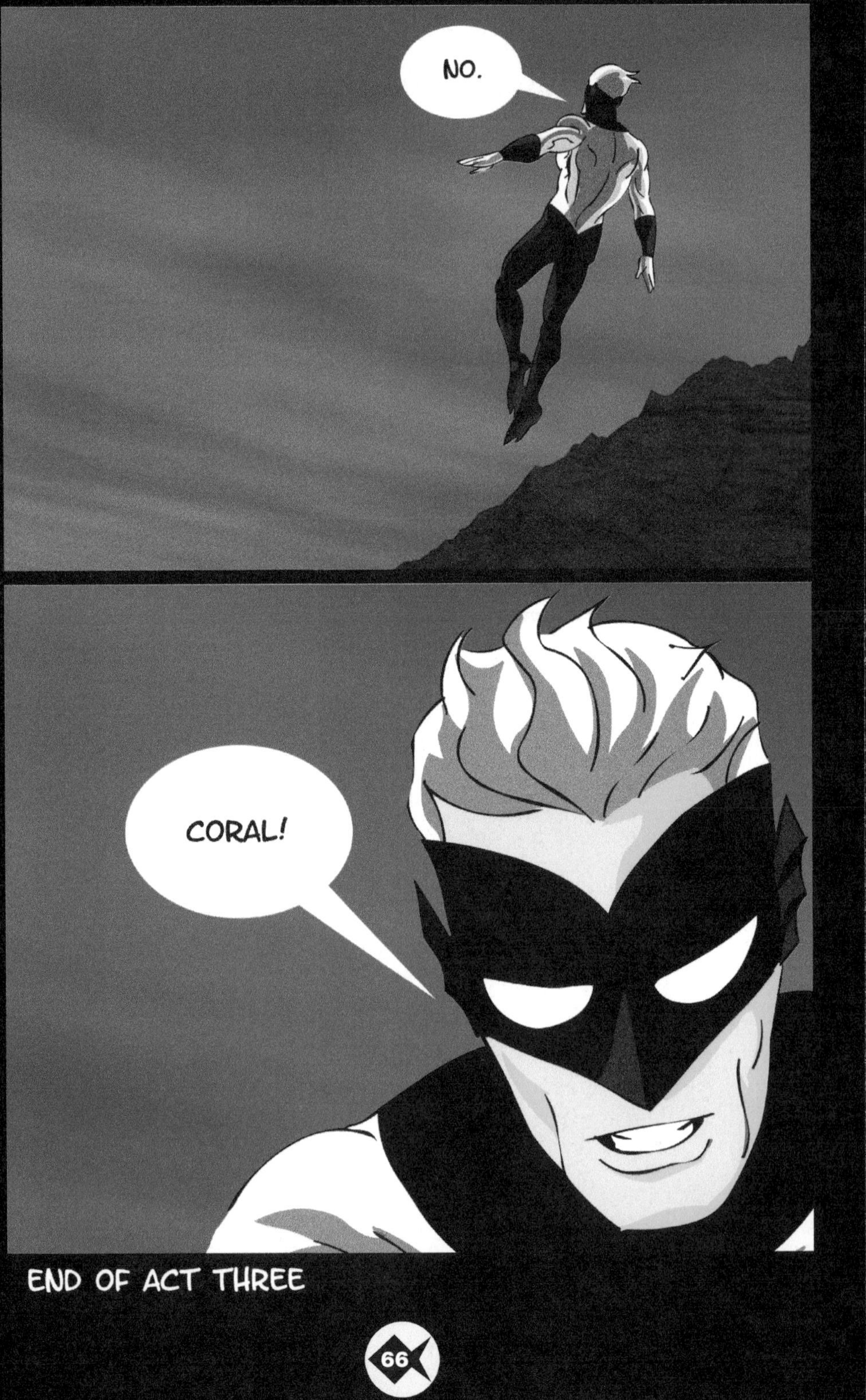
NO.
CORAL!

END OF ACT THREE

Act 4

Power Up

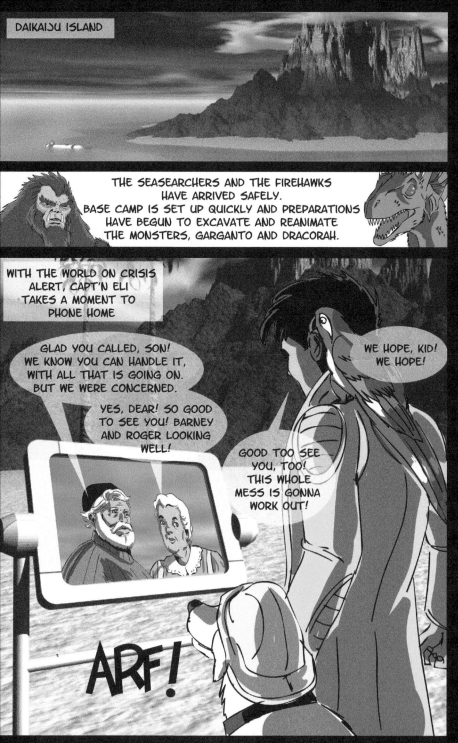

DAIKAIJU ISLAND

THE SEASEARCHERS AND THE FIREHAWKS HAVE ARRIVED SAFELY. BASE CAMP IS SET UP QUICKLY AND PREPARATIONS HAVE BEGUN TO EXCAVATE AND REANIMATE THE MONSTERS, GARGANTO AND DRACORAH.

WITH THE WORLD ON CRISIS ALERT, CAPT'N ELI TAKES A MOMENT TO PHONE HOME

GLAD YOU CALLED, SON! WE KNOW YOU CAN HANDLE IT, WITH ALL THAT IS GOING ON. BUT WE WERE CONCERNED.

WE HOPE, KID! WE HOPE!

YES, DEAR! SO GOOD TO SEE YOU! BARNEY AND ROGER LOOKING WELL!

GOOD TOO SEE YOU, TOO! THIS WHOLE MESS IS GONNA WORK OUT!

ARF!

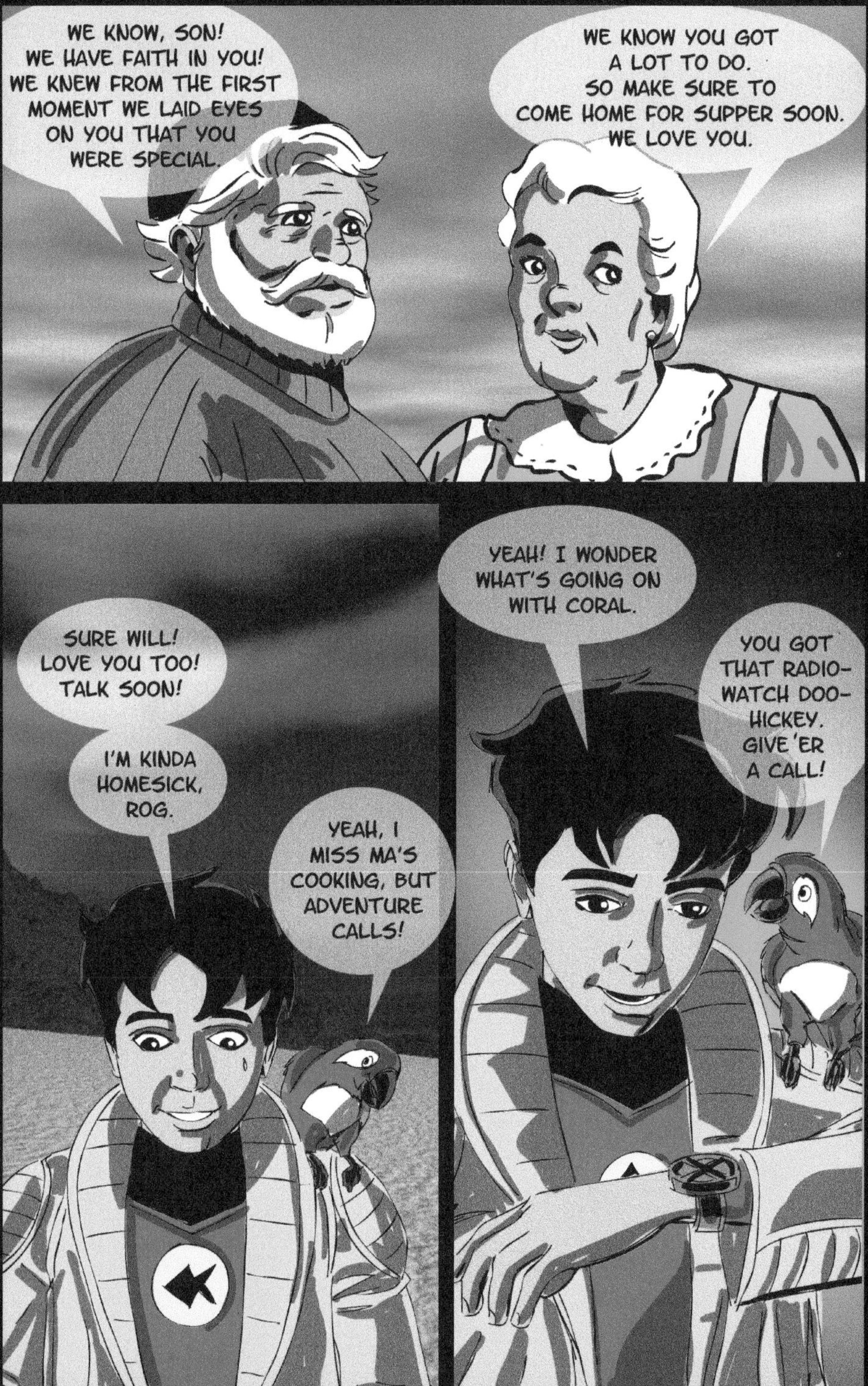
WE KNOW, SON! WE HAVE FAITH IN YOU! WE KNEW FROM THE FIRST MOMENT WE LAID EYES ON YOU THAT YOU WERE SPECIAL.
WE KNOW YOU GOT A LOT TO DO. SO MAKE SURE TO COME HOME FOR SUPPER SOON. WE LOVE YOU.
SURE WILL! LOVE YOU TOO! TALK SOON!
I'M KINDA HOMESICK, ROG.
YEAH, I MISS MA'S COOKING, BUT ADVENTURE CALLS!
YEAH! I WONDER WHAT'S GOING ON WITH CORAL.
YOU GOT THAT RADIO-WATCH DOO-HICKEY. GIVE 'ER A CALL!

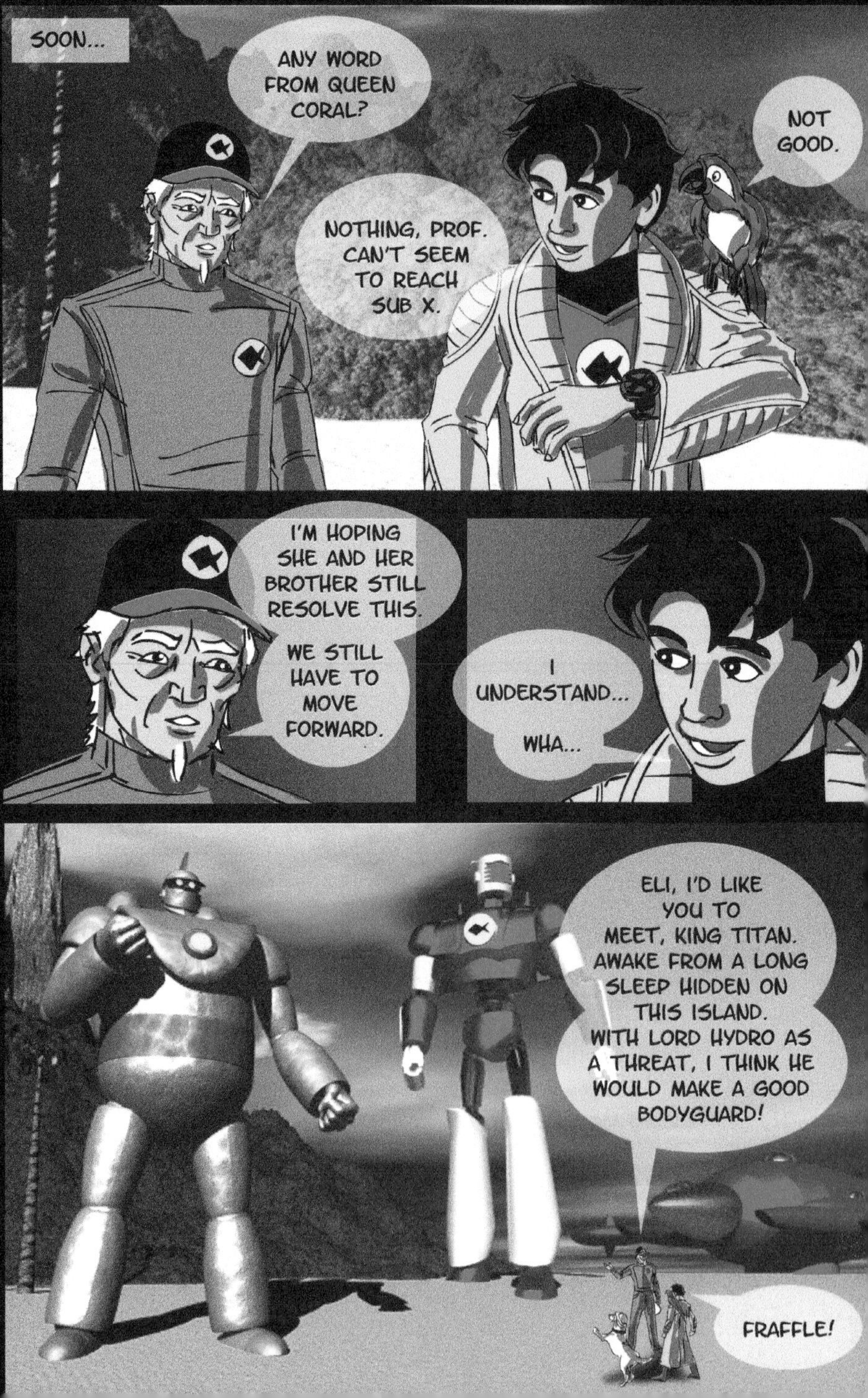
SOON...
ANY WORD FROM QUEEN CORAL?
NOTHING, PROF. CAN'T SEEM TO REACH SUB X.
NOT GOOD.
I'M HOPING SHE AND HER BROTHER STILL RESOLVE THIS.
WE STILL HAVE TO MOVE FORWARD.
I UNDERSTAND...
WHA...
ELI, I'D LIKE YOU TO MEET, KING TITAN. AWAKE FROM A LONG SLEEP HIDDEN ON THIS ISLAND. WITH LORD HYDRO AS A THREAT, I THINK HE WOULD MAKE A GOOD BODYGUARD!
FRAFFLE!

ACT 4 - POWER UP

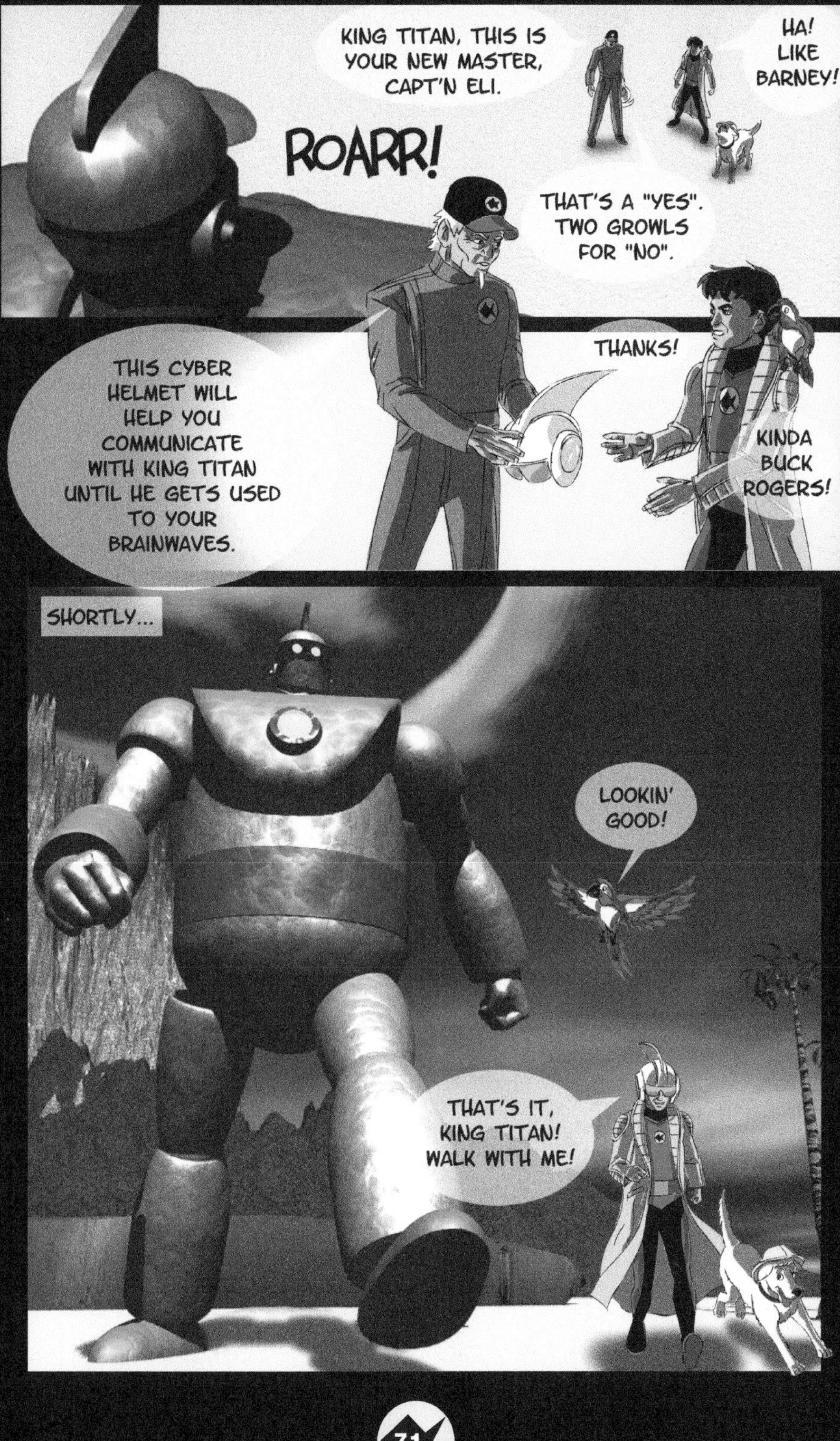
KING TITAN, THIS IS YOUR NEW MASTER, CAPT'N ELI.
HA! LIKE BARNEY!
ROARR!
THAT'S A "YES". TWO GROWLS FOR "NO".
THIS CYBER HELMET WILL HELP YOU COMMUNICATE WITH KING TITAN UNTIL HE GETS USED TO YOUR BRAINWAVES.
THANKS!
KINDA BUCK ROGERS!
SHORTLY...
LOOKIN' GOOD!
THAT'S IT, KING TITAN! WALK WITH ME!

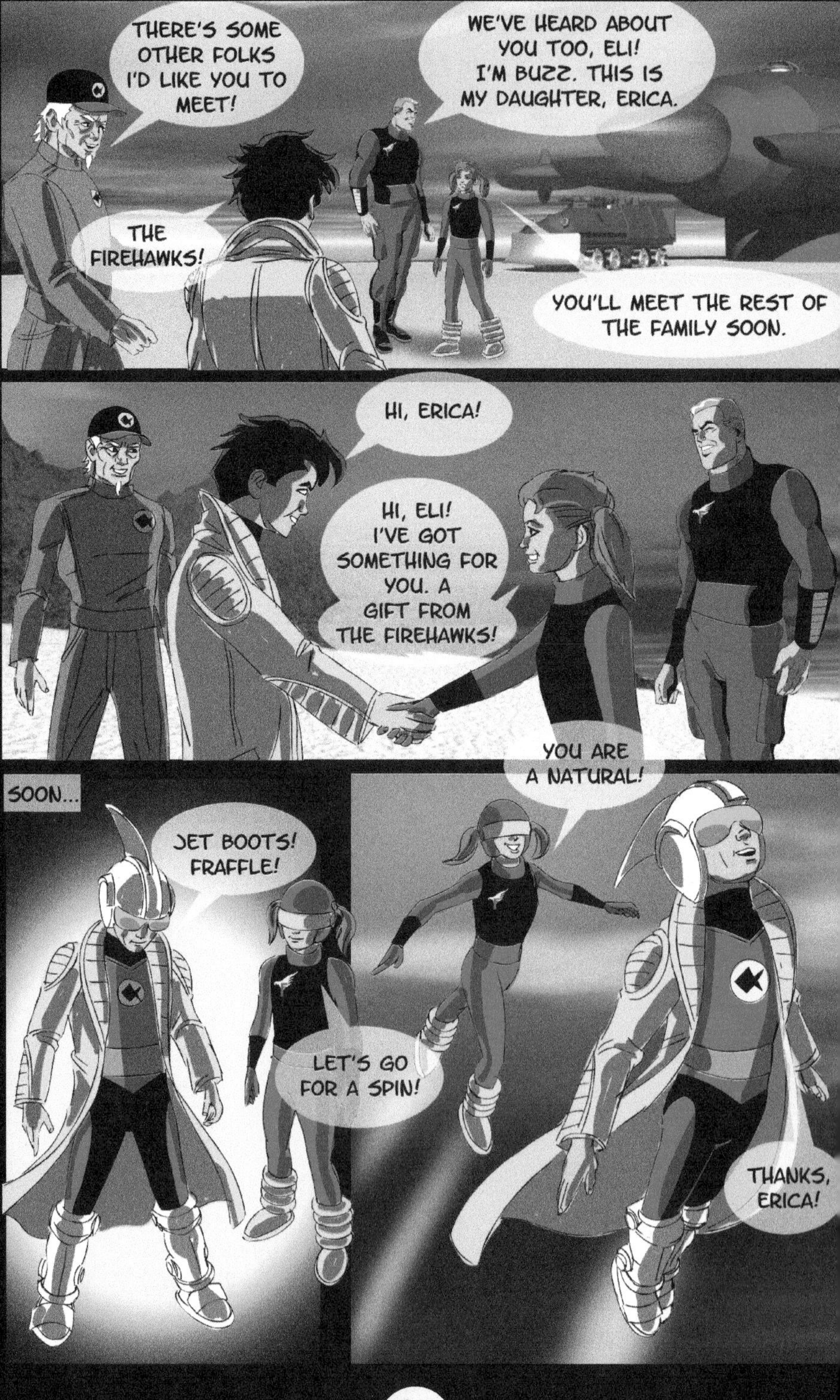
THERE'S SOME OTHER FOLKS I'D LIKE YOU TO MEET!
WE'VE HEARD ABOUT YOU TOO, ELI! I'M BUZZ. THIS IS MY DAUGHTER, ERICA.
THE FIREHAWKS!
YOU'LL MEET THE REST OF THE FAMILY SOON.
HI, ERICA!
HI, ELI! I'VE GOT SOMETHING FOR YOU. A GIFT FROM THE FIREHAWKS!
SOON...
JET BOOTS! FRAFFLE!
LET'S GO FOR A SPIN!
YOU ARE A NATURAL!
THANKS, ERICA!

Act 4 - Power Up

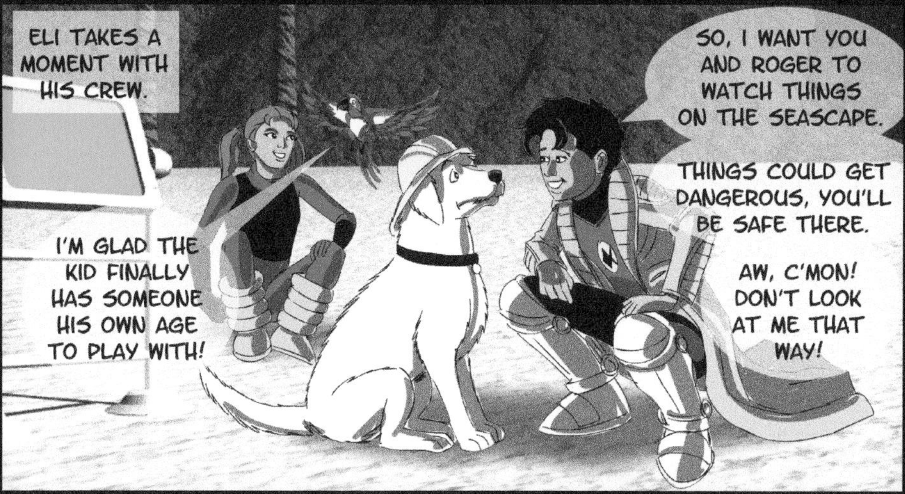
ELI TAKES A MOMENT WITH HIS CREW.
SO, I WANT YOU AND ROGER TO WATCH THINGS ON THE SEASCAPE.
THINGS COULD GET DANGEROUS, YOU'LL BE SAFE THERE.
I'M GLAD THE KID FINALLY HAS SOMEONE HIS OWN AGE TO PLAY WITH!
AW, C'MON! DON'T LOOK AT ME THAT WAY!

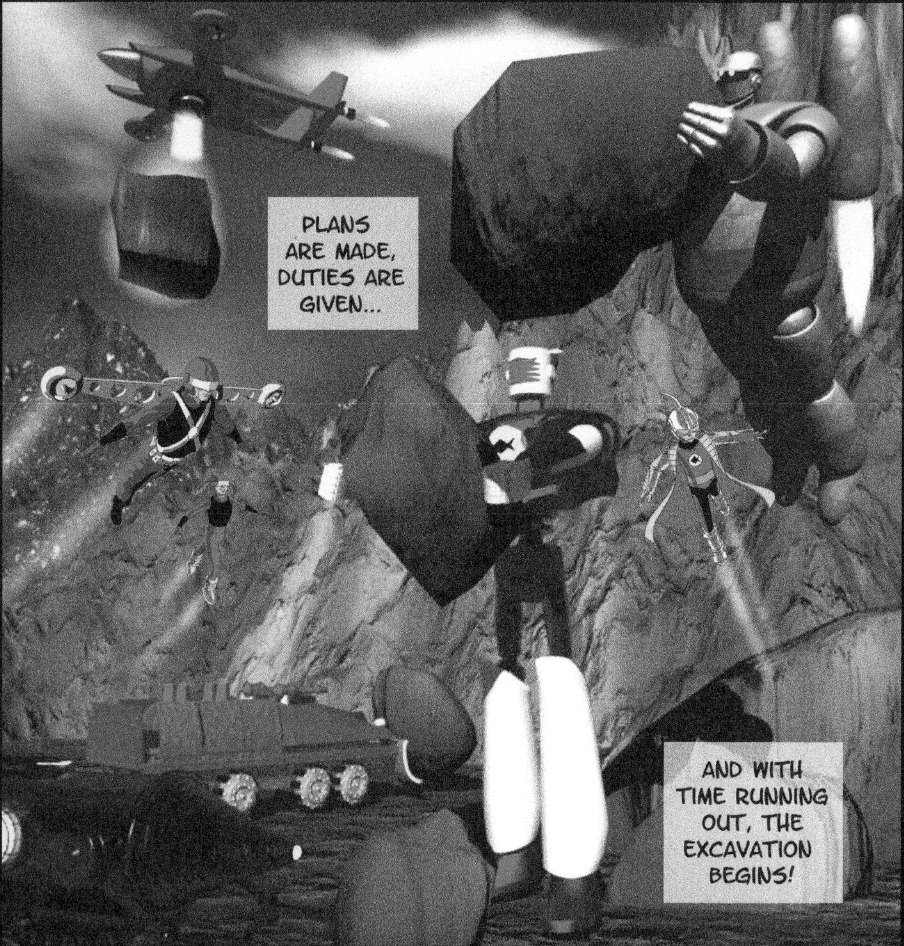
PLANS ARE MADE, DUTIES ARE GIVEN...
AND WITH TIME RUNNING OUT, THE EXCAVATION BEGINS!

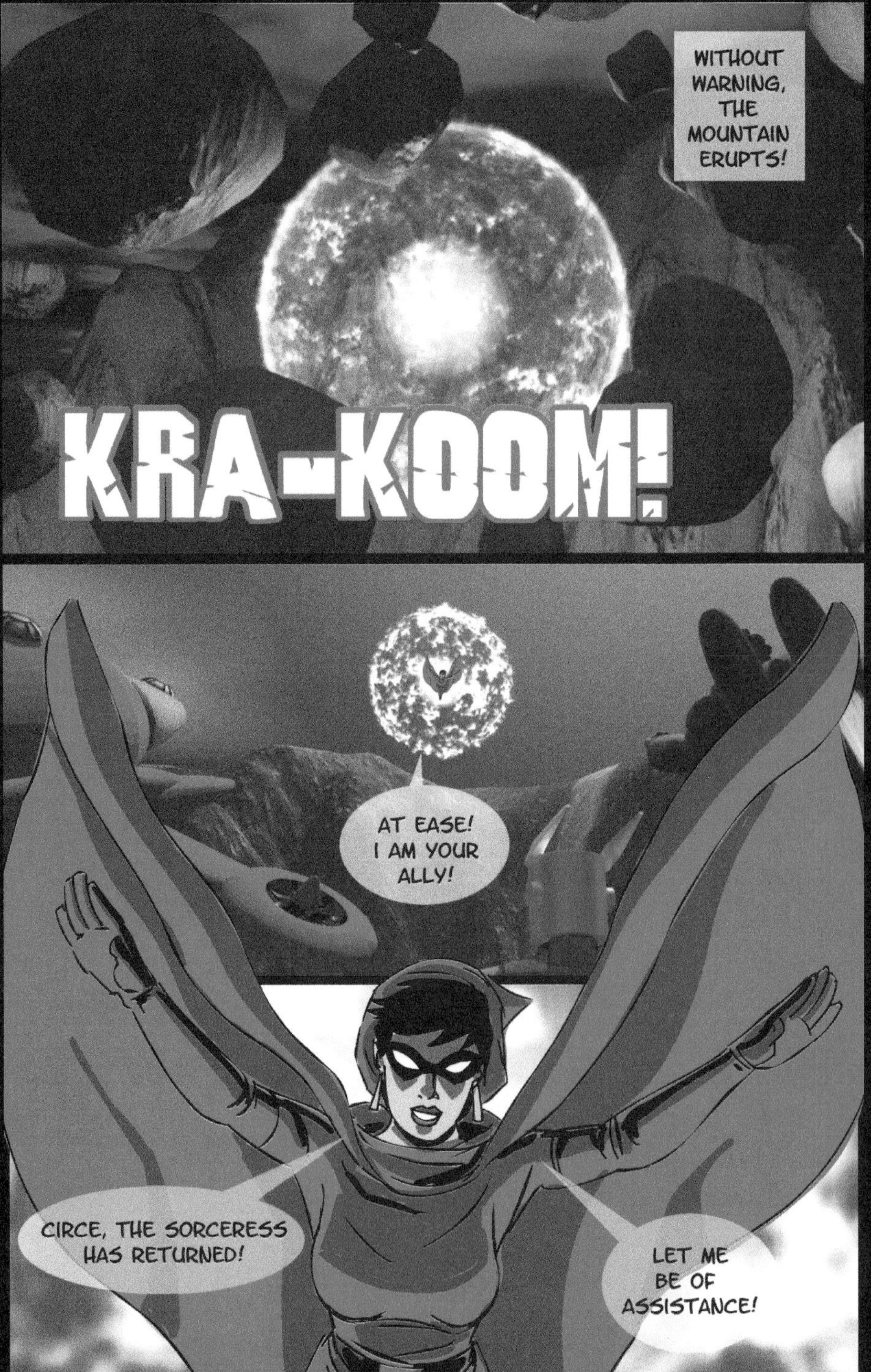
WITHOUT WARNING, THE MOUNTAIN ERUPTS!
KRA-KOOM!
AT EASE! I AM YOUR ALLY!
CIRCE, THE SORCERESS HAS RETURNED!
LET ME BE OF ASSISTANCE!

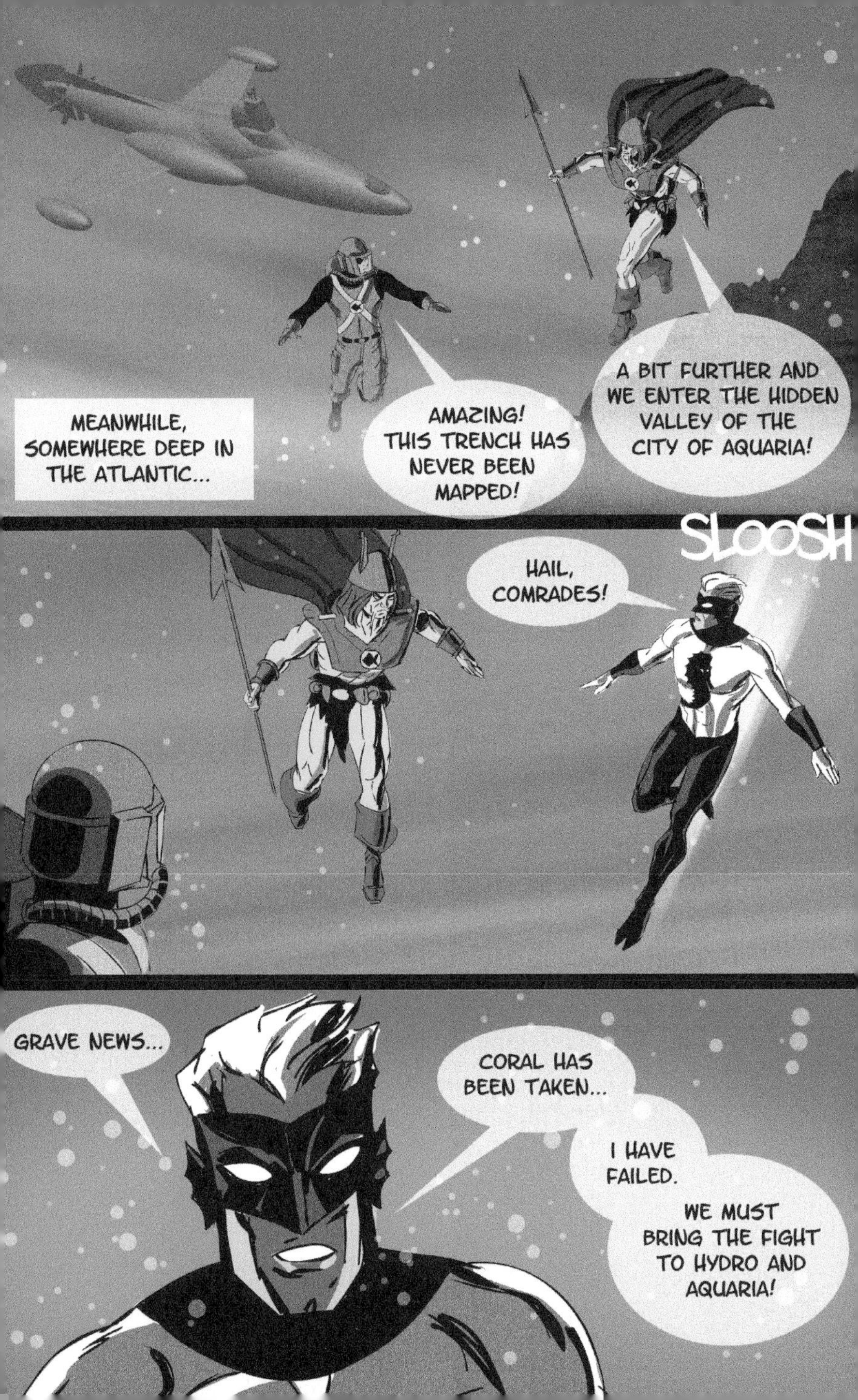
MEANWHILE, SOMEWHERE DEEP IN THE ATLANTIC...
AMAZING! THIS TRENCH HAS NEVER BEEN MAPPED!
A BIT FURTHER AND WE ENTER THE HIDDEN VALLEY OF THE CITY OF AQUARIA!
SLOOSH
HAIL, COMRADES!
GRAVE NEWS...
CORAL HAS BEEN TAKEN...
I HAVE FAILED.
WE MUST BRING THE FIGHT TO HYDRO AND AQUARIA!

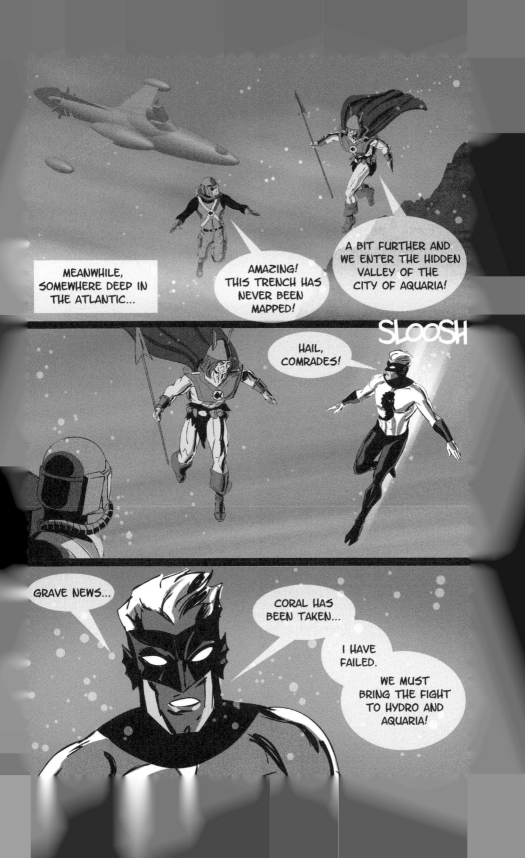

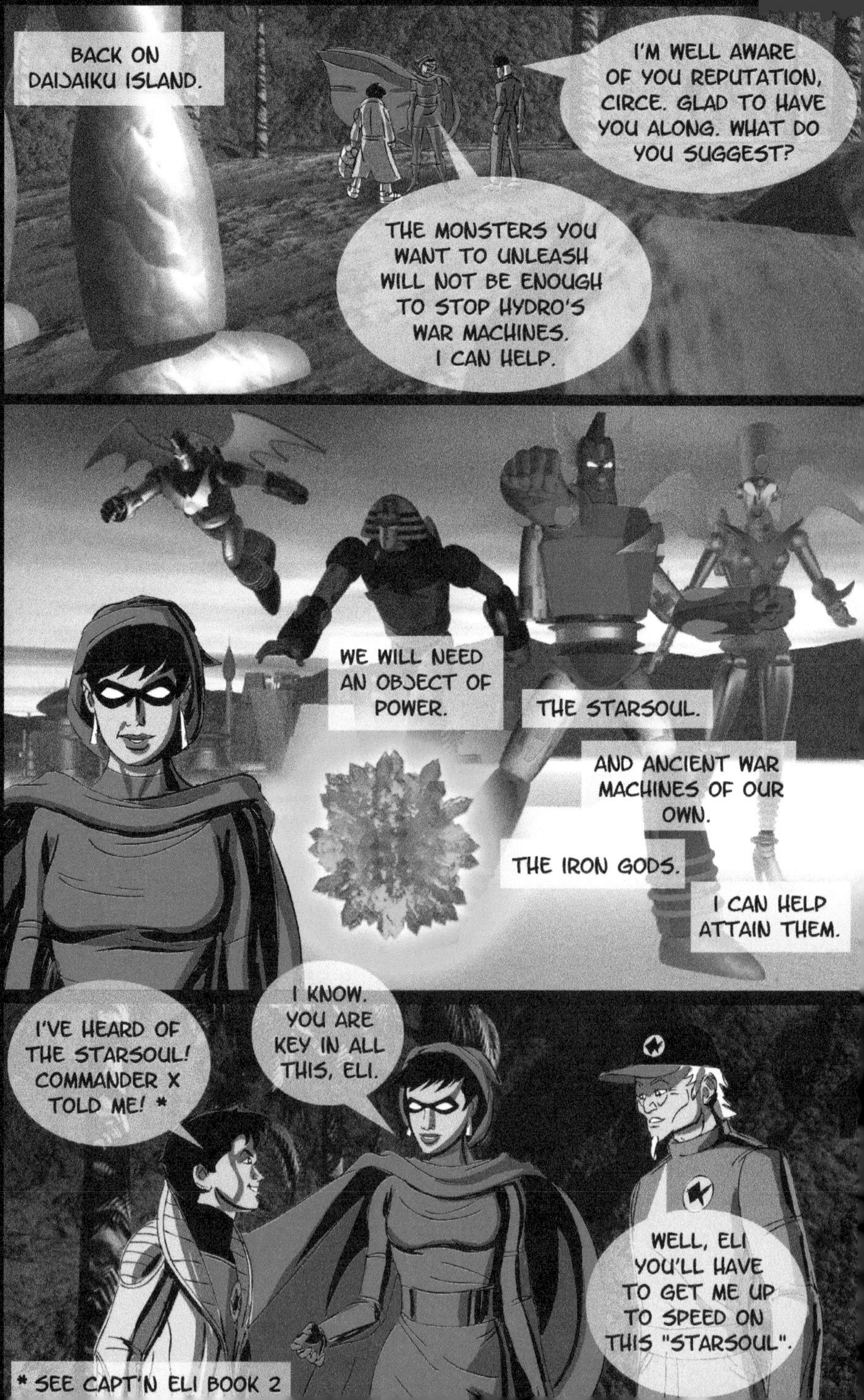
BACK ON DAIJAIKU ISLAND.
I'M WELL AWARE OF YOU REPUTATION, CIRCE. GLAD TO HAVE YOU ALONG. WHAT DO YOU SUGGEST?
THE MONSTERS YOU WANT TO UNLEASH WILL NOT BE ENOUGH TO STOP HYDRO'S WAR MACHINES. I CAN HELP.
WE WILL NEED AN OBJECT OF POWER.
THE STARSOUL.
AND ANCIENT WAR MACHINES OF OUR OWN.
THE IRON GODS.
I CAN HELP ATTAIN THEM.
I'VE HEARD OF THE STARSOUL! COMMANDER X TOLD ME! *
I KNOW. YOU ARE KEY IN ALL THIS, ELI.
WELL, ELI YOU'LL HAVE TO GET ME UP TO SPEED ON THIS "STARSOUL".
* SEE CAPT'N ELI BOOK 2

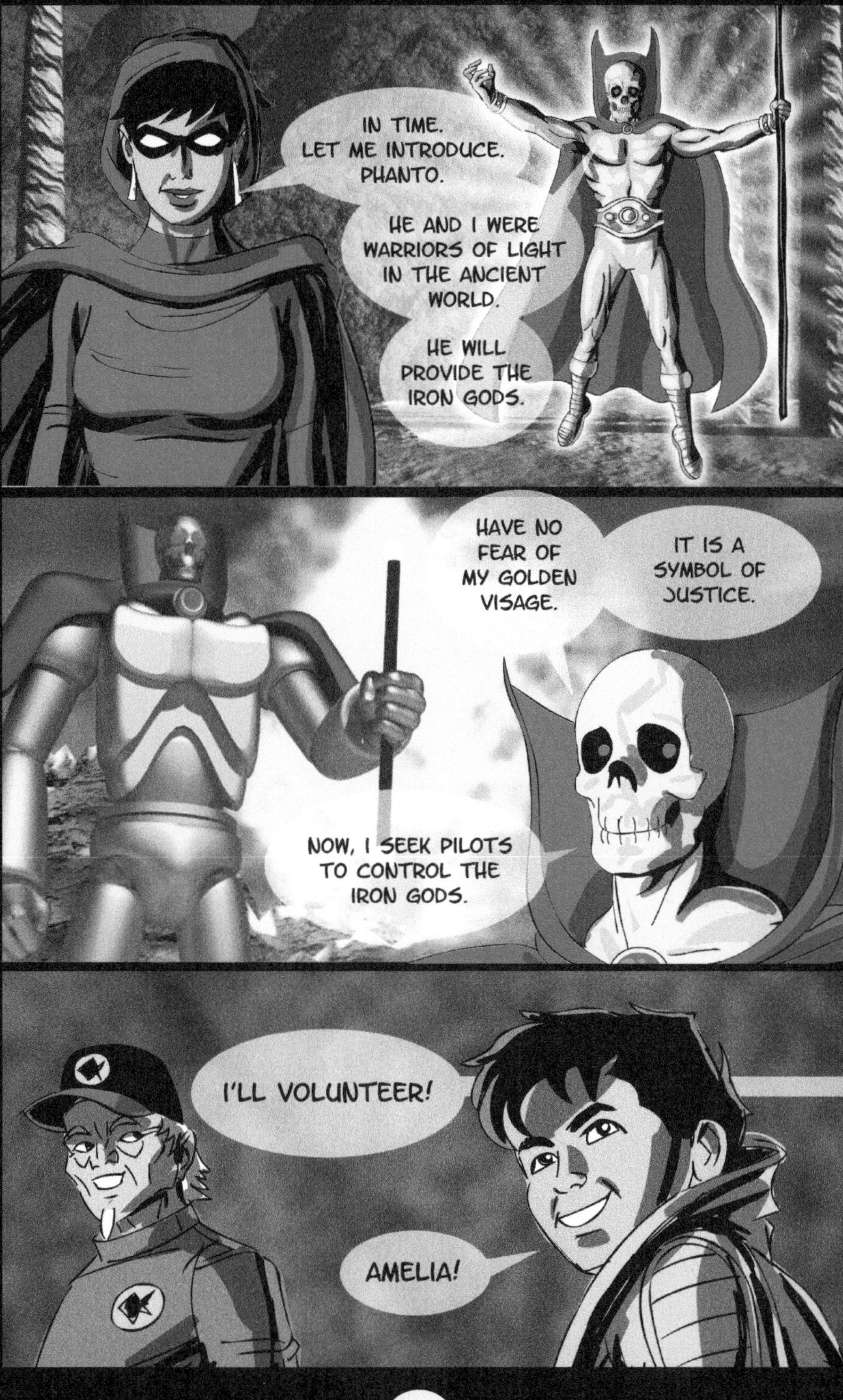
IN TIME.
LET ME INTRODUCE.
PHANTO.
HE AND I WERE WARRIORS OF LIGHT IN THE ANCIENT WORLD.
HE WILL PROVIDE THE IRON GODS.
HAVE NO FEAR OF MY GOLDEN VISAGE.
IT IS A SYMBOL OF JUSTICE.
NOW, I SEEK PILOTS TO CONTROL THE IRON GODS.
I'LL VOLUNTEER!
AMELIA!

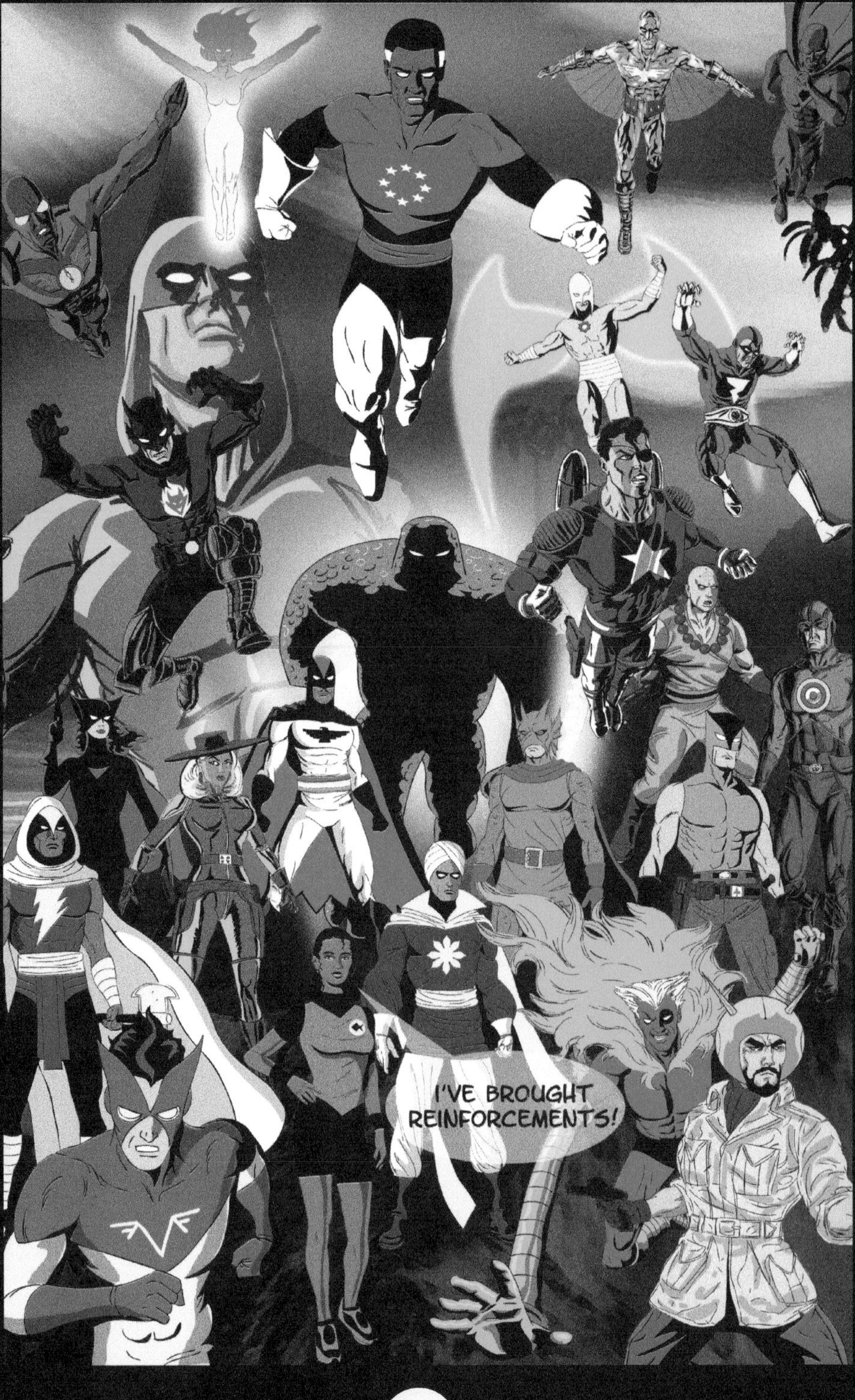
I'VE BROUGHT REINFORCEMENTS!

ACT 4 – POWER UP

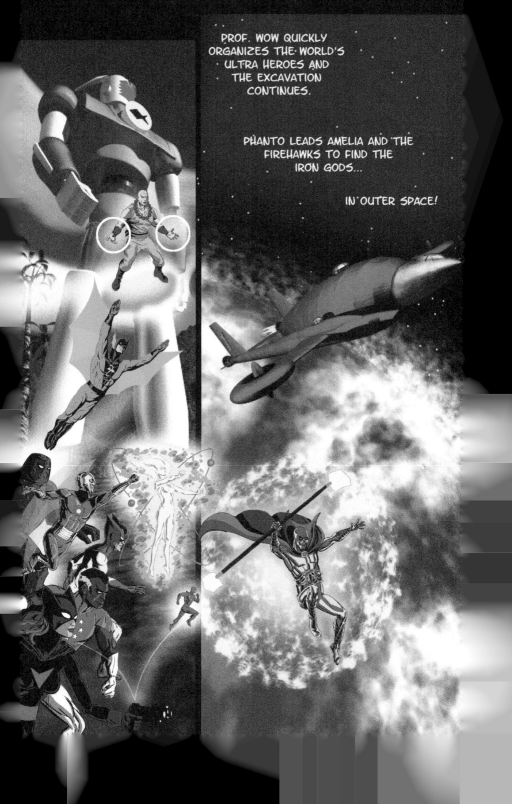

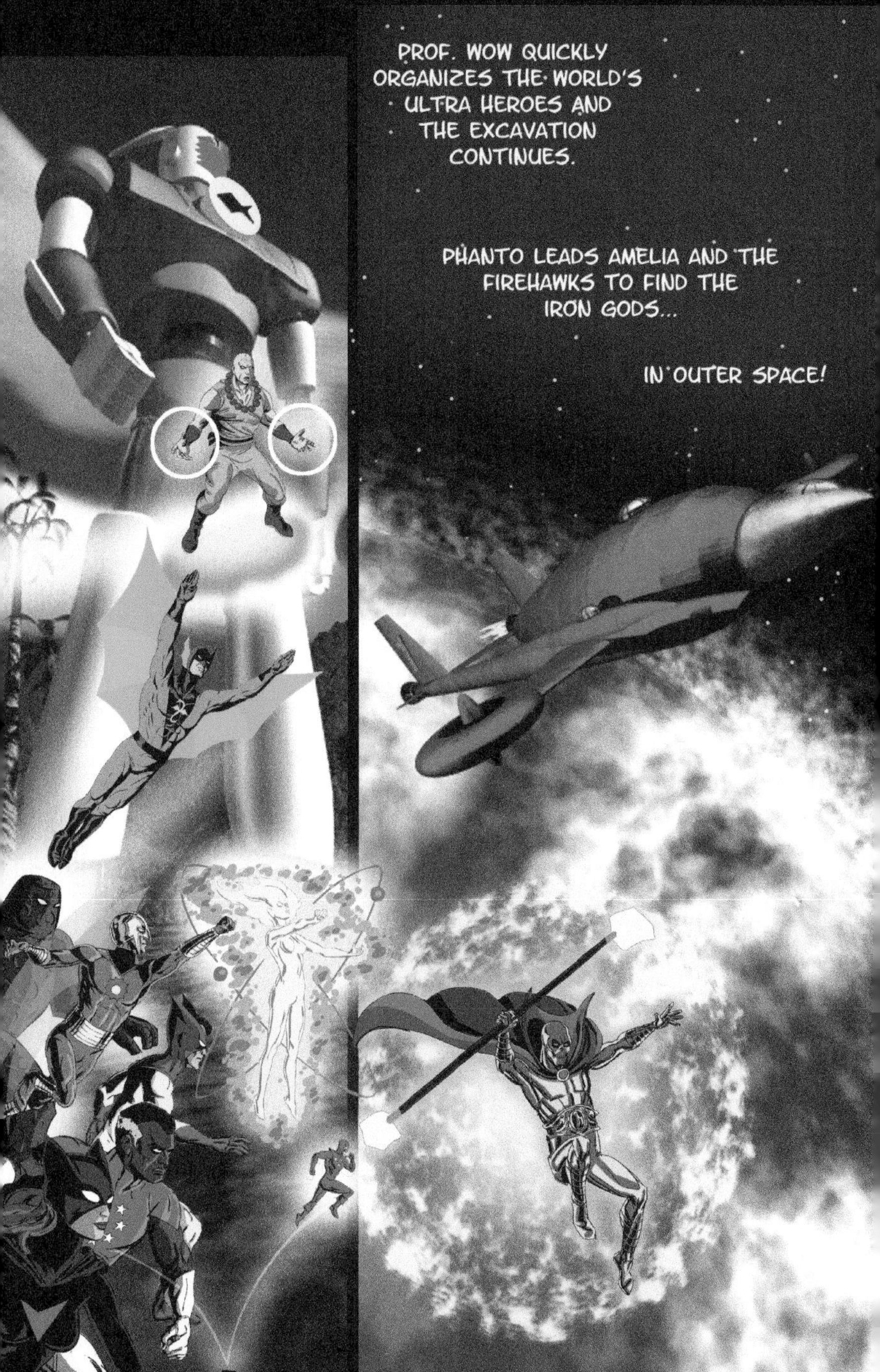
PROF. WOW QUICKLY ORGANIZES THE WORLD'S ULTRA HEROES AND THE EXCAVATION CONTINUES.
PHANTO LEADS AMELIA AND THE FIREHAWKS TO FIND THE IRON GODS...
IN OUTER SPACE!

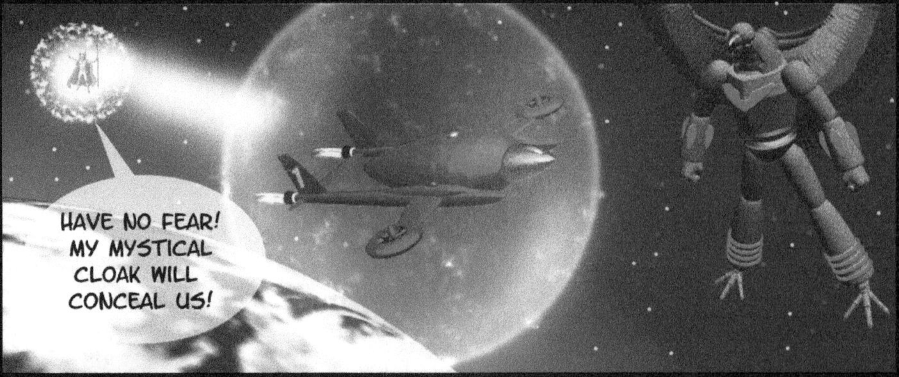
HAVE NO FEAR!
MY MYSTICAL
CLOAK WILL
CONCEAL US!

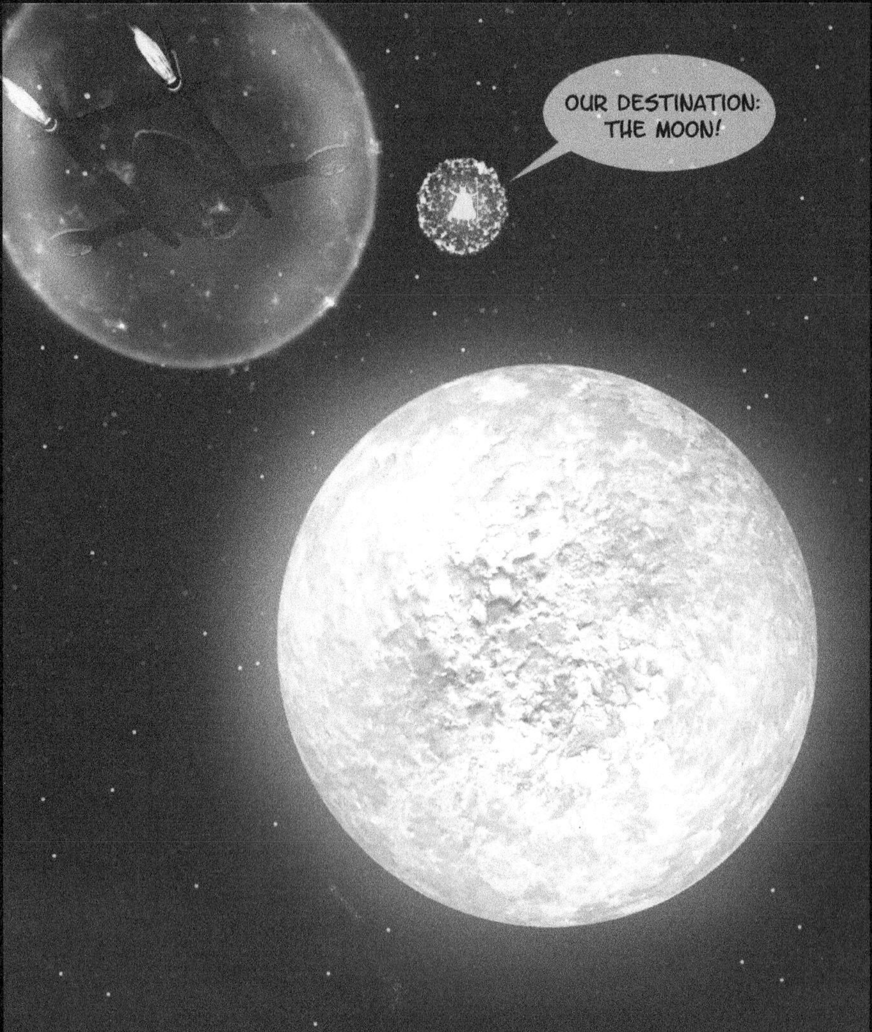
OUR DESTINATION:
THE MOON!

ACT 4 - POWER UP

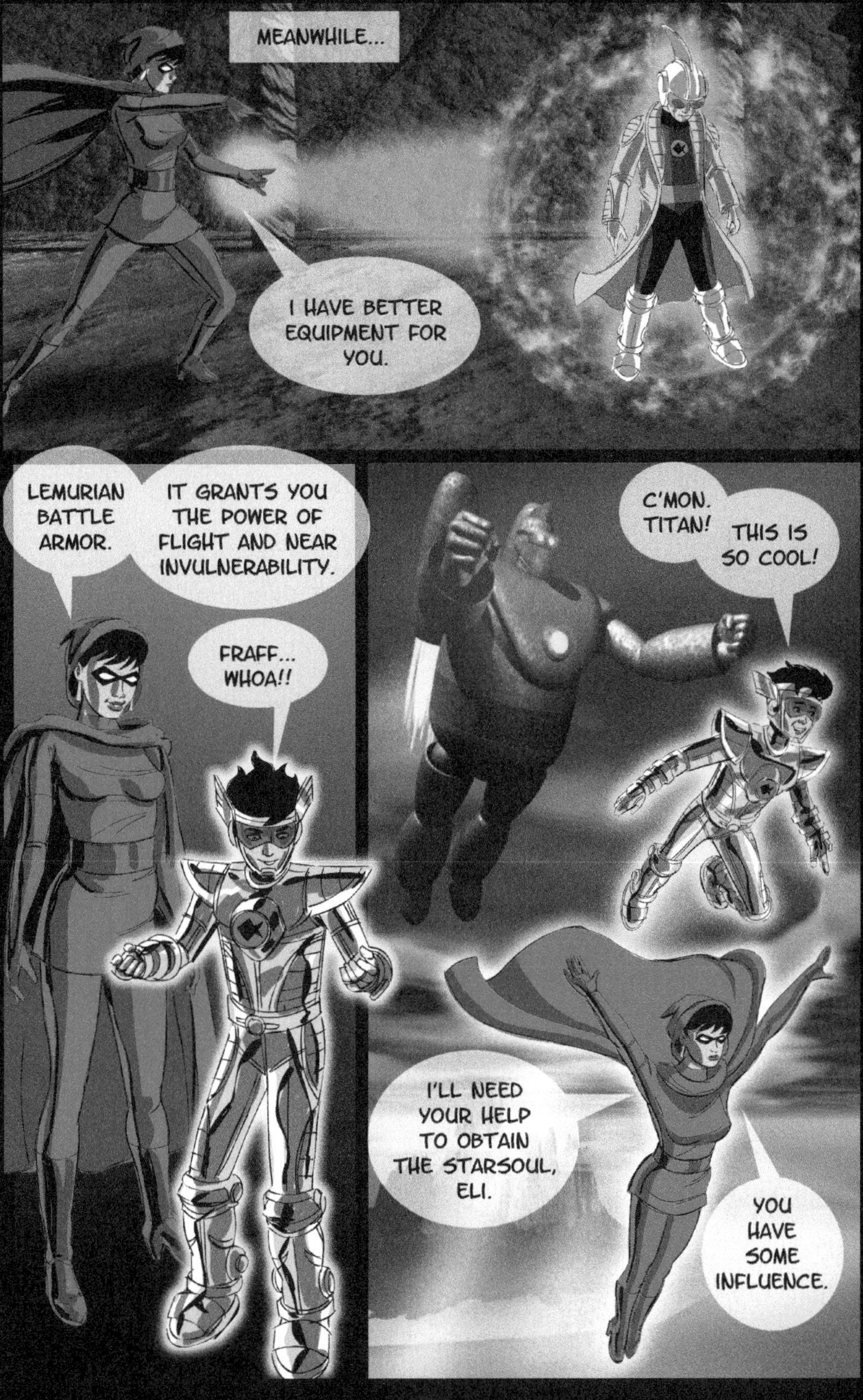
MEANWHILE...
I HAVE BETTER EQUIPMENT FOR YOU.
LEMURIAN BATTLE ARMOR.
IT GRANTS YOU THE POWER OF FLIGHT AND NEAR INVULNERABILITY.
FRAFF... WHOA!!
C'MON. TITAN!
THIS IS SO COOL!
I'LL NEED YOUR HELP TO OBTAIN THE STARSOUL, ELI.
YOU HAVE SOME INFLUENCE.

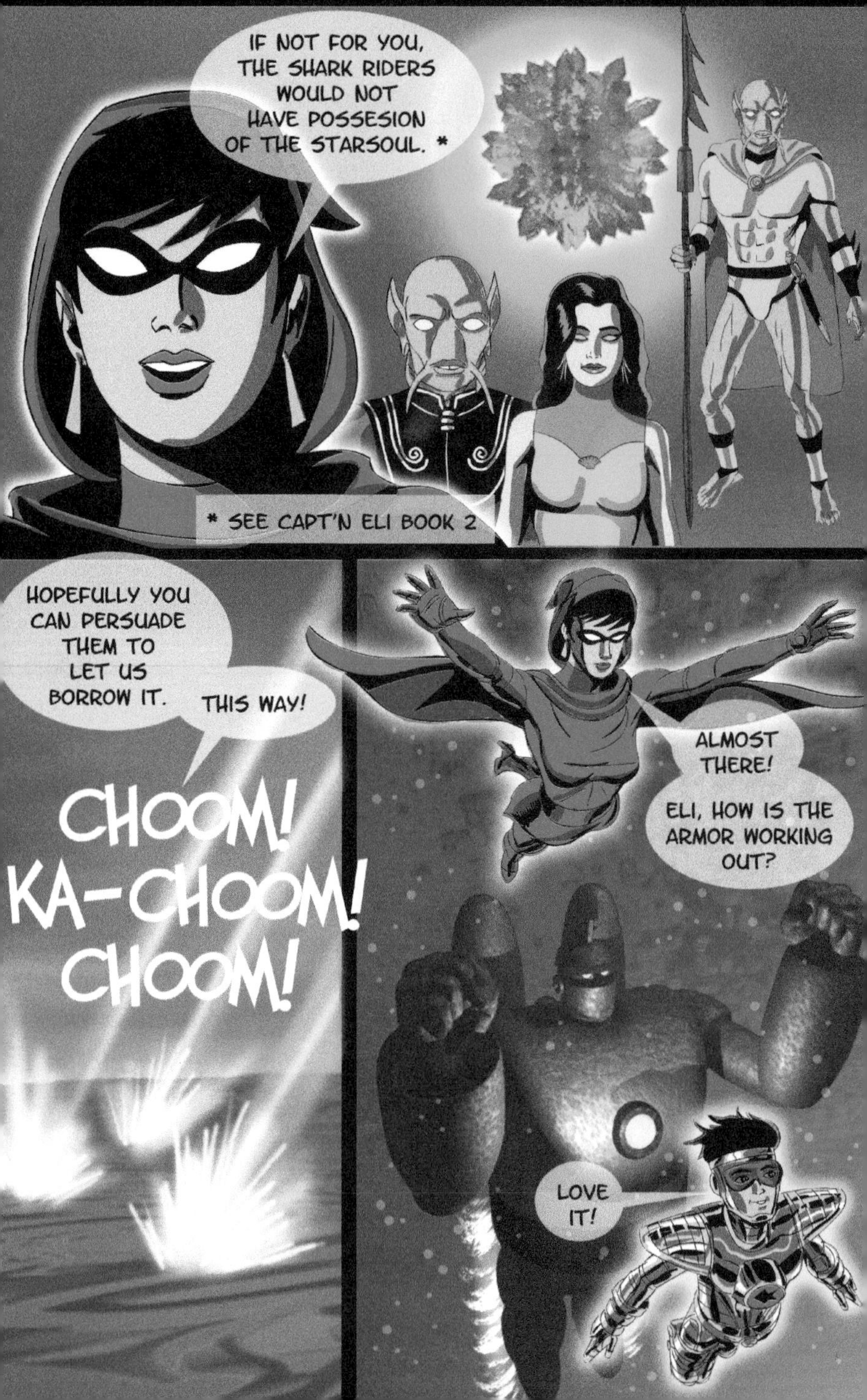
IF NOT FOR YOU, THE SHARK RIDERS WOULD NOT HAVE POSSESION OF THE STARSOUL. *
* SEE CAPT'N ELI BOOK 2
HOPEFULLY YOU CAN PERSUADE THEM TO LET US BORROW IT.
THIS WAY!
CHOOM! KA-CHOOM! CHOOM!
ALMOST THERE!
ELI, HOW IS THE ARMOR WORKING OUT?
LOVE IT!

Act 4 - Power Up

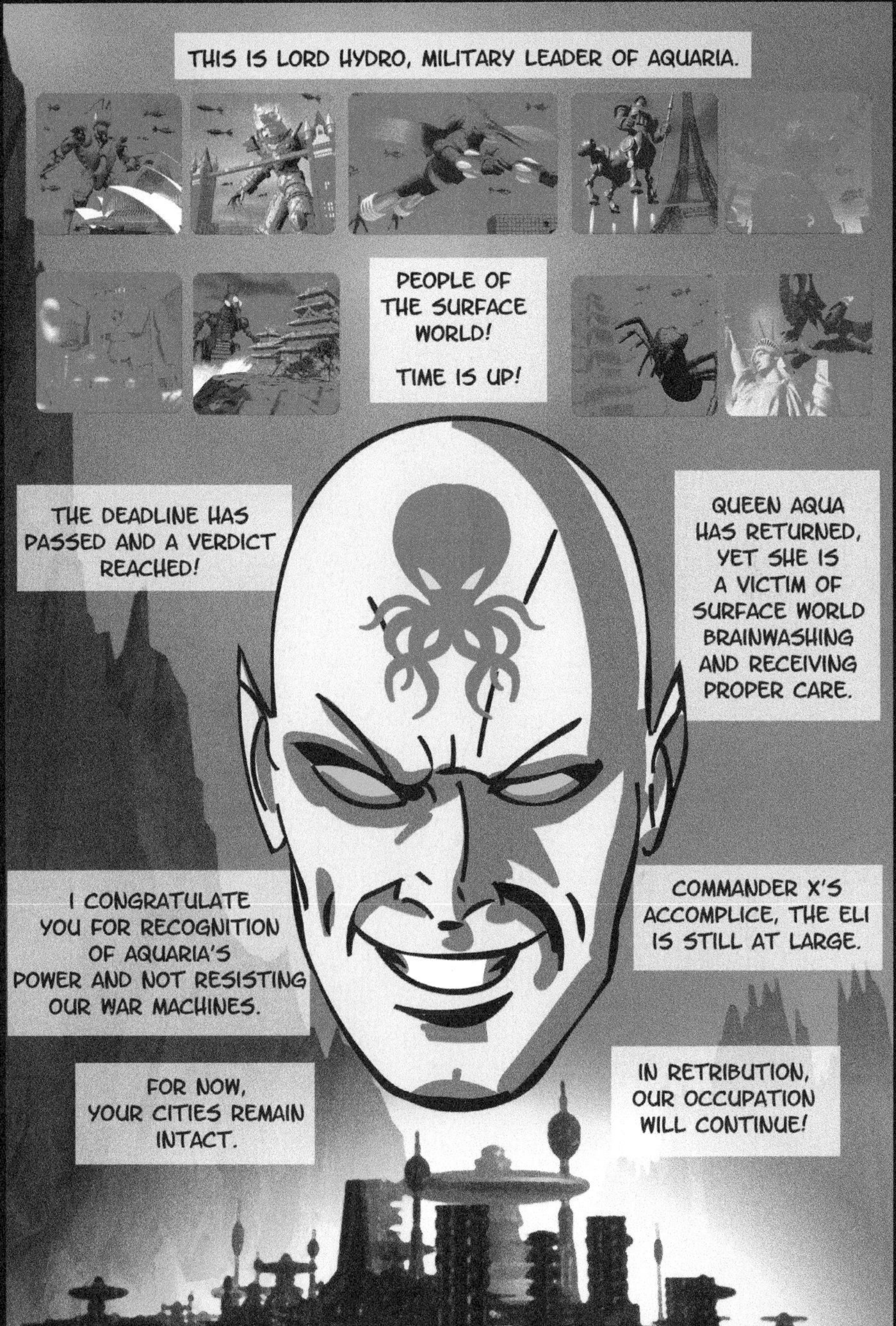
THIS IS LORD HYDRO, MILITARY LEADER OF AQUARIA.
PEOPLE OF THE SURFACE WORLD!
TIME IS UP!
THE DEADLINE HAS PASSED AND A VERDICT REACHED!
QUEEN AQUA HAS RETURNED, YET SHE IS A VICTIM OF SURFACE WORLD BRAINWASHING AND RECEIVING PROPER CARE.
I CONGRATULATE YOU FOR RECOGNITION OF AQUARIA'S POWER AND NOT RESISTING OUR WAR MACHINES.
COMMANDER X'S ACCOMPLICE, THE ELI IS STILL AT LARGE.
FOR NOW, YOUR CITIES REMAIN INTACT.
IN RETRIBUTION, OUR OCCUPATION WILL CONTINUE!

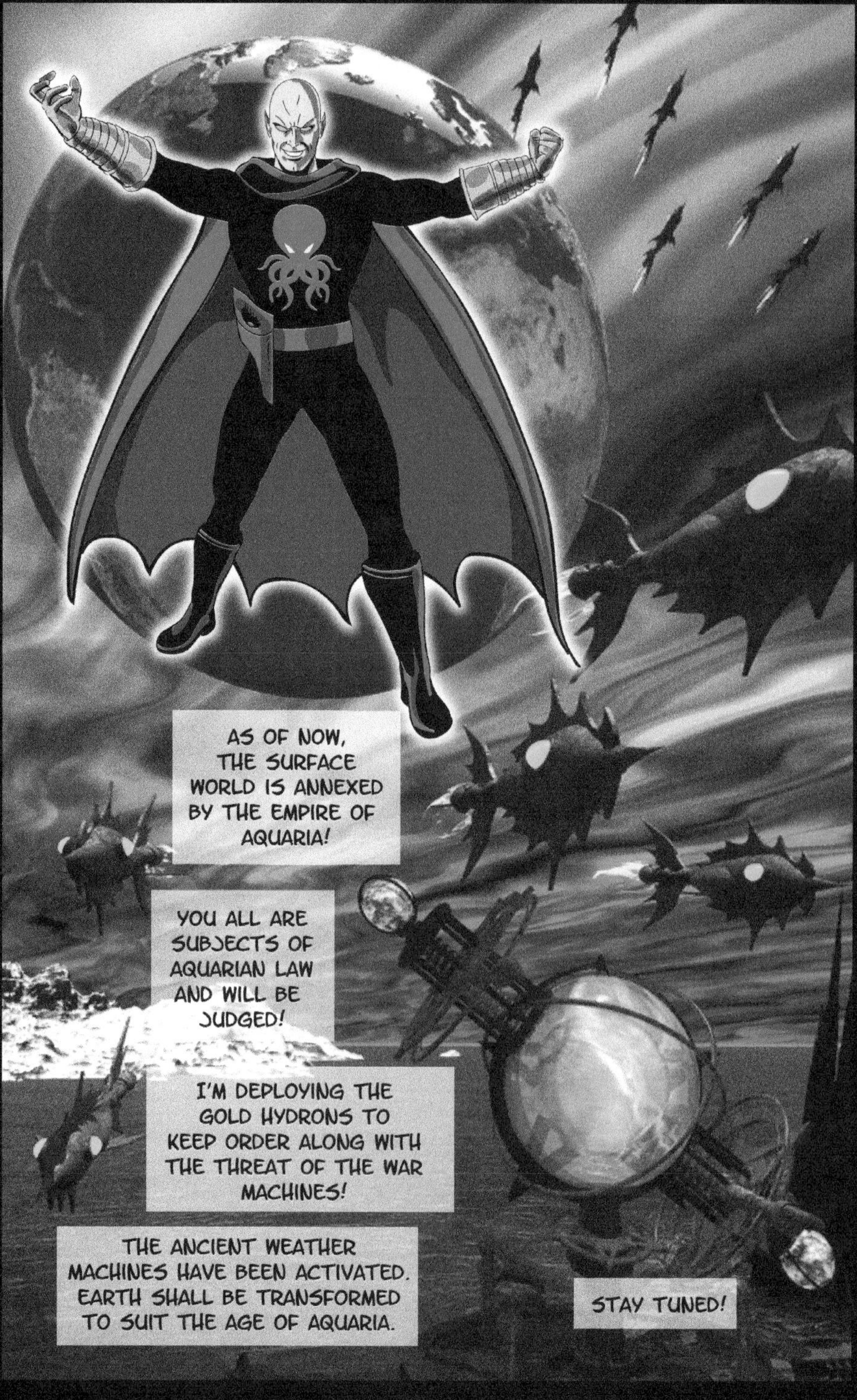
AS OF NOW, THE SURFACE WORLD IS ANNEXED BY THE EMPIRE OF AQUARIA!
YOU ALL ARE SUBJECTS OF AQUARIAN LAW AND WILL BE JUDGED!
I'M DEPLOYING THE GOLD HYDRONS TO KEEP ORDER ALONG WITH THE THREAT OF THE WAR MACHINES!
THE ANCIENT WEATHER MACHINES HAVE BEEN ACTIVATED. EARTH SHALL BE TRANSFORMED TO SUIT THE AGE OF AQUARIA.
STAY TUNED!

ACT 4 - POWER UP

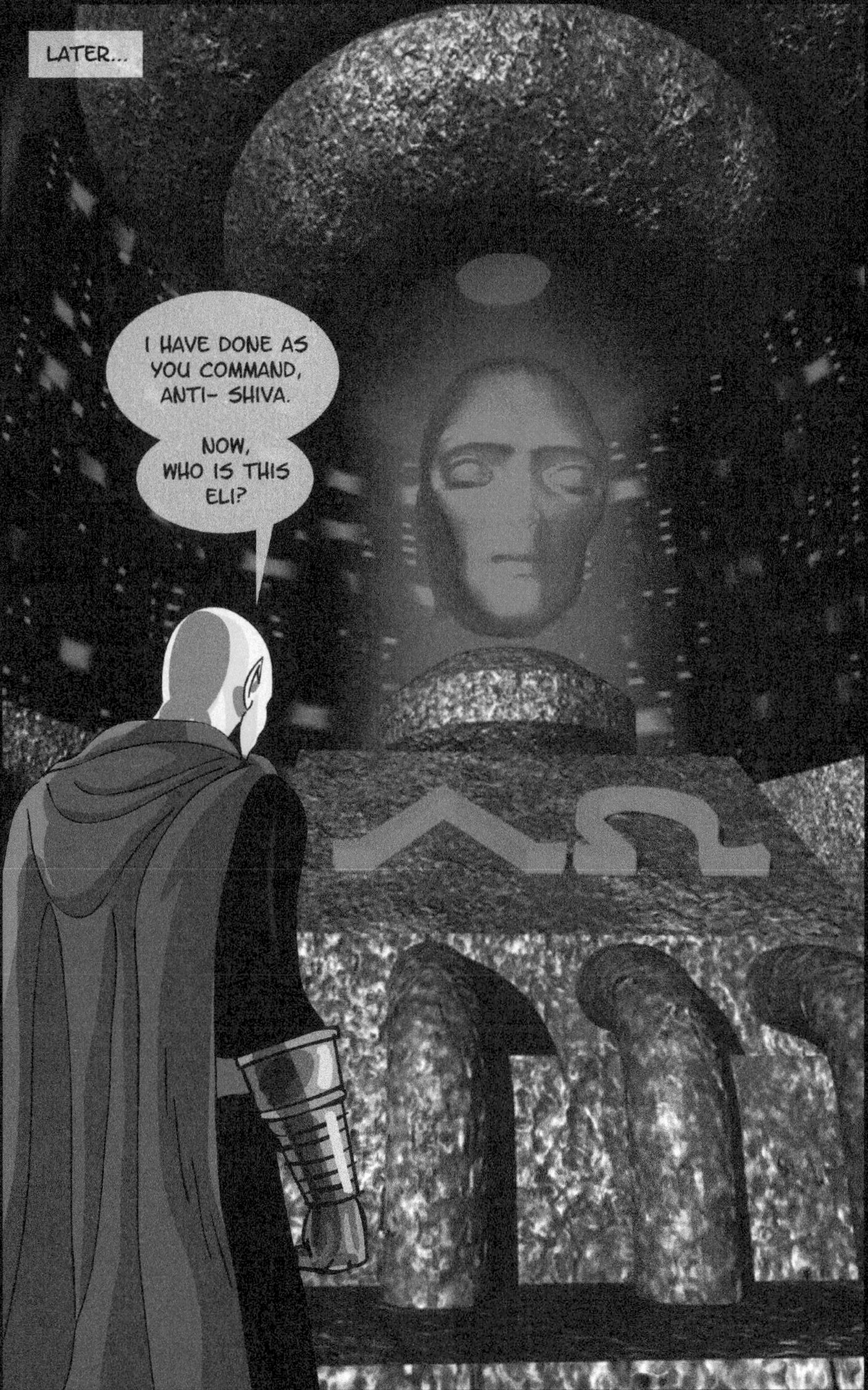
LATER...
I HAVE DONE AS YOU COMMAND, ANTI- SHIVA.
NOW, WHO IS THIS ELI?

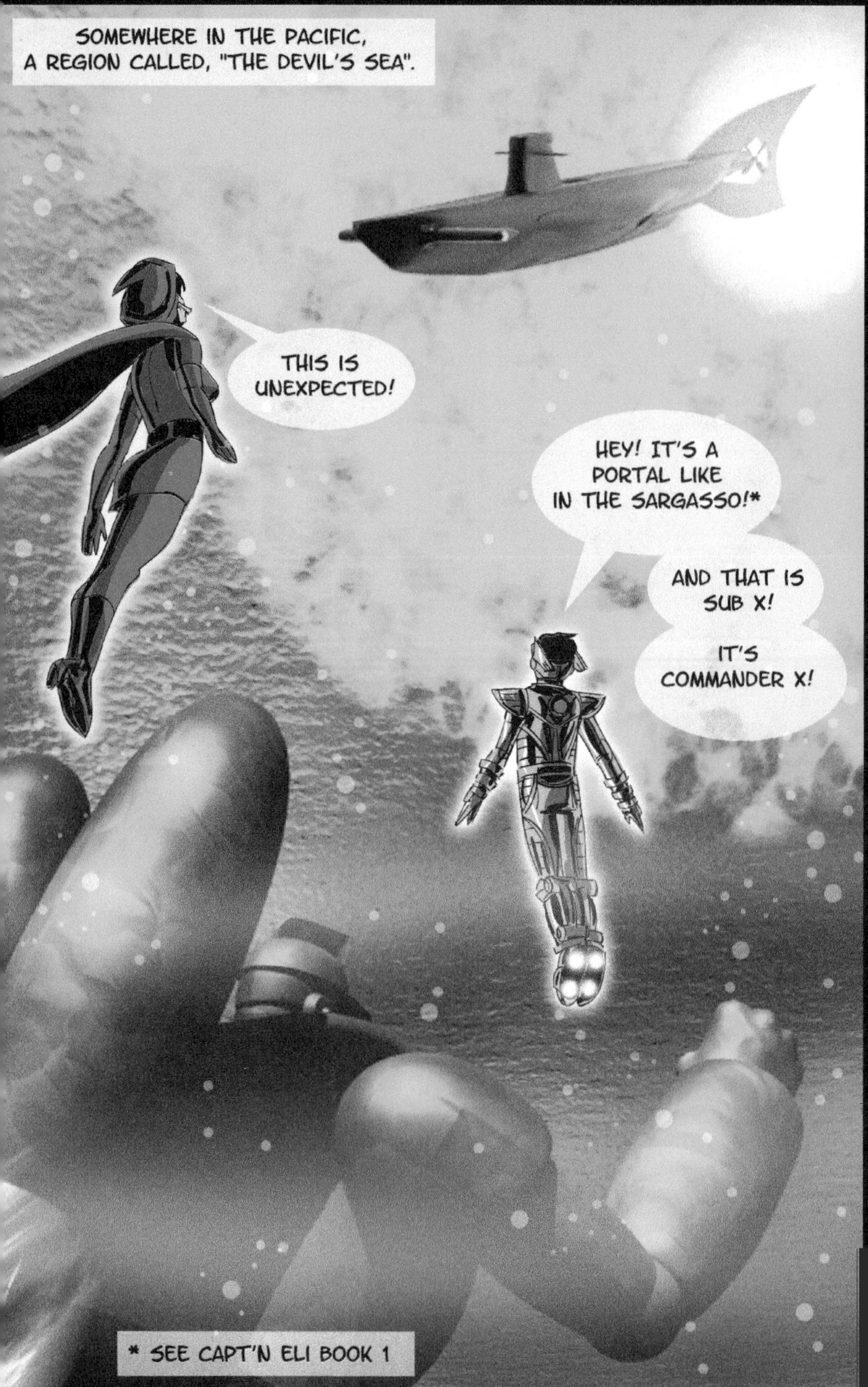
SOMEWHERE IN THE PACIFIC, A REGION CALLED, "THE DEVIL'S SEA".
THIS IS UNEXPECTED!
HEY! IT'S A PORTAL LIKE IN THE SARGASSO!*
AND THAT IS SUB X!
IT'S COMMANDER X!
* SEE CAPT'N ELI BOOK 1

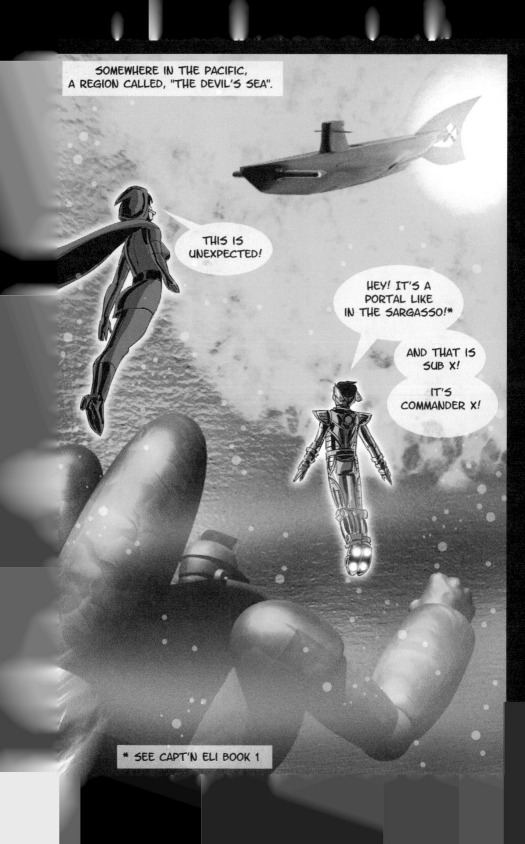

ACT 4 - POWER UP

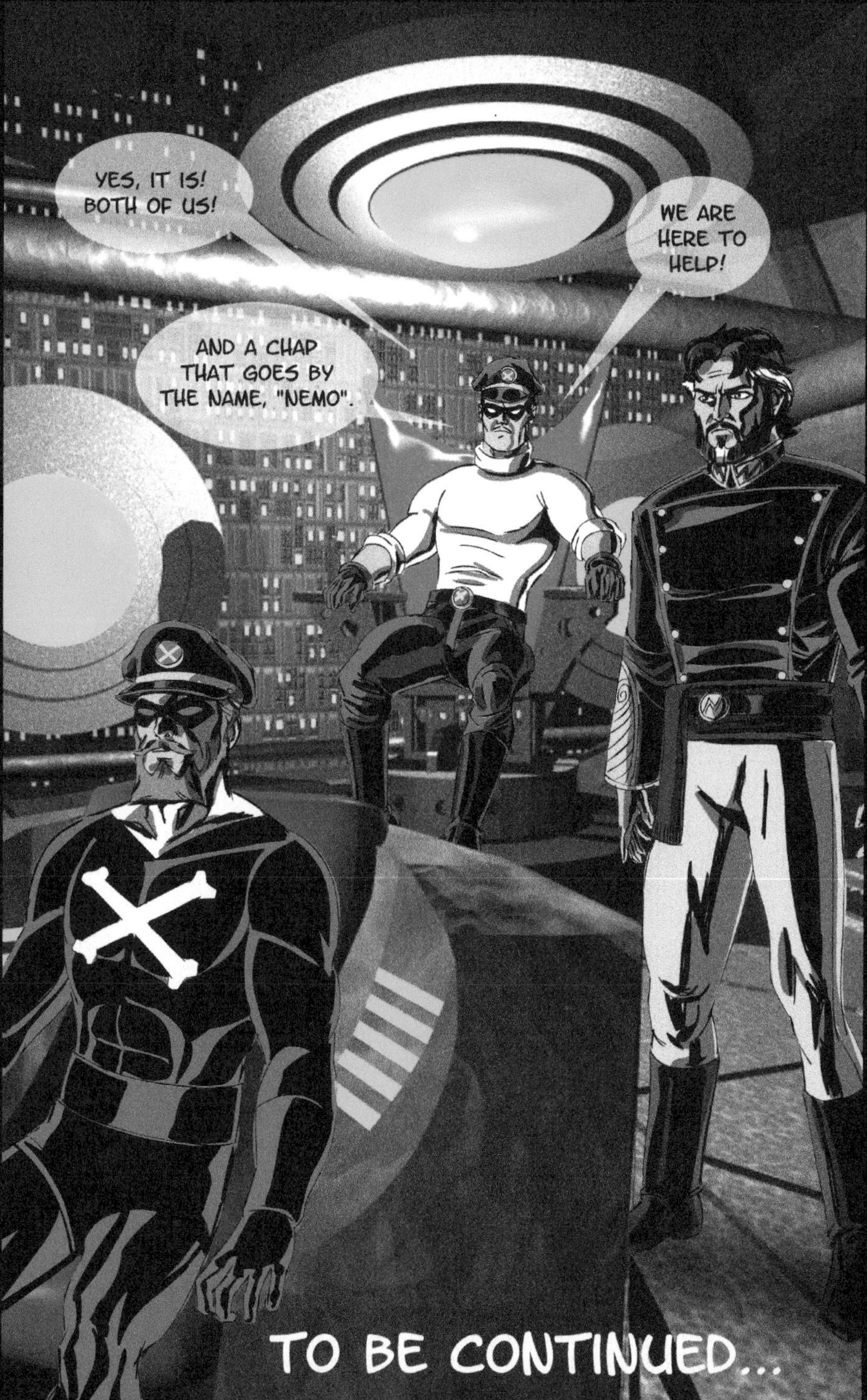
YES, IT IS! BOTH OF US!
AND A CHAP THAT GOES BY THE NAME, "NEMO".
WE ARE HERE TO HELP!
TO BE CONTINUED...

COMMANDER X

SHIVA 99

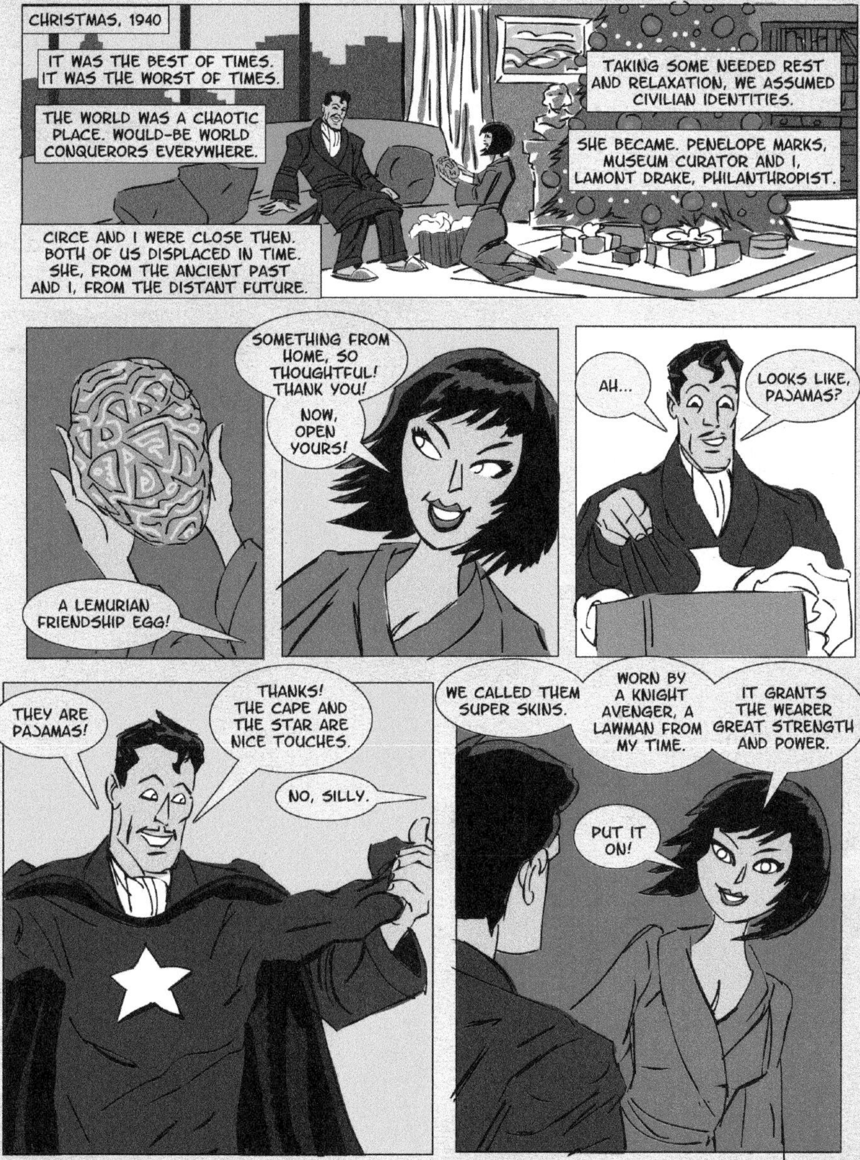
CHRISTMAS, 1940
IT WAS THE BEST OF TIMES. IT WAS THE WORST OF TIMES.
THE WORLD WAS A CHAOTIC PLACE. WOULD-BE WORLD CONQUERORS EVERYWHERE.
CIRCE AND I WERE CLOSE THEN. BOTH OF US DISPLACED IN TIME. SHE, FROM THE ANCIENT PAST AND I, FROM THE DISTANT FUTURE.
TAKING SOME NEEDED REST AND RELAXATION, WE ASSUMED CIVILIAN IDENTITIES.
SHE BECAME. PENELOPE MARKS, MUSEUM CURATOR AND I, LAMONT DRAKE, PHILANTHROPIST.
A LEMURIAN FRIENDSHIP EGG!
SOMETHING FROM HOME, SO THOUGHTFUL! THANK YOU!
NOW, OPEN YOURS!
AH...
LOOKS LIKE, PAJAMAS?
THEY ARE PAJAMAS!
THANKS! THE CAPE AND THE STAR ARE NICE TOUCHES.
NO, SILLY.
WE CALLED THEM SUPER SKINS.
WORN BY A KNIGHT AVENGER, A LAWMAN FROM MY TIME.
IT GRANTS THE WEARER GREAT STRENGTH AND POWER.
PUT IT ON!

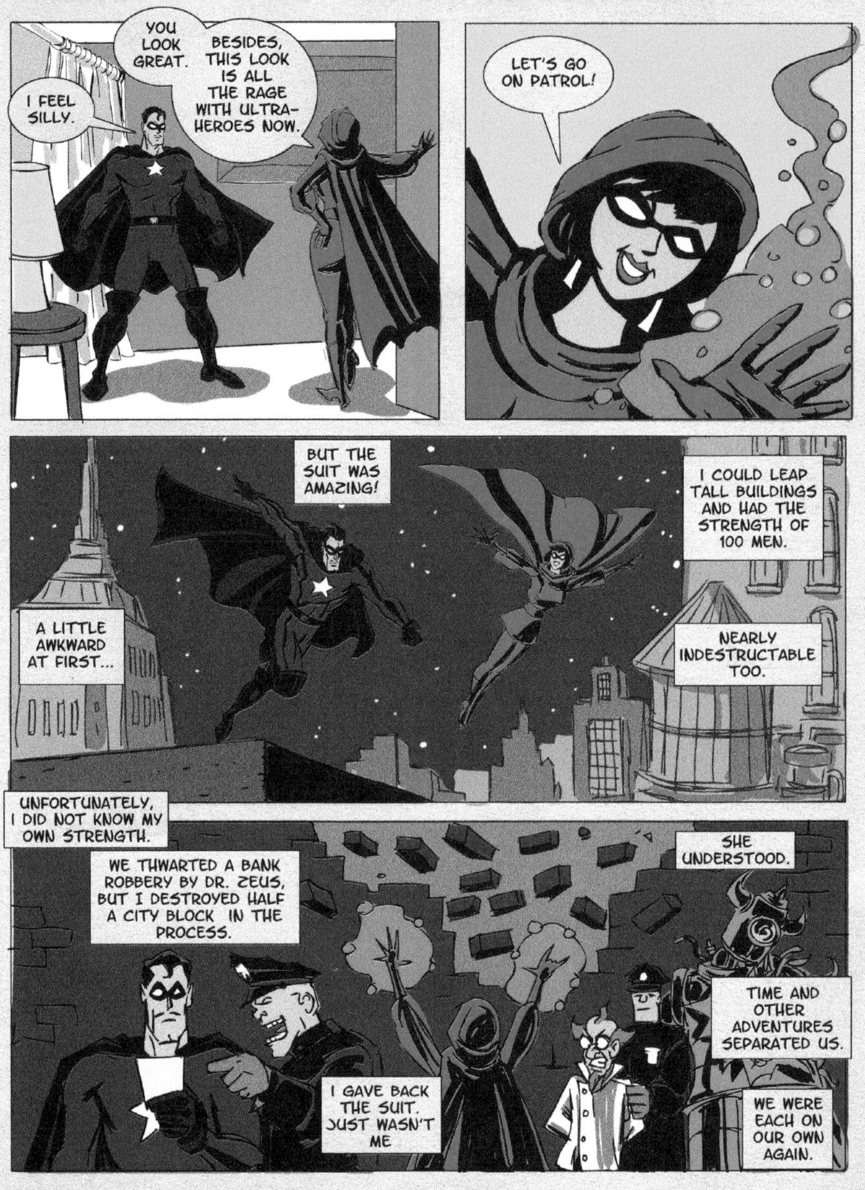
I FEEL SILLY.
YOU LOOK GREAT.
BESIDES, THIS LOOK IS ALL THE RAGE WITH ULTRA-HEROES NOW.
LET'S GO ON PATROL!
A LITTLE AWKWARD AT FIRST...
BUT THE SUIT WAS AMAZING!
I COULD LEAP TALL BUILDINGS AND HAD THE STRENGTH OF 100 MEN.
NEARLY INDESTRUCTABLE TOO.
UNFORTUNATELY, I DID NOT KNOW MY OWN STRENGTH.
WE THWARTED A BANK ROBBERY BY DR. ZEUS, BUT I DESTROYED HALF A CITY BLOCK IN THE PROCESS.
SHE UNDERSTOOD.
I GAVE BACK THE SUIT. JUST WASN'T ME
TIME AND OTHER ADVENTURES SEPARATED US.
WE WERE EACH ON OUR OWN AGAIN.

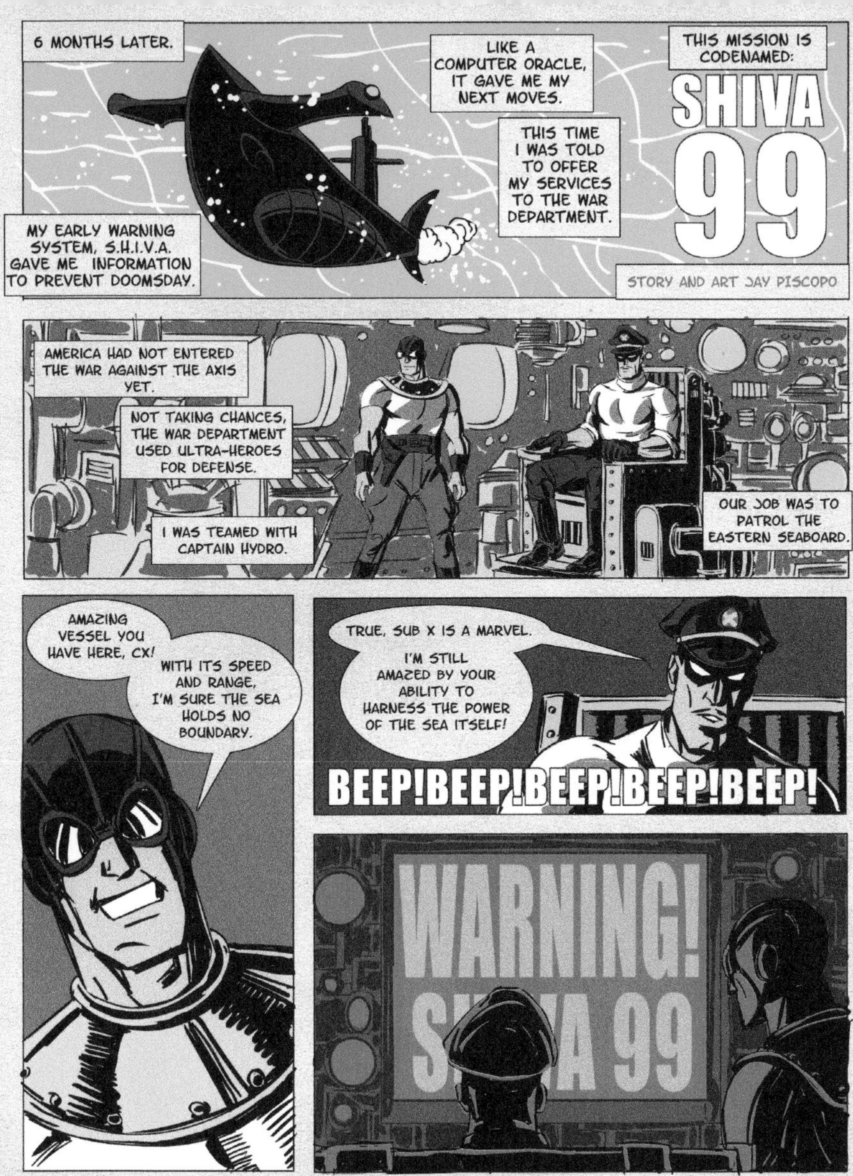
6 MONTHS LATER.
LIKE A COMPUTER ORACLE, IT GAVE ME MY NEXT MOVES.
THIS MISSION IS CODENAMED:
SHIVA 99
THIS TIME I WAS TOLD TO OFFER MY SERVICES TO THE WAR DEPARTMENT.
MY EARLY WARNING SYSTEM, S.H.I.V.A. GAVE ME INFORMATION TO PREVENT DOOMSDAY.
STORY AND ART JAY PISCOPO
AMERICA HAD NOT ENTERED THE WAR AGAINST THE AXIS YET.
NOT TAKING CHANCES, THE WAR DEPARTMENT USED ULTRA-HEROES FOR DEFENSE.
I WAS TEAMED WITH CAPTAIN HYDRO.
OUR JOB WAS TO PATROL THE EASTERN SEABOARD.
AMAZING VESSEL YOU HAVE HERE, CX!
WITH ITS SPEED AND RANGE, I'M SURE THE SEA HOLDS NO BOUNDARY.
TRUE, SUB X IS A MARVEL.
I'M STILL AMAZED BY YOUR ABILITY TO HARNESS THE POWER OF THE SEA ITSELF!
BEEP!BEEP!BEEP!BEEP!BEEP!
WARNING!

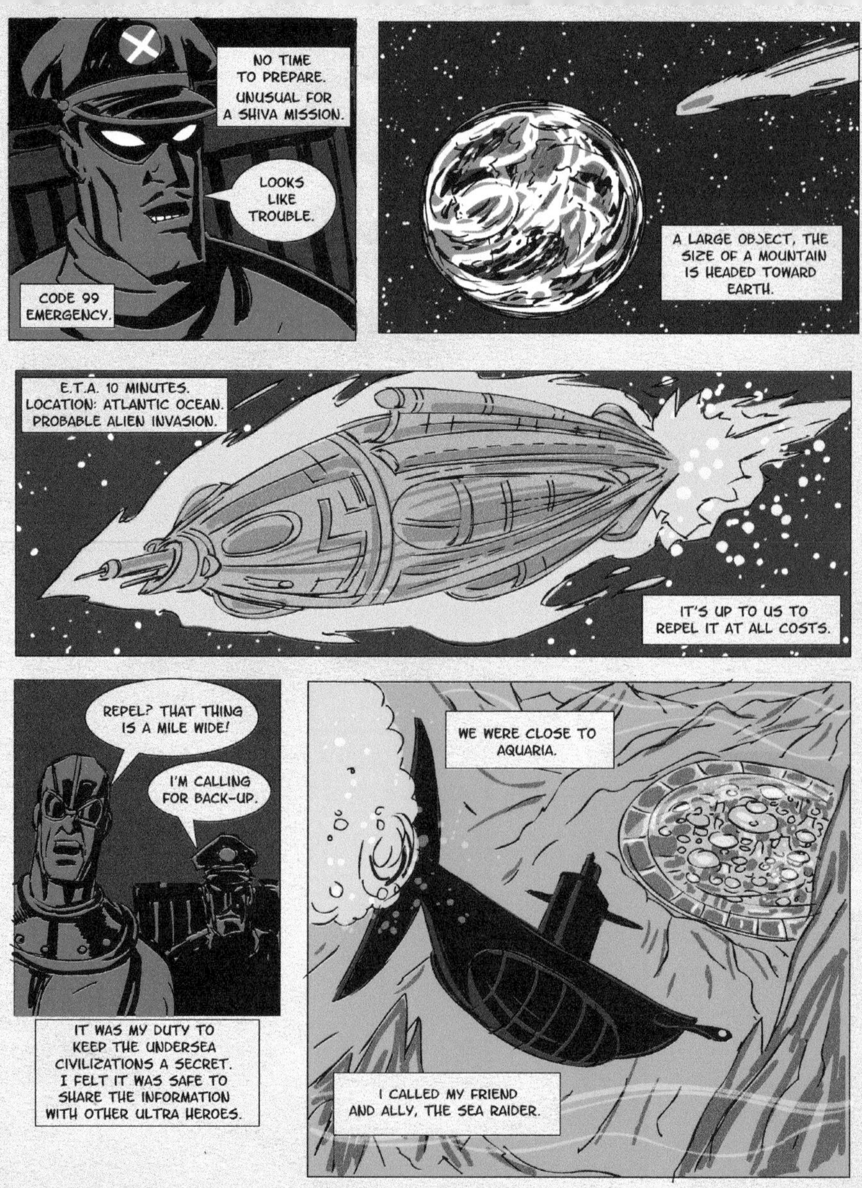
NO TIME TO PREPARE. UNUSUAL FOR A SHIVA MISSION.
LOOKS LIKE TROUBLE.
CODE 99 EMERGENCY.
A LARGE OBJECT, THE SIZE OF A MOUNTAIN IS HEADED TOWARD EARTH.
E.T.A. 10 MINUTES. LOCATION: ATLANTIC OCEAN. PROBABLE ALIEN INVASION.
IT'S UP TO US TO REPEL IT AT ALL COSTS.
REPEL? THAT THING IS A MILE WIDE!
I'M CALLING FOR BACK-UP.
IT WAS MY DUTY TO KEEP THE UNDERSEA CIVILIZATIONS A SECRET. I FELT IT WAS SAFE TO SHARE THE INFORMATION WITH OTHER ULTRA HEROES.
WE WERE CLOSE TO AQUARIA.
I CALLED MY FRIEND AND ALLY, THE SEA RAIDER.

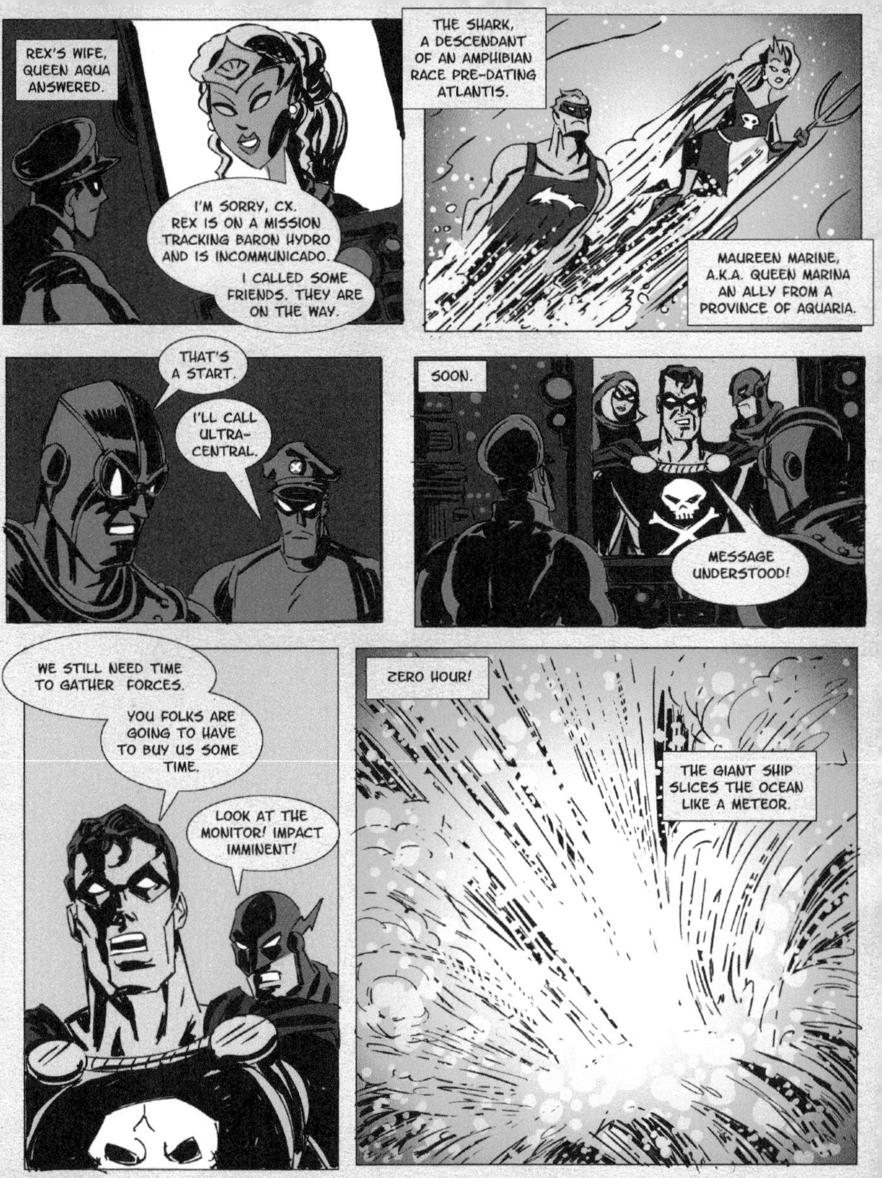
REX'S WIFE, QUEEN AQUA ANSWERED.
I'M SORRY, CX. REX IS ON A MISSION TRACKING BARON HYDRO AND IS INCOMMUNICADO.
I CALLED SOME FRIENDS. THEY ARE ON THE WAY.
THE SHARK, A DESCENDANT OF AN AMPHIBIAN RACE PRE-DATING ATLANTIS.
MAUREEN MARINE, A.K.A. QUEEN MARINA AN ALLY FROM A PROVINCE OF AQUARIA.
THAT'S A START.
I'LL CALL ULTRA-CENTRAL.
SOON.
MESSAGE UNDERSTOOD!
WE STILL NEED TIME TO GATHER FORCES.
YOU FOLKS ARE GOING TO HAVE TO BUY US SOME TIME.
LOOK AT THE MONITOR! IMPACT IMMINENT!
ZERO HOUR!
THE GIANT SHIP SLICES THE OCEAN LIKE A METEOR.

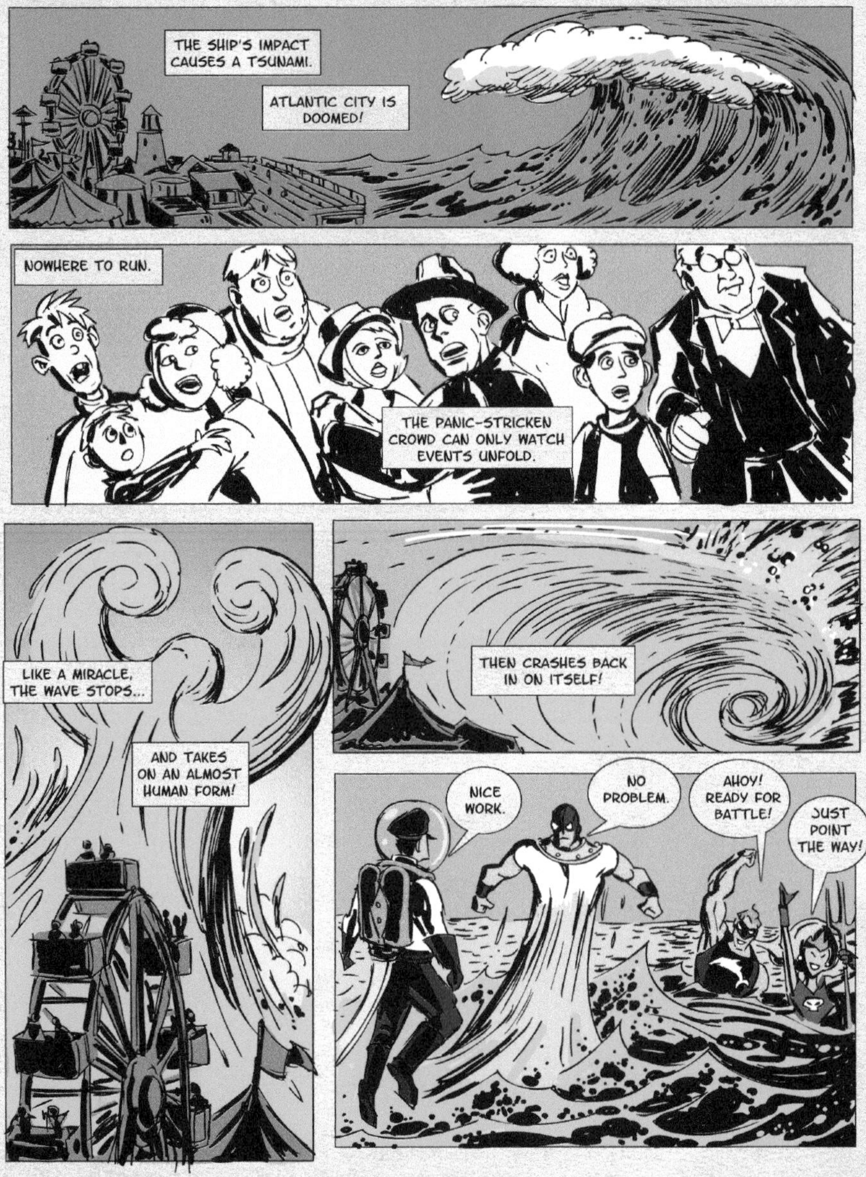
THE SHIP'S IMPACT CAUSES A TSUNAMI.
ATLANTIC CITY IS DOOMED!
NOWHERE TO RUN.
THE PANIC-STRICKEN CROWD CAN ONLY WATCH EVENTS UNFOLD.
LIKE A MIRACLE, THE WAVE STOPS...
AND TAKES ON AN ALMOST HUMAN FORM!
THEN CRASHES BACK IN ON ITSELF!
NICE WORK.
NO PROBLEM.
AHOY! READY FOR BATTLE!
JUST POINT THE WAY!

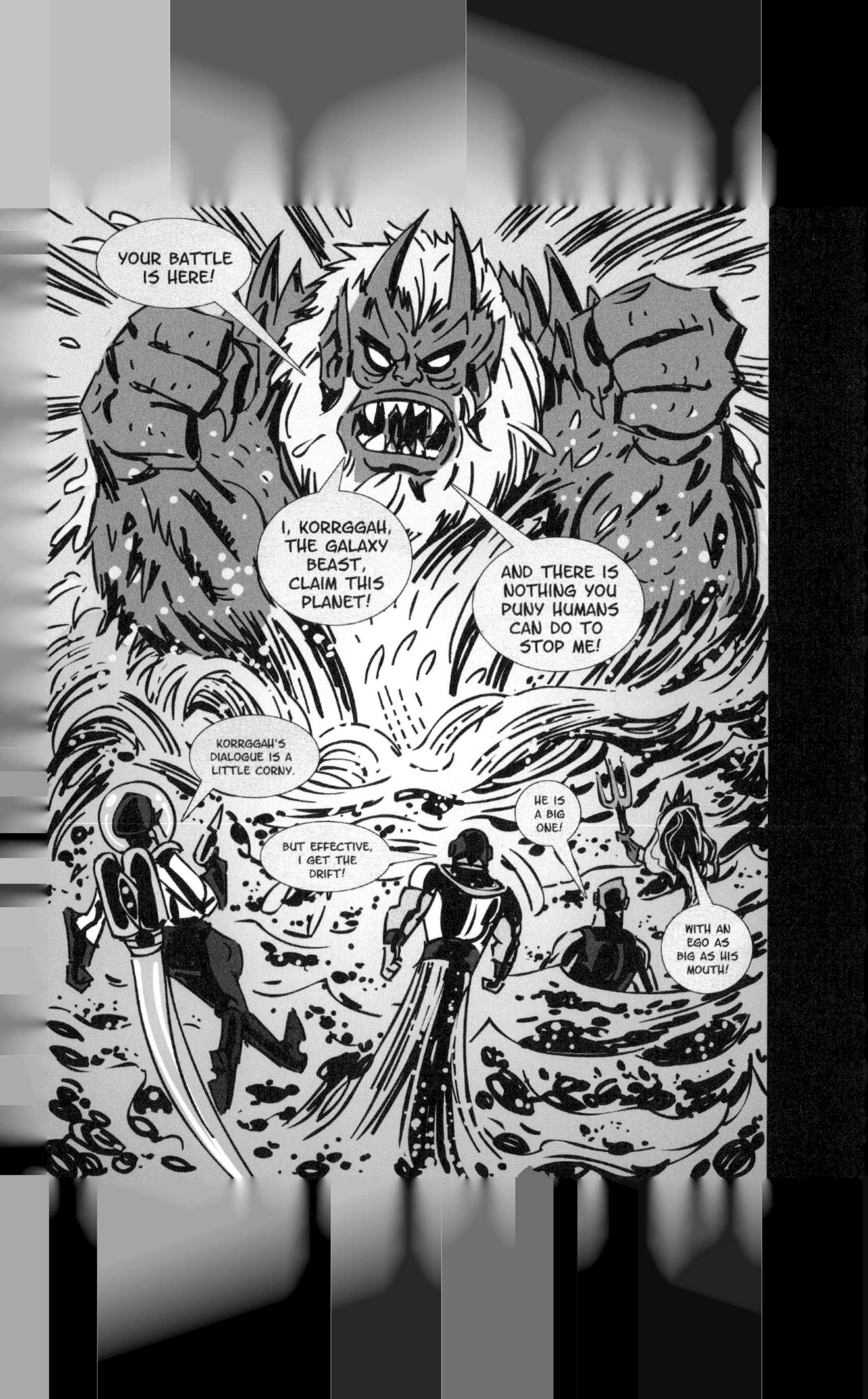
YOUR BATTLE IS HERE!
I, KORRGGAH, THE GALAXY BEAST, CLAIM THIS PLANET!
AND THERE IS NOTHING YOU PUNY HUMANS CAN DO TO STOP ME!
KORRGGAH'S DIALOGUE IS A LITTLE CORNY.
BUT EFFECTIVE, I GET THE DRIFT!
HE IS A BIG ONE!
WITH AN EGO AS BIG AS HIS MOUTH!

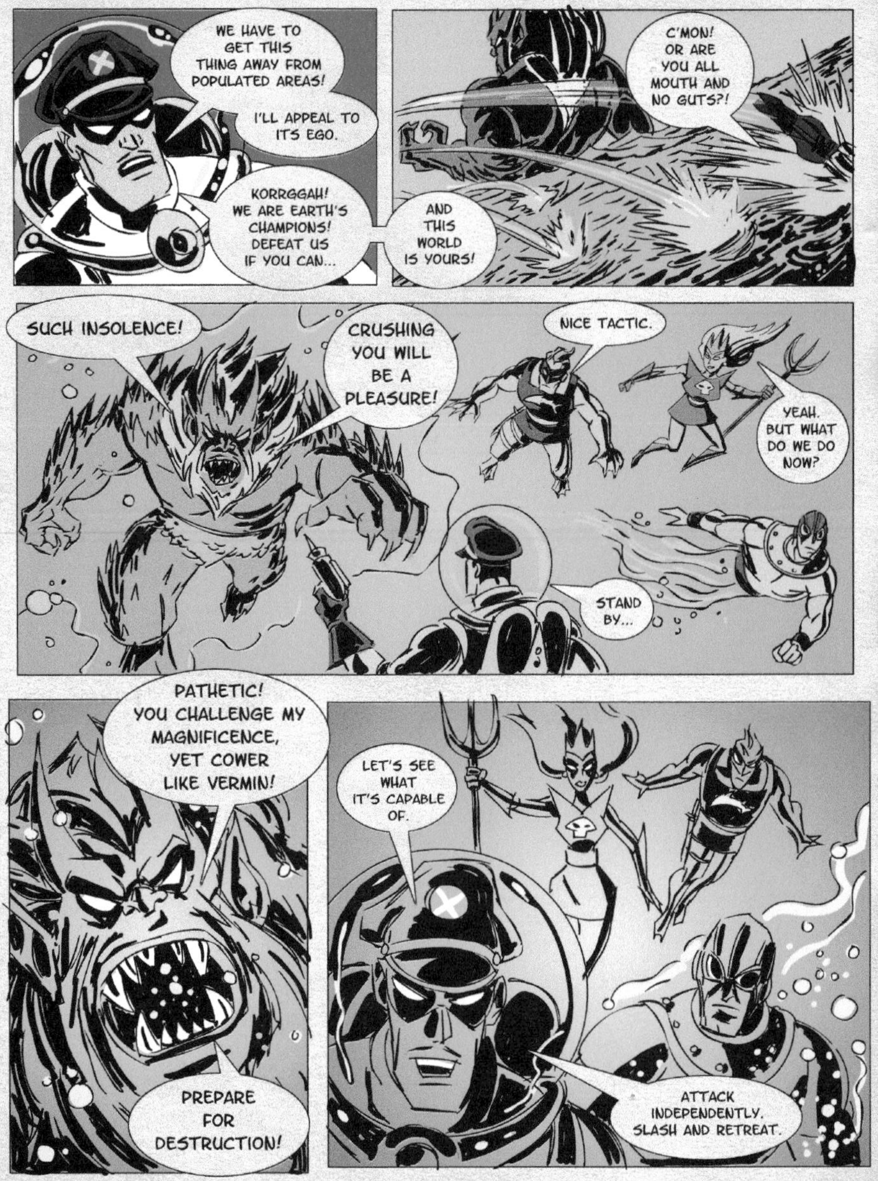
WE HAVE TO GET THIS THING AWAY FROM POPULATED AREAS!
I'LL APPEAL TO ITS EGO.
KORRGGAH! WE ARE EARTH'S CHAMPIONS! DEFEAT US IF YOU CAN...
AND THIS WORLD IS YOURS!
C'MON! OR ARE YOU ALL MOUTH AND NO GUTS?!
SUCH INSOLENCE!
CRUSHING YOU WILL BE A PLEASURE!
NICE TACTIC.
YEAH. BUT WHAT DO WE DO NOW?
STAND BY...
PATHETIC! YOU CHALLENGE MY MAGNIFICENCE, YET COWER LIKE VERMIN!
PREPARE FOR DESTRUCTION!
LET'S SEE WHAT IT'S CAPABLE OF.
ATTACK INDEPENDENTLY. SLASH AND RETREAT.

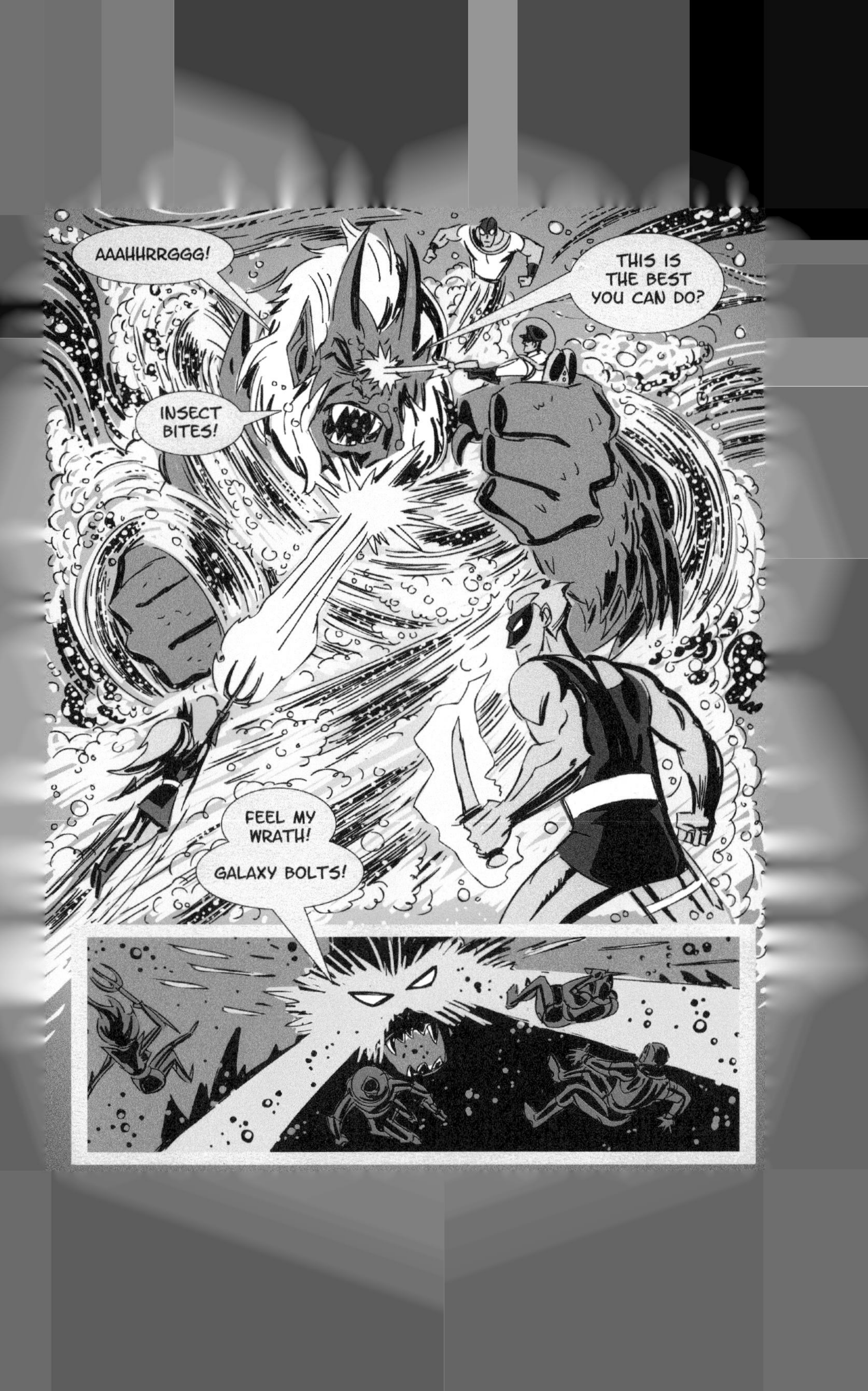
AAAHHRRGGG!
THIS IS THE BEST YOU CAN DO?
INSECT BITES!
FEEL MY WRATH!
GALAXY BOLTS!

COMMANDER X

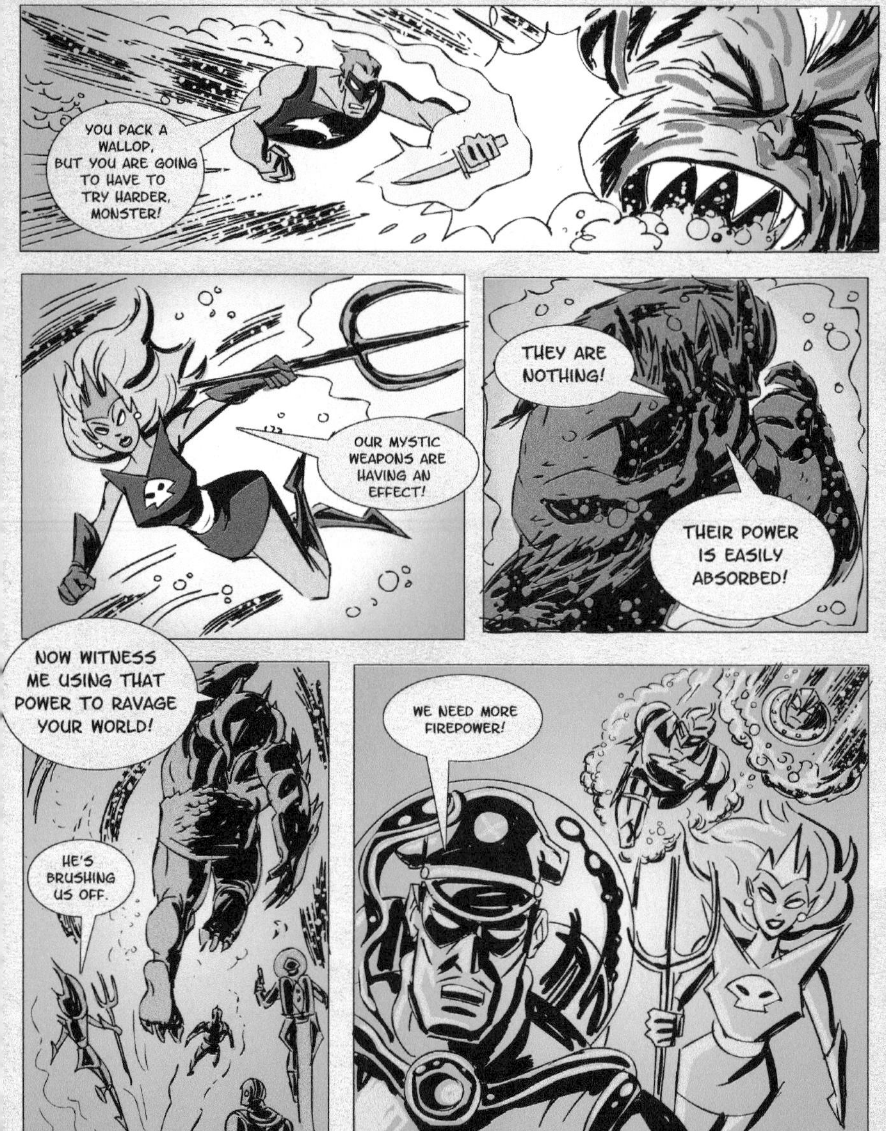
YOU PACK A WALLOP, BUT YOU ARE GOING TO HAVE TO TRY HARDER, MONSTER!
OUR MYSTIC WEAPONS ARE HAVING AN EFFECT!
THEY ARE NOTHING!
THEIR POWER IS EASILY ABSORBED!
NOW WITNESS ME USING THAT POWER TO RAVAGE YOUR WORLD!
HE'S BRUSHING US OFF.
WE NEED MORE FIREPOWER!

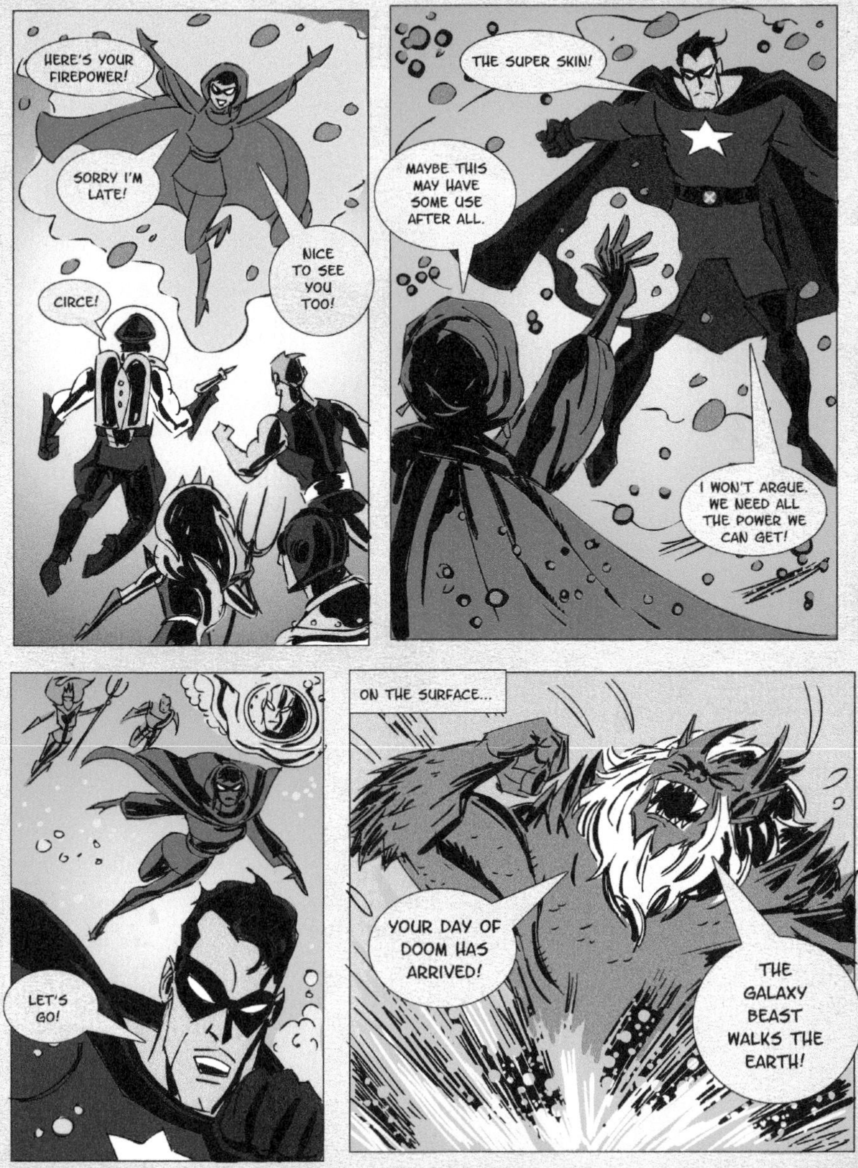
HERE'S YOUR FIREPOWER!
SORRY I'M LATE!
CIRCE!
NICE TO SEE YOU TOO!
THE SUPER SKIN!
MAYBE THIS MAY HAVE SOME USE AFTER ALL.
I WON'T ARGUE. WE NEED ALL THE POWER WE CAN GET!
LET'S GO!
ON THE SURFACE...
YOUR DAY OF DOOM HAS ARRIVED!
THE GALAXY BEAST WALKS THE EARTH!

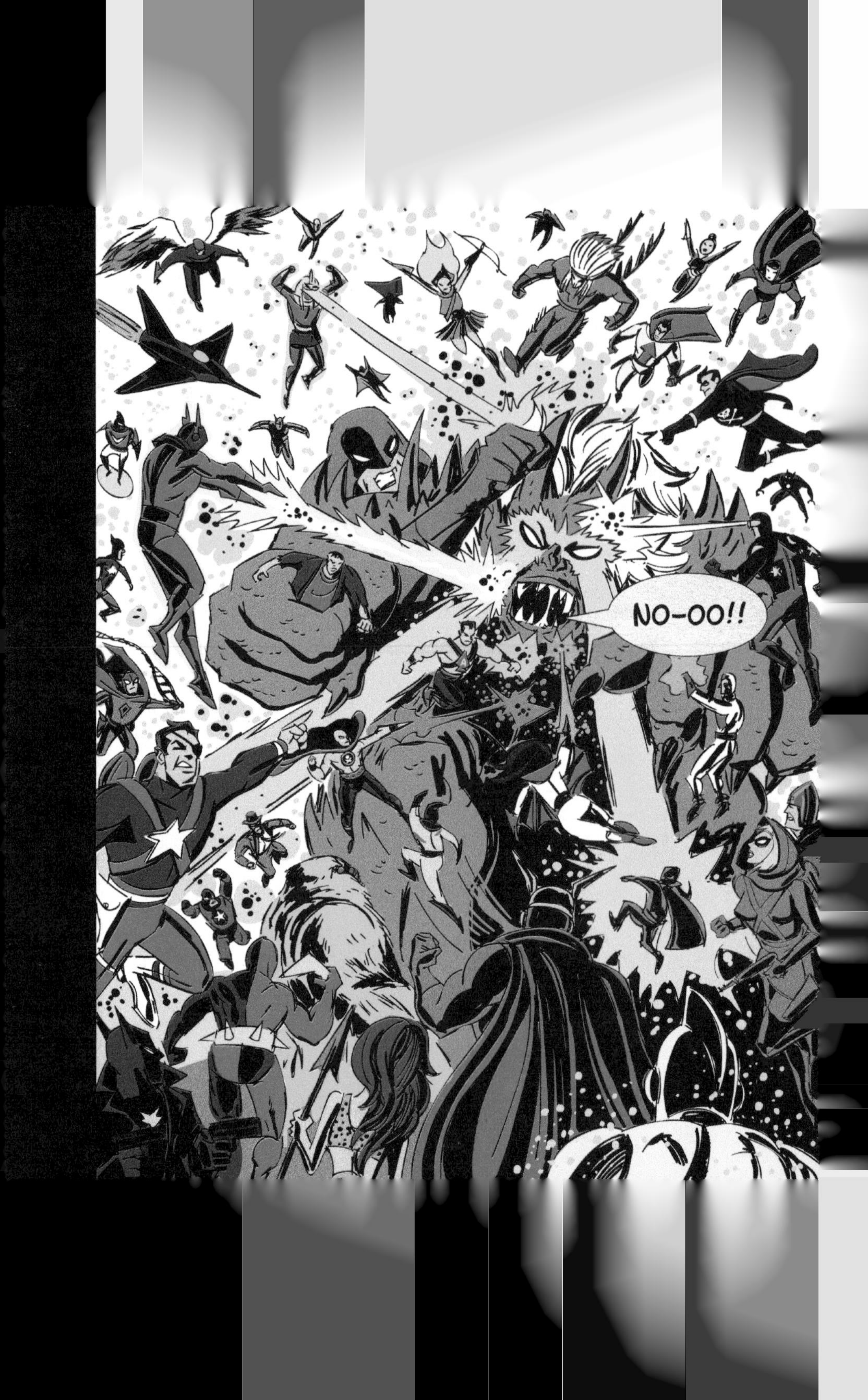
NO-OO!!

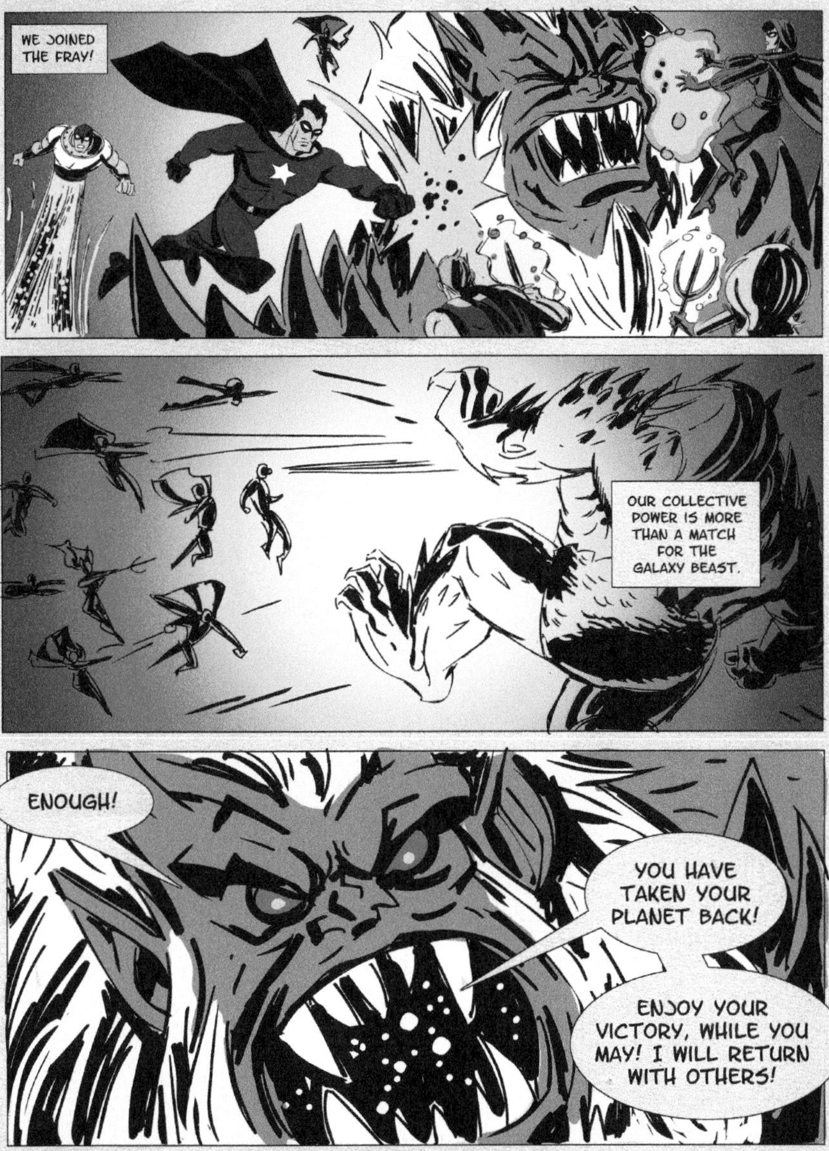
WE JOINED THE FRAY!
OUR COLLECTIVE POWER IS MORE THAN A MATCH FOR THE GALAXY BEAST.
ENOUGH!
YOU HAVE TAKEN YOUR PLANET BACK!
ENJOY YOUR VICTORY, WHILE YOU MAY! I WILL RETURN WITH OTHERS!

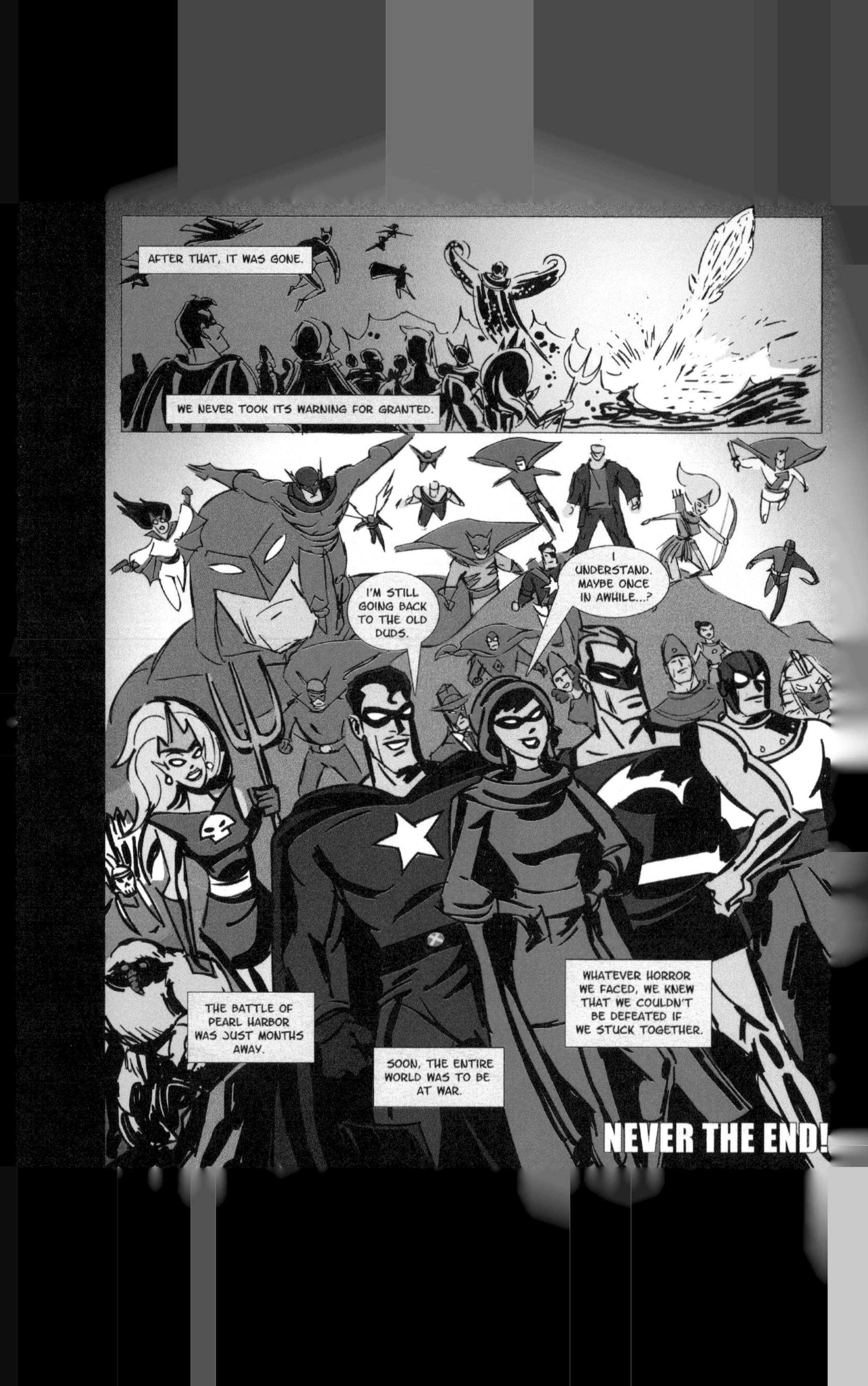
AFTER THAT, IT WAS GONE.
WE NEVER TOOK ITS WARNING FOR GRANTED.
I'M STILL GOING BACK TO THE OLD DUDS.
I UNDERSTAND. MAYBE ONCE IN AWHILE...?
THE BATTLE OF PEARL HARBOR WAS JUST MONTHS AWAY.
SOON, THE ENTIRE WORLD WAS TO BE AT WAR.
WHATEVER HORROR WE FACED, WE KNEW THAT WE COULDN'T BE DEFEATED IF WE STUCK TOGETHER.
NEVER THE END!

THE STORY BEHIND THE STORY

A kid in a raincoat, in a rowboat, with a parrot.

You've got to be kidding.

That was my first reaction when I was asked to work with Capt'n Eli. Luckily, in spite of my reservations, I looked deeper and discovered a whole other universe and the opportunity to create an odyssey. But I'm getting ahead of myself. Let's start at the beginning.

Capt'n Eli is a namesake. It affectionately honors Eli Forsley of Gray, Maine. He was known as Dr. Eli and, in his time, he was that and more. He served in the U.S. Navy in the Pacific during World War II. After the war, he earned his master's degree in social work and a doctorate of education. He was a pioneer in providing mentally ill and disabled veterans a home where they could be a part of the community.

Before I get even further, I should tell you that Capt'n Eli is also a brand. A brand of soda that includes Eli Forsley's root beer. Yup, an old family recipe. You probably think I'll say it's the best I ever tasted. You'd be right and I wouldn't be lying!

Fred Forsley, Eli's son, named his own son Eli. Around the time his son was born he decided he wanted to bring the family root beer to the world – or at least to his home state of Maine. So, in honor of his Dad, Capt'n Eli's Root Beer was created. The soda label (featuring a kid in a raincoat, in a rowboat, with a parrot) was designed and a recipe for success was created!

Since the beginning, Fred saw the potential of Capt'n Eli to be more than just a brand mascot. His father was known as a great storyteller and for his spirit of fun. That sense of fun was expressed in his root beer and Fred felt this same sense of fun could be instilled in an adventure story. Combing the two E's – entertainment and education – he saw how Capt'n Eli could be a positive addition to the world of children's entertainment. He hoped the character could be developed into an animated TV show for kids.

This is where I came in.

A kid in a raincoat, in a rowboat, with a parrot.

It didn't really sound as silly as I first let on (no sillier than other stuff I'd worked on!). But I still had my doubts. Could we create something that stood on its own? I gave it some more thought. The Lone Ranger, The Green Hornet and Captain Midnight were all created to entertain and sell a product. Why not Capt'n Eli?

"Let's make a pilot," Fred said. We decided to start with an activity placemat with games and comics for families to enjoy while waiting for their meals to arrive at a restaurant.

Then we decided to create a book. At first, we thought a storybook fantasy approach might work, a la Dr. Seuss. I suggested we add Barney (I love dogs!) and name the parrot Jolly Roger. Capt'n Eli had a crew and we were off!

Capt'n Eli as a detective and inventor intrigued me. While many adore the adventures of a boy on a broomstick, The Hardy Boys and Tom Swift were the adventures of my childhood. I thought about seafaring stories, Captain Nemo, and old adventure comic strips. I thought about Eli Forsley. I though about fathers and sons. I though about heroes, real and imagined. I thought about Jonny Quest, Aquaman, the Sub-Mariner and every cartoon and comic I ever loved. *The Undersea Adventures of Capt'n Eli* began to form and grew into this series of books.

Thanks for reading and drop me a note anytime at jaypiscopo@captneli.com.

Until then, ***STAND BY FOR ADVENTURE!***

-JAY

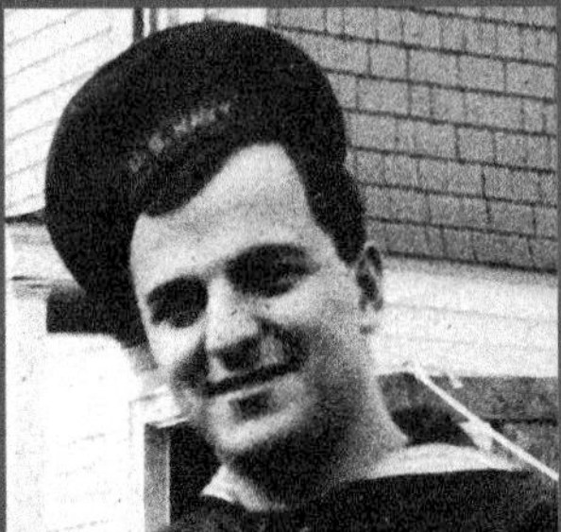

Eli Forsley, 1943

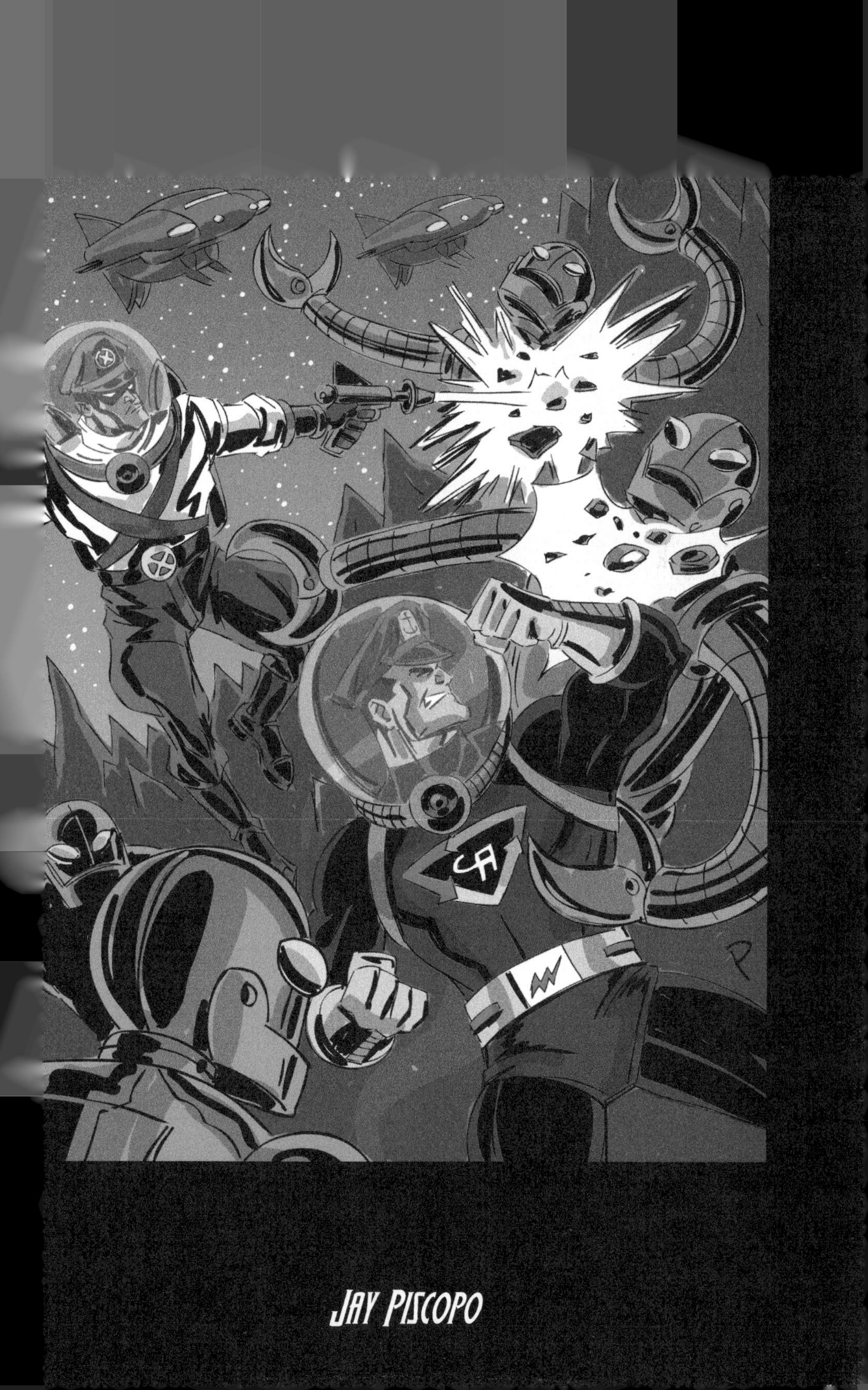

JAY PISCOPO

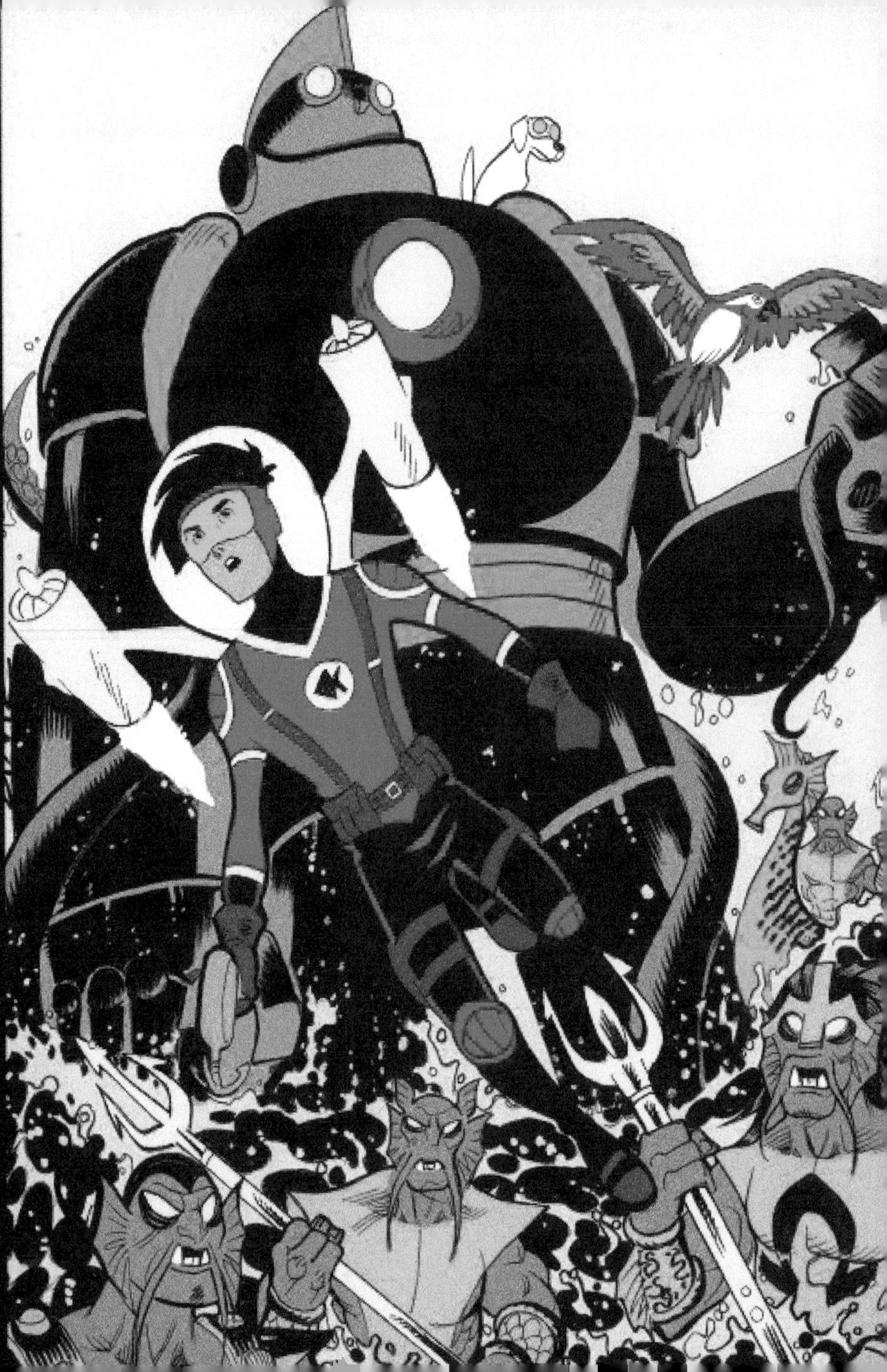

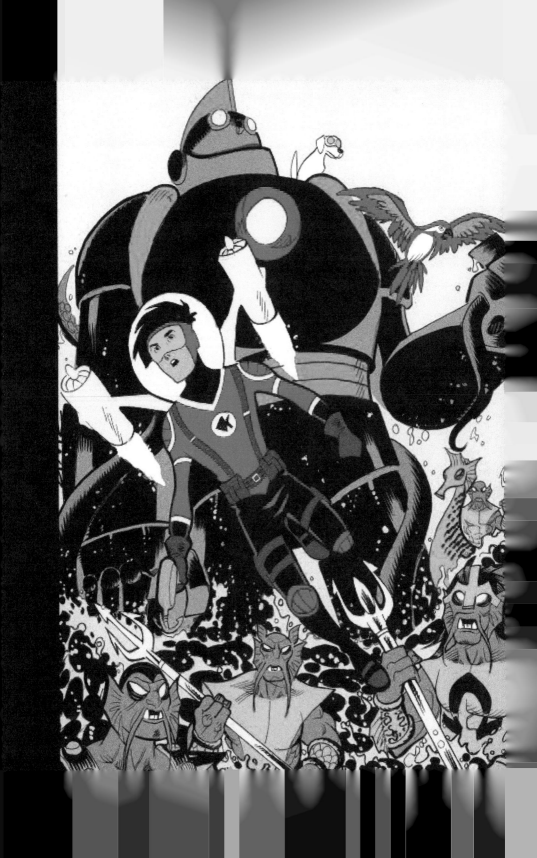

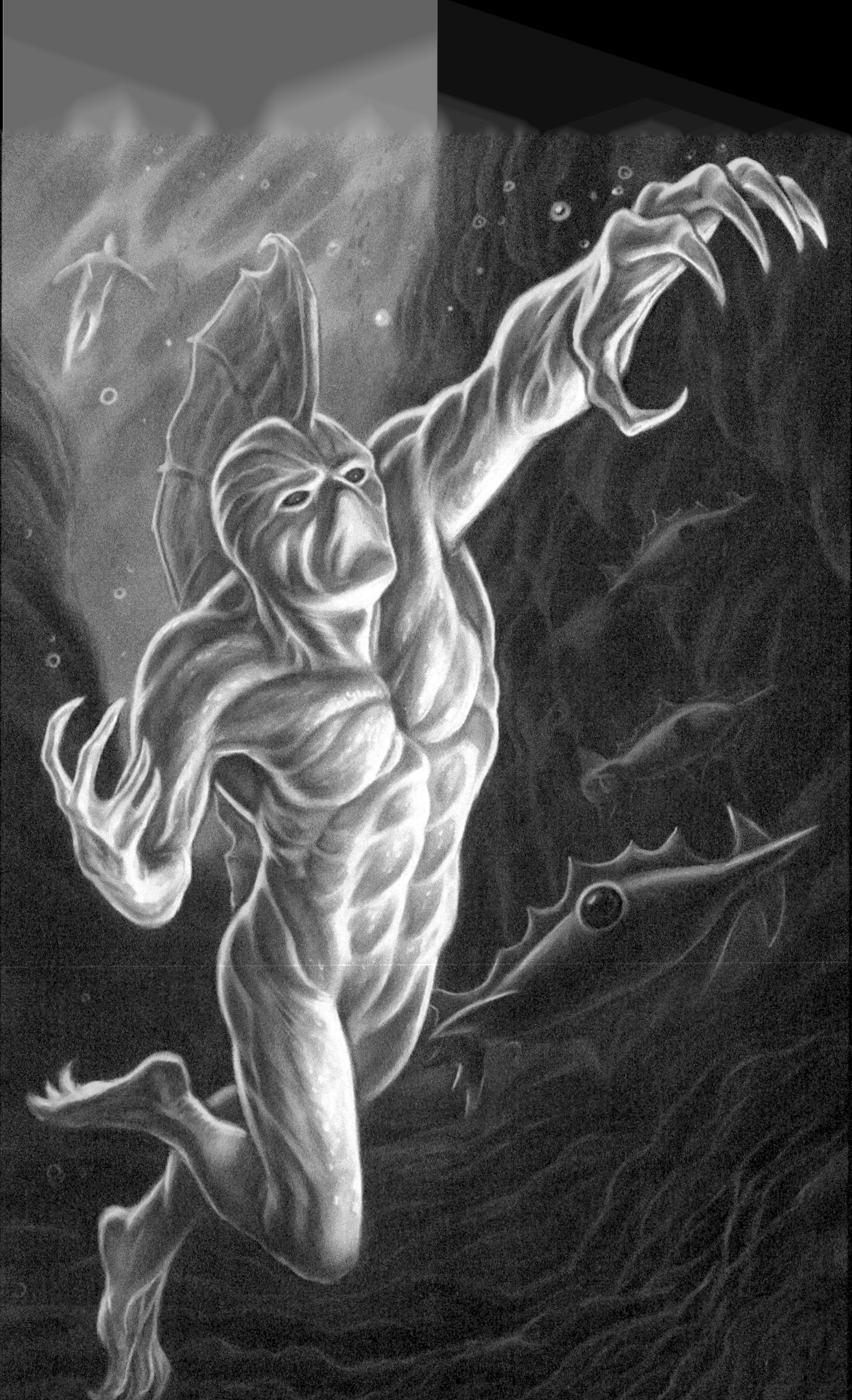
MCHUGH

JEREMY MCHUGH

RICK PARKER